at your doorstep

Premium serviced apartments offering health club access, indoor/outdoor pool, award winning restaurants, designer retail, salons, supermarket and deli, international medical and dental clinic, travel services, and more.
All in one central location, all at your doorstep.

Leasing enquiries (8621) 6279-8502.

SHANGHAI CENTRE

SUITE 710. NO.1376 NANJING ROAD WEST. SHANGHAI 200040, CHINA.
TEL: (8621) 6279-8600. LEASING@SHANGHAICENTRE.NET

WWW.SHANGHAICENTRE.COM

www.gloriahotels.com

Be it a business, or a leisure trip, your needs are the same - someone who understands you! From a hassle-free experience to multi-lingual staff and from centrally-located to value-for-money properties, there is always a Gloria International Hotel or Resort to suit your needs. From the north to the south of China, we are continuously improving ourselves to enthrall you. There is now a place where you will experience Chinese hospitality at its best with international flavor.

Gloria International Hotels . . . your prestige address!

Beijing • Dalian • Nanchang • Shenyang • Suzhou • Xi'an • Wanzhou, Chongqing • Harbin • Qingdao • Qinhuangdao • Sanya • Haikou

(86)10-6515 7878
Toll Free Hotline 800-810 8855 gih.beijing@gloriahotels.com

非凡汇聚
商务之最
Where Business Blossoms

花园酒店
THE GARDEN HOTEL
GUANGZHOU

368 Huanshi Dong Lu, Guangzhou, 510064.
The People's Republic of China.
中华人民共和国广州市环市东路三六八号
邮政编码 510064
Tel:电话:(86-20) 83338989
Fax:传真:(86-20) 83350467
Website:www.thegardenhotel.com.cn

DGrosmangin/MCMorazzani

adler

Mémoires de Femmes · Mémoire du Monde

Zen : harmony and balance in a necklace woven in white gold
and diamonds, lit by brilliantly coloured briolette-cut sapphires.

adler, jewellers since 1886.

www.adler.ch

GENEVE 23, rue du Rhône Tél 022 819 80 26 Hotel Noga Hilton 022 819 80 40 . **GSTAAD** Parkstrasse Tel 033 / 744 66 80 . **LONDON** 13, New Bond Street Tel 020 / 7409 2237
MOSCOW Petrovka Street Tel 095 730 44 90 Smolenskaya Place Tel 095 937 80 89 . **ST.PETERSBURG** Moyka emb. Taleon Club Tel 812 315 80 95
HONGKONG Mandarin Oriental Hotel Tel 23 66 66 16 . **TOKYO** Sun Motoyama Ginza, Namiki Street Tel 03 / 3573 0003

Our Service
我们的服务

Our Hotel
我们的酒店

Harbour View Hotel
Zhuhai

47 Middle Lover's Avenue, Zhuhai 519015 P. R. China
中国珠海吉大情侣中路47号 邮编：519015
Tel电话：(+86) 756 3322 888 Fax传真：(+86) 756 3371 385
Website酒店网址：www.harbourviewhotel.com
E-mail电子信箱：hvhbc@pub.zhuhai.gd.cn

HongKong office香港办事处：
Tel电话：(+852) 2541 9383 Fax传真：(+852) 2834 7137

www.harbourviewhotel.com

While you are in Hong Kong

Opal Brooch
澳宝石真金胸针

最佳礼物 Opal is a perfect gift

Opal Bangle
澳宝石真金手镯

Exclusively designed by

Opal Mine Ltd
Hong Kong

Shop G. Ground Floor, Burlington House, 92 Nathan Rd., Tsim Sha Tsui District, Kowloon, Hong Kong. Tel: 2721 9933
(Near Granville & Cameron Rd., Opposite the Islamic Mosque.)

本店属
优质旅游服务
计划认可商户
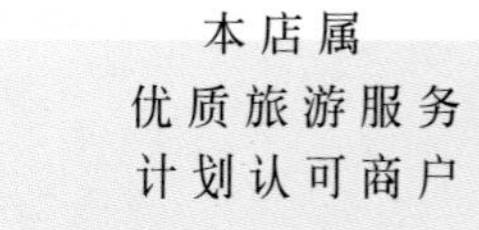

OPAL JEWELLERY ALSO FOR MEN

14Kt & 18Kt Gold & Silver
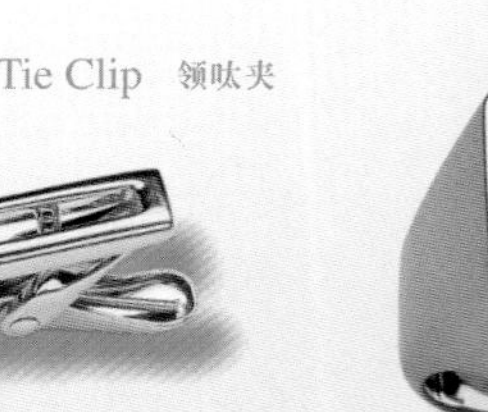
Tie Clip 领呔夹

Men's Ring
男装戒子

Cufflink
袖口钮

OPAL 澳宝石

澳大利亚国宝 — 世上最美的宝石

已流行欧美各国半个世纪

Opal Earring
澳宝石真金耳环

香港澳之宝 — 世界特级澳宝石集中地

Opal Earring
澳宝石真金耳环

Opal Pendant
澳宝石真金坠子

澳之宝

澳宝石 专门店

誉满全球的澳宝石专门店
满足你对澳宝石的一切需要

香港唯一矿洞式澳宝石专门店
访香港时请到本店一游（免费进场参观）
香港,九龙,尖沙咀区 弥敦道92号华敦大厦地下
（尖沙咀区 回教寺斜对面 接近：加连威老道口）

Opal Brooch
澳宝石真金胸针

Opal Bracelet
澳宝石真金手链

Opal Earring
澳宝石真金耳环

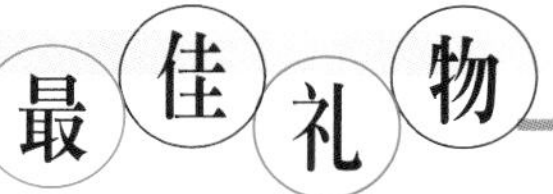

真金澳宝石首饰
请到香港 澳之宝 选购

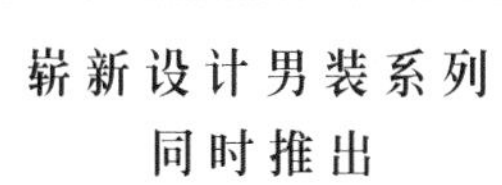

OPAL
Australia's Native Gemstone

Men's Ring
男装戒子

Cufflink 袖口钮

FOR ANY PURCHASE GETS A FREE OPAL

Opal Jewellery Gold & Silver

任何顾客
均可获赠澳宝石一粒

澳宝石最佳礼物

真金澳宝石首饰

Take Home a Beautiful Opal

It's a perfect gift

Our price are much lower

than those you'll find in USA or Australia

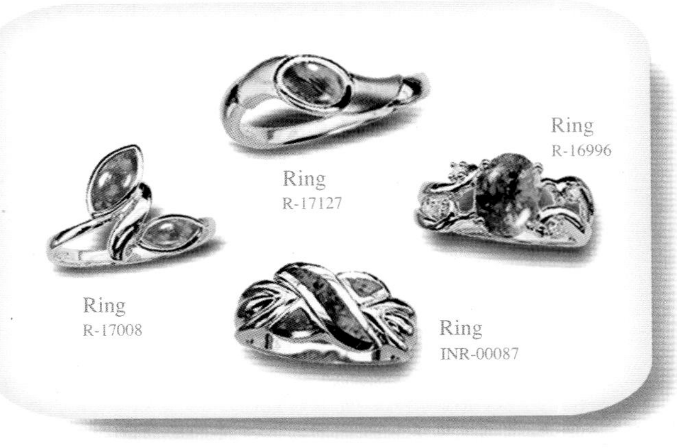

澳宝石是当今世上最美丽的宝石

营业时间
每天开放

上午九时半
至晚上七时

欢迎使用人民币

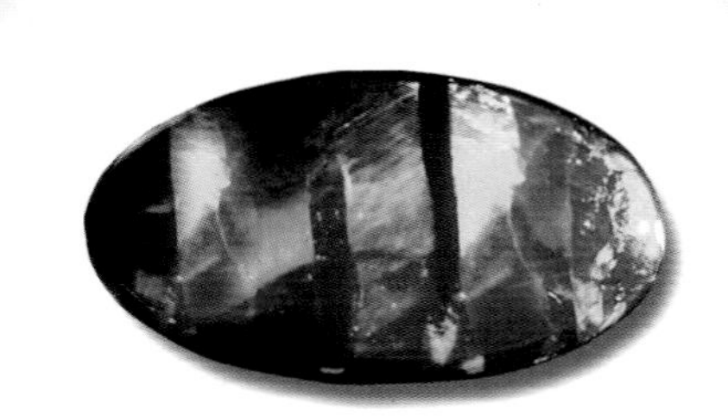

本店属
优质旅游服务
计划商户

香港 澳之宝 专门店

享誉世界的澳宝石供应商

由开采澳宝矿石至琢磨及镶作，均由本集团直接经营，大量减低成本，故售价方面可大幅度低於原产地澳大利亚，欢迎选购．

欢迎中国及香港同胞光临

香港 九龙 尖沙咀区 弥敦道92号华敦大厦地下
回教寺斜对面 接近：加连威老道口

click **www.opalnet.com** 网上资讯

With catalogue & price list, mail orders accepted.

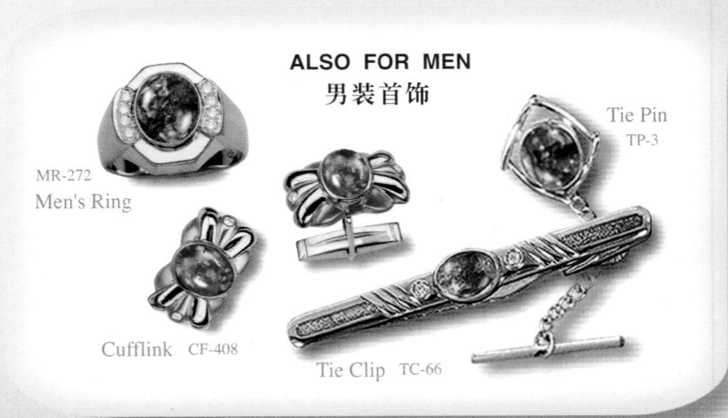

Visit The Opal Mine

While you're in Hong kong

Opal Lovers' Paradise

Buyers from all over the world to buy their Opals
▼ at the Opal Mine Showroom in Hong Kong

Study Area

▲ Our opal specialists & gemologists would like to share their knowledge of opals with you.
店内设有学习区教你如何分析澳宝石品质

▲ 来自世界各地的买家正在店内选购澳宝石

The Opal Mine

You are cordially invited to visit one of the world's largest opal showroom in a simulated opal mining cave. We mine opals, we cut opals and we sell opals, so our prices are much lower than those you'll find in the USA or Australia. Come and see uncut opals embedded in the mine's wall and learn more about this beautiful gemstone in our study area.

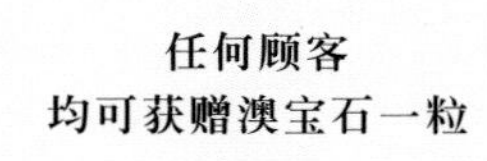

任何顾客
均可获赠澳宝石一粒

FOR ANY PURCHASE
GETS A FREE OPAL

每天营业时间由上午九时半至晚上七时
香港 九龙 尖沙咀区 弥敦道92号华敦大厦地下

Open Every Day 9:30am - 7:00pm

▼ Cutters at work

Workers skillfully cutting and polishing opals.
经验技师正在店内琢磨著澳宝石

Opal Mine Ltd

Internationally Renowned Opal Specialists

Shop G. & H. Ground Floor, Burlington House,
92 Nathan Rd., Tsim-Sha-Tsui District,
Kowloon, Hong Kong. Tel: 2721 9933
(Near Granville Road, opposite the Mosque.)

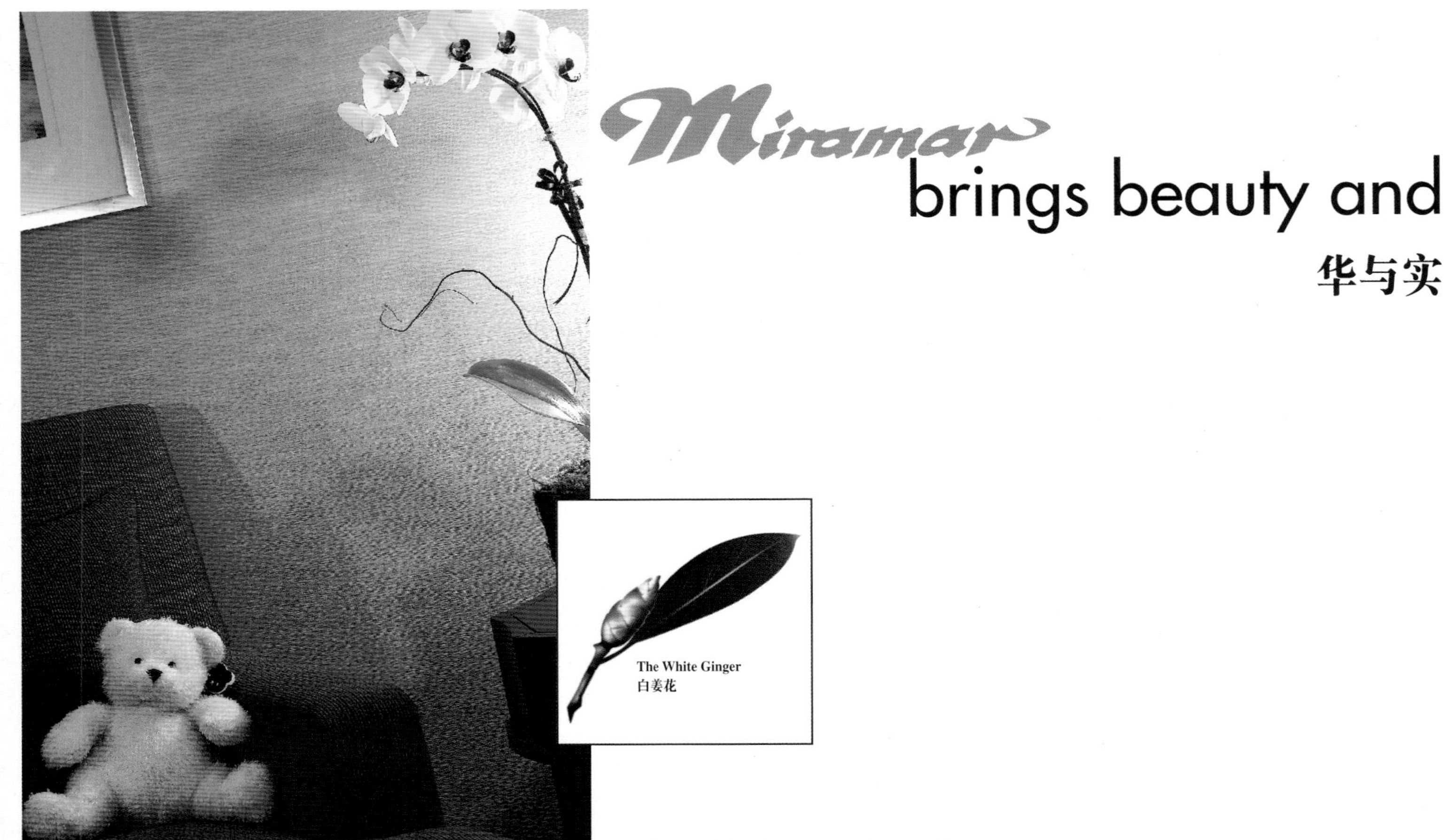

Hotel Miramar Hong Kong
美丽华酒店

Prime location in Tsim Sha Tsui with direct access to business, shopping and tourist landmarks • 525 guestrooms and suites • Miramar Club and business floors with broadband internet access for privileged travellers • Choices of renowned restaurants and bar • Meeting & conference venues including grand ballroom for 1,000 guests and 10 well-appointed function rooms • Other facilities: business centre, in-door heated swimming pool and fitness centre

酒店位于繁盛的尖沙咀，一个集商业、购物及旅游区的市中心。设525间宽敞豪华房间及套房，多家名闻遐迩的餐厅酒吧提供中西佳肴美酒，顶层宴会厅可容纳多至千位宾客，与及十间多功能会议厅，适合各类型宴会及商务会议。另设现代化商务中心、室内暖水泳池及健身中心。

118-130 Nathan Road, Tsim Sha Tsui, Kowloon, Hong Kong
香港九龙尖沙咀弥敦道118-130号
Tel 电话：(852) 2368-1111
Fax 传真：(852) 2369-1788
E-mail 电邮：miramarhk@mihmc.com
Website 网址：http://www.miramarhk.com

Hotels Managed by Miramar International Hotel Management Corporation S. A.

Hong Kong	Shenzhen	Shanghai
Hotel Miramar Hong Kong	Nan Hai Hotel	Miramar Apartment
Pinnacle Apartment	Shekou Haitao Hotel	Ruitai Jingan Hotel
Silvermine Beach Hotel		Ruitai Hongqiao Hotel

The White Ginger
洋葱花

Nan Hai Hotel 南海酒店

5-star resort hotel for leisure and business travellers • Convenient location in Shenzhen • Close to Shekou Passenger Pier, Shenzhen Airport and Shenzhen Train Station • Easy access to the nearby tourist attractions and golf clubs • 396 guestrooms and suites • Broadband internet access for all guestrooms • Other facilities: multi-purposed function rooms, business centre, restaurants, bar & lounge and recreational facilities.

五星级度假酒店，消闲或商务会议皆宜。邻近蛇口码头、深圳机场及深圳火车站，来往旅游景点及高尔夫球会所方便快捷。设396间舒适房间及套房，所有客房及商务楼层设宽频上网。酒店设施完善，客人可享用多功能会议室、商务中心、餐厅、酒吧及各式康乐设备。

1 Gong Ye 1st Road, Nanhai Blvd., Shekou, Shenzhen, China
中国深圳市蛇口南海大道工业一路一号
Tel 电话 ： (86-755) 2669-2888
Fax 传真 ： (86-755) 2669-2440
Postal Code 邮政编码：518069

nan hai hotel 南海酒店
Managed by Miramar International
美麗華國際酒店管理

Hong Kong Office 香港办事处
Tel 电话 ： (852) 2315-5388
Fax 传真 ： (852) 2311-7686
E-mail 电邮 ： hkoffice@nanhai-hotel.com
Website 网址 ： http://www.nanhai-hotel.com

Hong Kong Office
Tel ： (852) 2315-5618
Fax ： (852) 2367-5962

Beijing Office
Tel ： (86-10) 6515-6719
Fax ： (86-10) 6515-0134

Shanghai Office
Tel ： (86-21) 6270-5539
Fax ： (86-21) 6270-5486

Taipei Office
Tel ： (886-2) 8786-1618
Fax ： (886-2) 8786-1968

Miramar
Miramar International Hotel Management Corp. S.A.
美 麗 華 國 際 酒 店 管 理 有 限 公 司

CHAMPAGNE

Veuve Clicquot

凯歌皇牌香槟

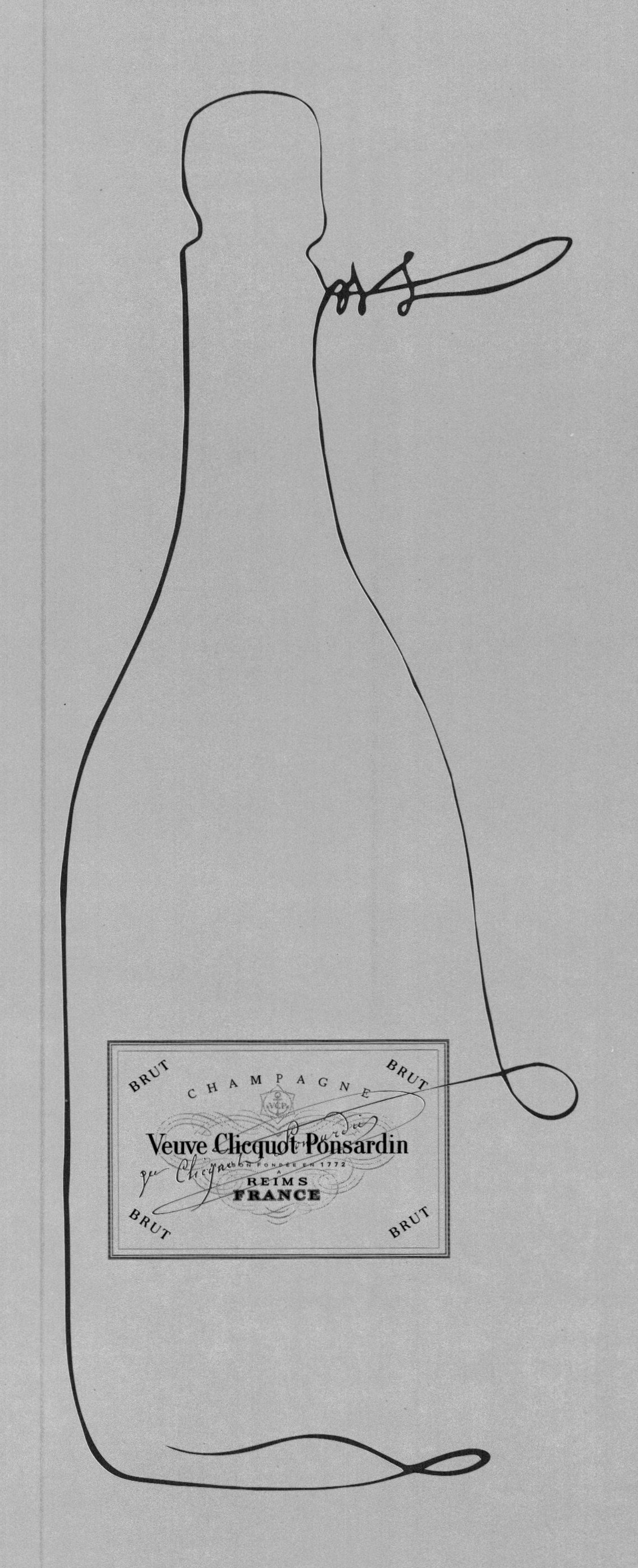

contents

features

cities and regions

CHINA WELCOMES YOU
Edition June 06 - 07

Published annually by Century Publishing Co. Ltd. of Shanghai - Lexicographical Publishing House for distribution in the guest rooms of international-standard hotels in China.

PRODUCER Minnie Yeung
ASSOCIATE PRODUCER Peggy Yu
MANAGING EDITOR Peter Hibbard (The Ginger Griffin)
CONTRIBUTING EDITORS Shamus Sillar, May Guan, Duncan, Natasha Dragun, Lees, Kristi Lanier
CHINESE EDITOR Wu Yaxian, Gao Bingqiang
PHOTOGRAPHY
Peter Hibbard, Panorama Stock Ltd, ChinaPic, Shanghai Top Photo Corp, Shamus Sillar, Steve Zhao, Chocolate George, Graham Uden, Christie's Hong Kong Ltd, Hong Kong Tourism Board, Macau Government Tourism Office, Jack Hollingworth, Richard Dobson, Imagine China, Photo Disc.
PRODUCTION MANAGER David Wang
PRODUCTION COORDINATORS Ivy Huang, Jean Cheng
DESIGNERS Tang Yi, Pippa Lamb, Amy Zhou
PRINTING C&C Joint Printing Co., (Guangdong) Ltd.

PUBLISHED BY:
SHANGHAI CENTURY PUBLISHING CO. LTD.,
LEXICOGRAPHICAL PUBLISHING HOUSE
457, Shaanxi Road (N.), 200040, Shanghai. China
Tel: (8621) 6247 2088, Fax: (8621) 6256 8566
E-mail: cishu@online.sh.cn

PRODUCED BY:
ISMAY PUBLICATIONS LTD
Head Office
20th Floor, Golden Centre, 188 Des Voeux Road Central, Hong Kong
Tel: (852) 2544 0360 Fax: (852) 2854 3761
Email: media@ismaychina.com

REPRESENTATIVE OFFICES:

BEIJING
1704, Building 2, Jian Wai Soho, 39 East 3rd Ring Road, Chaoyang District, 100022 Beijing. China
Tel: (8610) 5869 1894 Fax: (8610) 5869 1834
Email: ismaybj@ismaychina.com

SHANGHAI
1112 Central Plaza, 227 Huangpi Road (N.), 200003 Shanghai. China
Tel: (8621) 6375 8231/32 Fax: (8621) 6375 8233
Email: media@ismaychina.com

GUANGZHOU
1316 Main Tower, Guangdong International Hotel,
339 Huanshi Road East, 510098 Guangzhou. China
Tel: (8620) 8331 3037 Fax: (8620) 8331 0137
Email: ismaygz@pub.guangzhou.gd.cn

This publication, its text, maps and designs are protected by international copyright laws. All rights reserved. No part of the publication may be reproduced, stored in a retrieval system, or transmitted in any form by any means, electronic, photocopying, recording of or otherwise, without the prior and explicit permission in writing of Ismay Publications Ltd. Fashion Front and Painted Faces WestEast magazine. All reasonable efforts have been made to identify copyright holders.

Every effort has been made to ensure that all the factual content of this book is correct at time of going to press, but as the pace of change is fast it is suggested that travellers consult airlines, consulates, travel agents etc. for current travel advice. The publishers and all those associated with the publication cannot accept legal responsibility for any errors, however caused. The views and opinions expressed in this publication are not necessarily those of the publisher.

Ismay Publications Ltd. also produces the monthly city living magazines - Beijing Talk, Shanghai Talk, South China CityTalk and the bi-monthly Macau Talk.

©2006 Shanghai Lexicographical Publishing House

ISBN 962-684-111-7

Front cover image: courtesy of WestEast Magazine [WE]

PRICE: US$ 40.00 ¥ 332.00

图书在版编目（CIP）数据

中国欢迎您 /《中国欢迎您》编写组编．—上海：上海辞书出版社，2006.6
ISBN 7-5326-1187-6

Ⅰ．中…　Ⅱ．中…　Ⅲ．旅游资源—概况—中国—汉、英
Ⅳ．F592

中国版本图书馆 CIP 数据核字（2006）第 135875 号

CHANGIN
CHINA

Happy With Friends Coming From Afar

If you have visited China before, whether it was 10 years of even six months ago, you will probably have remarked on how it has miraculously changed since the last time you were here. If it's your first time, more than likely your preconceived ideas of what the country was like bear little semblance to the reality. The way the country views itself, as well as the way in which it views the outside world is changing in a monumental manner. And, just around the corner, with the world looking on, China will take the world stage as host to the 2008 Olympics in Beijing and the World Expo 2010 in Shanghai. Whilst many historical legacies live on, China looks to the future with an enthusiasm never witnessed in the history of mankind.

Welcome!

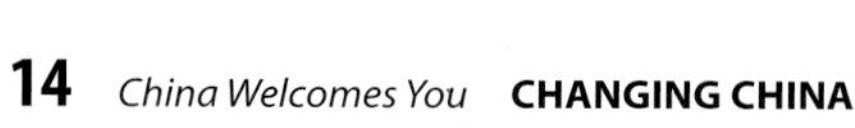

G

Within the last two decades China has reinvented her economy and society in a fashion hitherto unseen. With unfurling prosperity, relentless ambition and membership of the WTO, China's future is destined to be even more remarkable than her past. The effects of opening to the outside world have been dramatic and whilst a Communist orthodoxy still prevails, most Chinese value spending power over political power. The 'iron rice bowl' system wherein the government took care of all peoples' needs from cradle to grave has been shattered into unrecognisable pieces.

Deng Xiaoping ignited the flame of reform - setting up coastal zones for economic development and promoting private enterprise. His famous saying 'it doesn't matter what the colour the cat is as long as it catches mice' set the mood for a modernisation policy based on 'socialism with Chinese characteristics,' where making money was glorious. Following his death in 1997, Jiang Zemin presided over the radical restructuring of industry, rapid urbanisation and the nation's integration into the world's political and economic scene.

With the standing down of the old guard, ratified at the 16th Party Congress in November 2002, a younger group of new leaders headed by Hu Jintao have been installed. Their plain economic objectives to quadruple the 2002 gross domestic product by the year 2020 and to manage the development of a 'well-off' society. Affluence is clearly visible in China's major cities where the physical and social landscape has changed spectacularly over the last decade.

The Nineties nestled a massive consumer revolution in everything from food and fashion to high-tech goods and houses. Just decade old dreams of owning a colour TV or a washing machine became distant, as modern aspirations, including home and car ownership and exotic vacations become attainable for a growing middle class, expected to envelop more than twenty percent of the expanding urban population by 2010. 'Civilised' and 'sanitised' city centres carry an endless stream of purchasing pilgrims, surfacing for Cokes, Starbucks coffee or Big Macs, between dips into the sea of plenty. Huge national retail chains have emerged and the luxury market is super-buoyant in the main cities.

Paralleling the colossal change in outward appearance, a remarkable transformation in living conditions has swept the landscape. A lucrative home furnishing industry has developed with crystal-laden lighting emporia, huge furnishing stores, delightfully intimate interior design shops and a rising tide of DIY stores appearing in areas where it used to be difficult to find a 60-watt light bulb. Modern well-appointed apartment blocks and villas are appearing everywhere to satisfy fast-growing needs for a modern lifestyle. The dream of property ownership is well within the grasp of many, even though prices in some major cities such as Beijing and Shanghai are approaching, and sometimes exceeding, those in the West. With rising incomes, car ownership is becoming a priority for many.

There is perhaps no more salient illustration of China's determination to emerge as a powerful and progressive economy than its launch of the Shenzhou 5 space capsule, which orbited the Earth 14 times in October, 2003. China is on the move in a monumental manner and it may not be too long until it becomes the centre of the world yet again.

in the face of tradition

With 1.3 billion people spread across a vast chameleon-like landscape it is hard to define what constitutes an average Chinese citizen. Over 90% of the population are of Han ethnicity, named after the dynasty that ruled from 206 BC to AD 220, originating in the Yellow River basin. The remainder of the population is made up of 55 distinct nationality groups that largely inhabit the country's resource rich but economically backward western region. China's five autonomous regions - Guangxi, Xinjiang, Tibet, Inner Mongolia and Ningxia are still home to many of these minority people who have experienced a massive rise in living standards in recent years due to the central government's western economic enrichment initiative. Preferential social policies, including exemption from the one child per family rule, also assure the procreation of a multi-cultural Chinese nation.

The Zhuang minority is the largest group with 15 million members inhabiting the southwest region. Most minorities adhere to traditional customs and beliefs, though the encroachment of modern consumer society and tourism has resulted in a change of lifestyle and dress for those most exposed. Meanwhile, in the remote landscapes of the north and west, traditional identities have been easier to preserve, despite a huge influx of Han Chinese over the last twenty years.

On the huge grasslands of Inner Mongolia, the sons of Genghis Khan retain their yurt encampments, equestrian extravaganzas and gargantuan barbecue feasts. Tribes in the north-eastern forests include the Daur with their animal-head hats and the dwindling Oroqen minority who use deerskin and birch bark for everything from tents to canoes. The great western deserts of Xinjiang are home to 13 ethnic minorities, notably seven million Uygurs who appear Caucasian, are practicing Muslims and speak a Turkish dialect. Semi-nomadic Kazakh and Mongol herdsmen roam Xinjiang's grasslands and mountains, while the Sibo are Manchu descendants who cling to their language, script and skills such as archery. Many Tibetans are still high-altitude herdsmen and make long pilgrimages to ancient Lama temples.

Thirteen ethnic groups populate the mountainous Guizhou region, with 2.5 million Bouyei aboriginals living in the southwest. They marry very young, dress in sombre clothes with colourful trimmings, and are skilled batik makers. To the southeast of the region a flamboyant mix of minorities make up over 70 per cent of the area's population. Many of China's 7.5 million Miao minority live here. The Miao are renowned for their detailed hand-embroidery and silver coil jewellery. Their neighbours, the Dong, varnish their indigo-dyed jackets with egg white to ward off mosquitoes.

Some six and a half million Yi live in south-western China upholding a unique form of shamanism. At festival times, women don embroidered jackets and black turbans, or twist their hair into horn shapes. On Hainan Island there are sizeable Miao and Li populations.

The highlands and valleys of Yunnan are home to a third of China's ethnic minorities - many of the 24 ethnic groups, including lesser-known hill tribes, still follow colourful ways of life. The town of Lijiang is the home of the Naxi people - descendants of matriarchal Tibetan nomads. Their womenfolk wear distinctive blue tops and trousers, blue or black aprons and embroidered capes.

Deep in the southwest, bordering Myanmar, the Xishuangbanna region contains a fantastic diversity of nationalities and small tribes. The delicate Dai people, the largest minority, bear many Thai characteristics. Their Buddhist temples and saffron-robed clergy are a common sight, and their festivals attract hordes of tourists. Dai women commonly dress in bright short blouses, printed sarongs and silver belts, whilst the males are commonly tattooed with animal motifs.

Many of the 55 minorities have their own languages that include Tibetan, Uygur and Korean. Although the majority of people can communicate in Mandarin it is not surprising that up to one-third of the population still regard it as a second language. Mandarin is historically a dialect of the Beijing area and was designated as the official Chinese language in 1912.

Although Mandarin is used as the basic medium in the Chinese education system, the use of local dialects and minority languages is widespread within the far-flung national borders. Natives of Shanghai, Guangzhou (Canton) and many other cities communicate amongst themselves in their distinctive local or regional dialects that are largely incomprehensible to pure Mandarin speakers. The differences between such dialects can sometimes be compared to those between Spanish, German and English.

Regardless of the differences in the spoken language it is consoling to find that the written script is uniform throughout China. The only quandary presented is that over 50,000 characters are entered in the largest dictionary! In practice, however, educated people ordinarily use just four to five thousand and basic newspaper reports can be grasped with an understanding of about one thousand characters. In an effort to reform the language and increase literacy rates, as well as to promote national unity, the Communist government introduced the Pinyin system in 1958. This allows an approach to the spoken language through the use of the Roman alphabet and its associated numerals. Around the same time, the written script was simplified with many characters being rewritten in a less complicated arrangement so as to make them easier to learn.

Just like the language Chinese religious life can appear complicated, with temples full of idols and ornaments and worshippers dividing their attention between Buddhism and Taoism. The Chinese language does not have a term for the concept of religion in the western sense - expressions such as school or teaching are used instead. Religion remains a very practical feature of everyday life and prayers are likely to be requests for benefits such as good health, prosperity, fertility and good luck in exams.

While many modern Chinese would deny any religious belief, most acknowledge the balancing power of yin and yang, the polar opposites in which all things can be classified, that make it possible to accept the bad times along with the good.

THE FACE

Ethereal and mystical - Chinese beauty trangresses time and nature

Images courtesy of *WestEast Magazine*

FASHION FRONT

tim yip

Tim Yip won the Oscar for Best Art Design in 2001 for his work on the phenomenal movie 'Crouching Tiger, Hidden Dragon' and was nominated for another for his costume design. He is renowned for crossing the boundaries of the classical and the avant-garde, for mixing both masculinity and femininity, as well as extravagance with prudence and putting East and West in direct contact. His recent work, "Rouge – The Art of Tim Yip" presented at la Maison de la Culture de Bourges, delivered a fantasy of colour and light, emblematic of Chinese culture on a global stage

Credit: All fashion and accessories by FENDI

Credit: Necklace by BVLGARI

PAINTING FACES

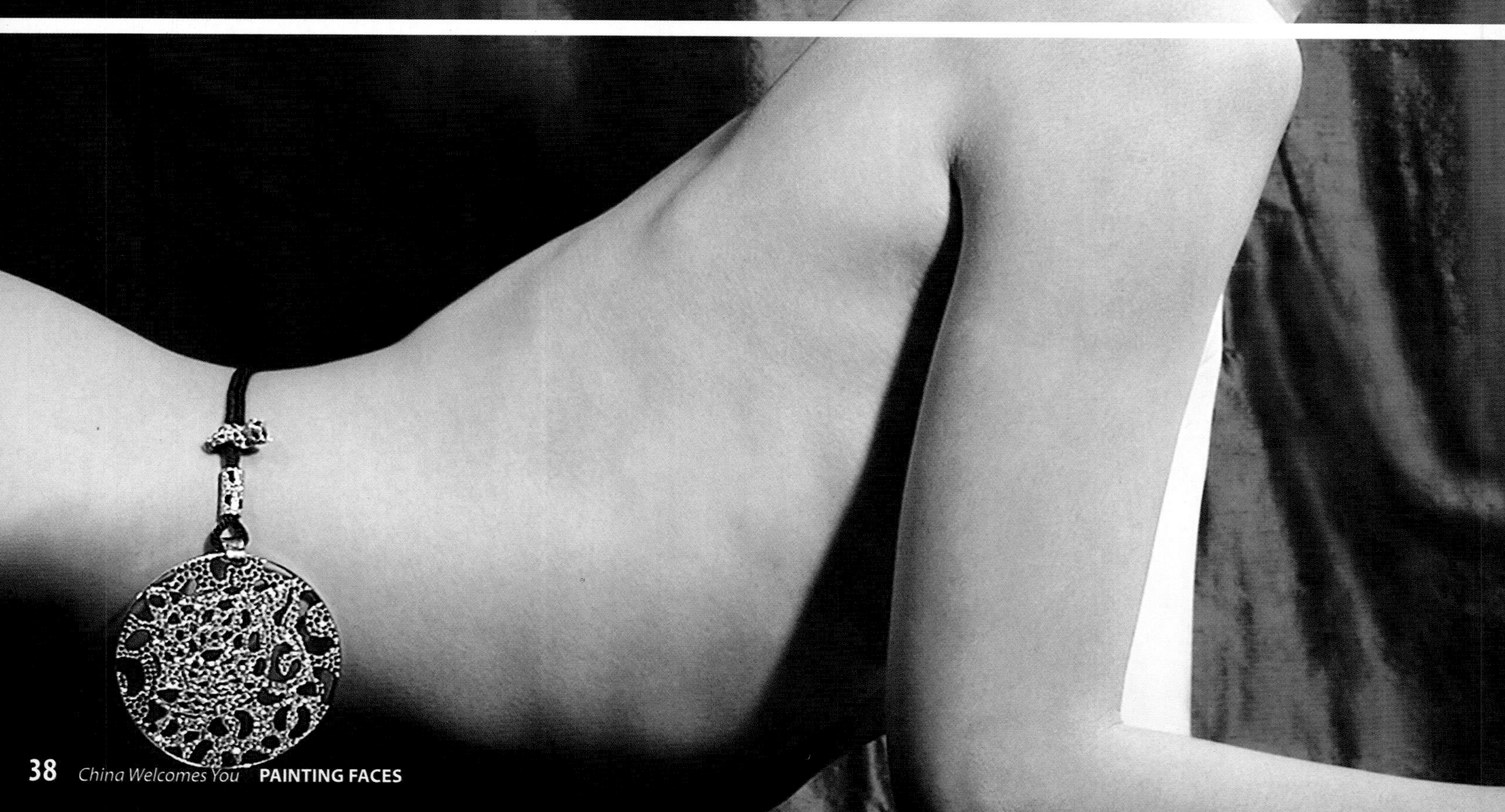

Images courtesy of WestEast Magazine
Photography & art direction by DC Chang @ Lightwarrior
Styling by Antonia Chang
Hair by Jane @ Indulge
Make-up by Sarah Tan @ Indulge
Models May @ Lightwarrior
Dog Dan & Santos @ Diva
All jewellery by Cartier - Le Baiser du Dragon Collection

MILESTONES IN JADE

For someone who thought, in his early years, that jade was old-fashioned and boring, Edward Chiu has passed mountainous milestones on his journey to the glittering pinnacle of his profession. He was quick to recognise the exciting design opportunities embedded in black and white jade and, exhibiting his exceptional creativity and extraordinary craftsmanship, he was the first in Hong Kong to use the stone in jewellery design. His contemporary and classic designs combine the essence of East-meets-West in the creation of dramatic and inspirational works of art that are both unique and highly individual. Each rare piece, tailor-made to his customer's personal taste and preferences, is a heart-felt expression of his own personal journey of spiritual inspiration. To universal acclaim, Edward Chiu's flagship store in the ifc Mall in Hong Kong opened in March 2006.

In classical Chinese culture more esteem was placed on jade than gold. Some 7000 years ago, Chinese craftsmen began manufacturing the first ritual objects out of the exquisite and exceptionally hard stone. The ancients believed that jade was a divine link between mortals and the gods and could repel evil spirits.

Jade's importance to the Chinese not only derives from its intrinsic value but also from associations with human virtues as it embodies qualities of beauty, hardness, durability and rareness.

SHANGHAI

the DESIGN STATE

Over the past 15 years Shanghai has leapfrogged from being a drab industrial centre to become China's most glamorous metropolis. Architects rush to array her in gleaming towers; artists and designers mention her alongside New York and Paris. Shanghai's meteoric rise as a great world city is again in the limelight, much as it was in days gone by. She knew how to be 'chic' long before today's trend-setters even dared. Whether its architecture or interiors, understanding Shanghai style requires looking back - back to the early 20th century when the city first began to seduce the globe.

From the time the British forcibly invited themselves to tea in the 1840s to 1949 when the People's Republic of China ushered everyone back out, Shanghai hosted a robust multicultural community. During the 'Concession era,' Europeans, Russians, Americans, Japanese and a host of others settled in the city, flooding it with ideas, customs and most visibly, architectural traditions. At the turn of the 20th century new architecture followed the patterns of historic European styles. But in the late 1920s everything changed. While America suffered from economic depression and fascism incubated in Europe, Shanghai began a decade of unprecedented political stability and wealth. For the well-heeled, Shanghai was an intoxicating swirl of high living. Called the Nanjing Decade, 1927 to 1937 saw a fever of activity. China's first generation of western-educated locals were returning to Shanghai with new ideas, a more varied design palette and the highbrow tastes and pocketbooks to make it all happen. At the same time more foreigners were arriving. They needed homes and they needed things to fill them with.

Out of this cauldron of influences and circumstances came a massive building effort. Shanghai's elite wanted luxuriant living and they wanted it au courant. They viewed themselves as the most

fashionable in Asia and lusted after the newest trends. Designers experimented with styles over the years, consequently imprinting the cityscape with a remarkable array of western architecture and design. By the advent of the 1930s they had turned heavily towards the trim lines of art deco. Characterised by a distinct group of decoration schemes (art deco literally means decorative arts), art deco appealed to Shanghai's chic populace for its edgy modernity. Starting with buildings like the Capitol Theatre in 1928 and the Peace Hotel in 1929, architects churned out art deco structures, furniture makers did the same, and people bought them.

While intense, Shanghai's building blitz didn't last long. The Sino-Japanese War, which began in 1937 halted new construction and gradually drained the city of its foreign population. But by then Shanghai had been permanently altered - its landscape parlayed into a rich canvas of Mediterranean villas, London-like row houses, neo-classical buildings, and scores of art deco apartment buildings.

In terms of design the Nanjing Decade gave Shanghai its singular style. Less tangibly but equally important, the era' s high-speed lifestyle came to define Shanghai. This spirit has escaped the wrecking ball and the dust of the decades and is at the core of the city today. As Shanghai stampedes into the 21st century her stylish present is inseparable from her stylish past and is the very thing that guides her future.

"Chinese style is most often associated with ornate carvings, complex patterns and a searing palette of rich reds and glitzy golds. But what is often overlooked is that there is a deep-rooted modernity inherent in Chinese design...."

CHINA STYLE, Periplus Editions. Text by Sharon Leece; photography by Michael Freeman. US$45.

Spencer Dodington

Architectural Renovator

As China lurched through the middle of the 20th century, its focus veered away from all things stylish and its architectural heritage suffered. In Shanghai, nightclubs and theatres closed and single-family homes were converted to house many. Ironically Shanghai has lost more Concession-era buildings to recent development than past neglect. Yet through it all she has kept her pizzazz and it was into this that Spencer Dodington stepped in 1995. A corporate executive, Dodington also had a lifelong passion for history and design and Shanghai's sultry 1930s style captivated him. 'The variety of design, it's romantic, and the fact that it was so brief and happened when the Japanese were at the gates,' he says referring to how Shanghai' s building boom occurred while Japan invaded China's north. 'Shanghai just turned me on.'

Dodington researched Shanghai style extensively, exploring every neighbourhood and taking over 10,000 photos. Ultimately he parlayed his passion into a career as an architectural renovator. Starting with the skeleton of a historic home, Dodington recreates the era's original look using materials, colours and design schemes sympathetic to the 1930s. Keeping it authentic means knowing what the era's homes looked like. Since most buildings have been retrofitted beyond recognition, Dodington had to piece together a "design palette" by snooping through countless old buildings and culling through the scant records available.

Typical Shanghai style incorporated several elements. First was the juxtaposition of colour. Pale yellow or grey walls were offset by solid, dark wood, warm lighting, and sharp colour accents. Dodington's own restored art deco flat features yellow walls and is filled with lustrous wood furniture, leather club chairs, and deep red accents. 'Style was all about colours and opulence, he says. The design scheme was also reflected in materials. Many buildings featured terrazzo, a tinted cement with marble chips, in floors; woodwork on doors, windows, and floors; and glazed tiles on exteriors and in mosaics.

In a sense, then, Dodington is a curator of a living museum. 'I'm restoring and preserving one residence at a time.'

" I'm restoring and preserving one residence at a time "

Hong Merchant

Chinese Antiques and Furniture Design

Concession-era Shanghai sometimes hogs too much attention. Mesmerized by the Bund, it's easy to forget that China had been producing its own exquisite designs long before the foreigners tumbled into town.

This fact did not escape collectors Jean-Philippe Weber and Pia Pierre. Using a restored 1930s long tang (lane) house as an exhibition space, the two have made a business of appreciating Chinese art and design. Their shop, Hong Merchant, is simultaneously an antiques dealership, design studio, art gallery and residence. Weber, a marketer turned collector, and Pierre, an archaeologist who runs a similar business in Bangkok, have filled the home with carefully chosen Ming and Qing-era antiques. In the large first floor parlour which opens onto a greenery-filled garden, cabinets, tables, desks, and chairs bask in tree-filtered light. Decorative pieces like statuary, jewellery boxes, and vases soften the surfaces. While some of the displayed pieces are available, they are exclusive and intended only for the serious collector.

In fact, their antique collection serves more for inspiration than as a core business. Pierre designs furniture using Ming and Qing styles, adapting it to a modern use. Examples include a cane-surfaced day bed redeployed as a coffee table and a small circular necklace box increased in proportion. 'A beautiful piece is a beautiful piece. You can change the proportion but the idea is already beautiful,' Weber says. We are asking 'why is it so beautiful?' Pierre takes the feeling and tries to extract it.

But if beautiful furnishings are the business's heart, its soul is the house. The Hong Merchant home is a graciously restored example of an era that fused Western and Eastern styles. In using an historic home as a canvas for their antiques and adaptive designs, they've fused styles again and with something old created something fresh, authentic, and beautiful.

" A beautiful piece is a beautiful piece. You can change the proportion but the idea is already beautiful "

The Yongfoo Elite

The Yongfoo Elite sits in the heart of Shanghai's former French Concession amidst leafy avenues populated by consular and government elites. Its magnificent 1930s garden villa, which once housed the British Consulate, today administers the finest hospitality, classic Shanghai gourmet cuisine, wine, cocktails and live music. The buildings are stocked with a huge collection of exquisite items collected over 20 years by its Shanghai-born American owner – ranging from a 600 year-old bed to a 1960s Gucci suite. Since opening in March 2004 the club has become a premier in its own inimitable right - being lauded with accolades including runner-up in 'Wallpaper' magazine's best club category.

"Runner-up in "Wallpaper" magazine's best club category"

CHINA'S CHANGING CITYSCAPES

The vision of China as a country full of architecture topped with upswept roofs, built around walled courtyards, connected to gardens full of tranquil lotus ponds by zigzag bridges is a little antiquated in the 21st century. While open-sided pavilions, temples and pagodas, moon gates and the like can still be found throughout China, such traditional edifices are now generally dressed up as sites for visiting tourists. Traditional temple and palace buildings typically feature circular columns linked by beams and a curved roofline with upturned eaves and ceramic tiles. From the 8th century on the eaves, featuring colourful sculpted animals and figures, became increasingly decorative.

In the south of China curves and ornamentation were more exaggerated, as in Guangdong's Foshan Ancestral Temple. Columns were carved in stone or painted with different colours denoting specific religions (bright red for Buddhists, black for Taoists), or the rank of palace occupants. Four-sided roofs, higher platforms or special yellow-glazed roof tiles, might distinguish imperial buildings. Occasionally, buildings broke away from convention in unique style, such as the circular-tiered buildings of the Temple of Heaven in Beijing. Like most important buildings in China, the temple was raised above ground level and built on a stone platform. Despite the oddity of that design, building materials and ground plans for traditional architecture have been strictly adhered to for countless generations.

Pagodas were originally introduced from India with Buddhism and intended to house saintly scriptures and relics, but were often used to guard cities. Most have a central stairway rising through an uneven number of storeys. Some survive from the Tang dynasty – like the twin Small and Large Wild Goose pagodas in Xi'an. As evidence of days when marauding bandits were the norm, defensive walls can still be found around some settlements. A 14 kilometre Ming dynasty city wall still encircles the centre of Xi'an and smaller rural walled villages can still be found, even in Hong Kong. Efforts are being made to recover and renovate parts of old city walls in many Chinese cities including Beijing and Nanjing.

Extremes of climate in the north spawned solidly insulated brick walls, while sub-tropical southern temperatures encouraged the use of open eaves, internal courtyards and wooden lattice screens. In the mountains of Guizhou and Guangxi, the Dong and Miao minorities still build large cedar wood houses, as well as drum towers and wind-and-rain bridges without nails. In Yunnan, Lijiang boasts hundreds of wooden homes – and classic Dai minority houses, to the south in Xishuangbanna, are built on stilts. Patches of traditional wooden architecture survive in other cities including Kunming and Chengdu.

The remnants of past architectural triumphs are now, more often than not, dwarfed by adjoining modern day skyscrapers soaring into the sky. China has enthusiastically embraced space-age architecture as a statement of its future ambition. The works of the world's most renowned architects, including I. M. Pei, John Portman, Michael Graves, Norman Foster, Richard Rogers, Paul Andreu and Jean-Marie Charpentier, are integral features of China's new cityscapes. The Jinmao Building in Shanghai, designed by Skidmore, Owings and Merrill and the tallest in China, demonstrates how an international look can incorporate Oriental characteristics with dazzling results. Its cavernous atrium, part of the highest hotel in the world – spirals spectacularly upwards over 33 floors. However space-age buildings may become, though, the traditional Chinese consideration of feng shui generally remains very important.

On the east coast, remnants of European and Japanese colonial architecture give the former treaty ports a very distinctive look. Shanghai paraded styles of architecture from all over the world in the 1930s. On the Shanghai Bund, the Zhongshan Circle in Dalian and the Qingdao waterfront, steel-and-glass skyscrapers vividly offset the former neo-classical and art deco splendour.

The past and present collide in many Chinese cities imbued with a rich architectural heritage, as the demands of modernisation and property speculation take precedence. Whilst some of the grander buildings may escape the bulldozer, huge tracts of housing embodying the quintessential character of cities like Beijing and Shanghai have been razed. In Beijing the traditional 'siheyuan' or four-sided courtyard dwellings, set in mazes of small lanes, or 'hutongs,' are under threat of annihilation. In Shanghai the very distinctive 'shikumen' or stone-framed door dwellings, a British-style terrace with Chinese characteristics, face a similar fate.

a fresh canvas

Chinese contemporary art

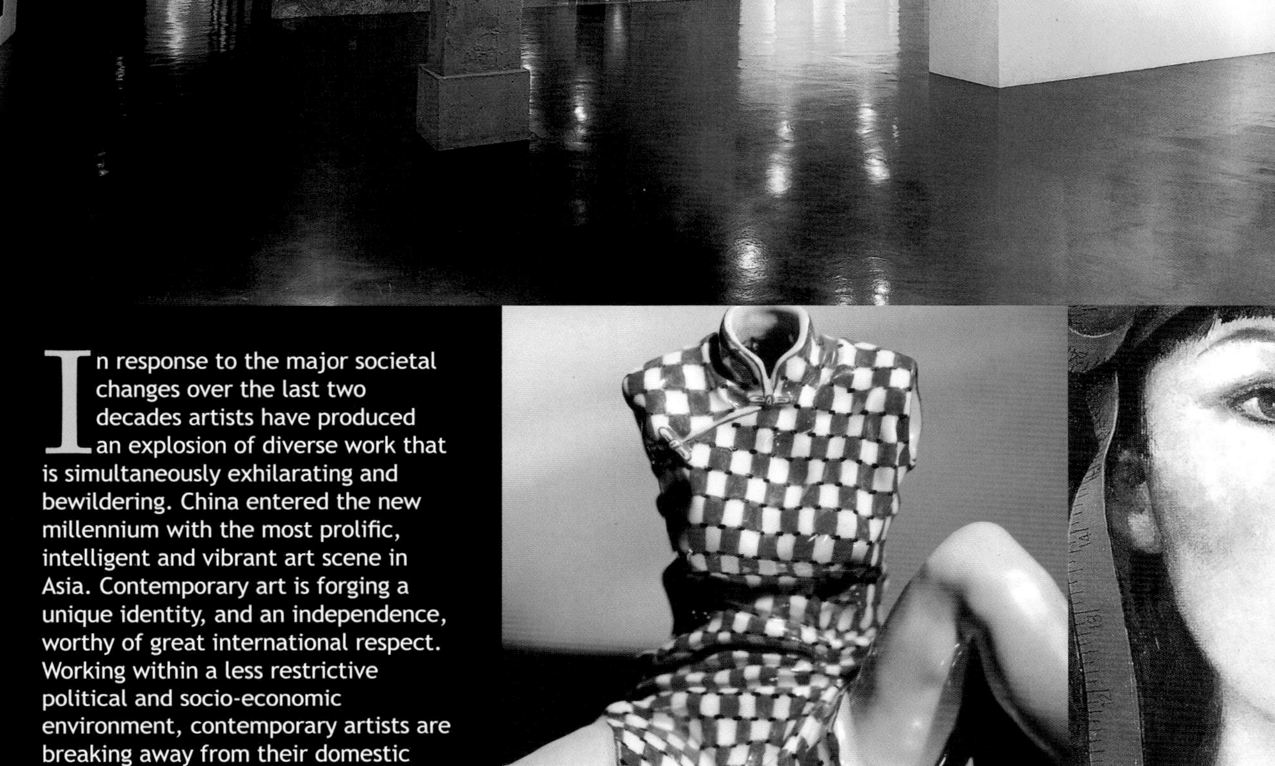

In response to the major societal changes over the last two decades artists have produced an explosion of diverse work that is simultaneously exhilarating and bewildering. China entered the new millennium with the most prolific, intelligent and vibrant art scene in Asia. Contemporary art is forging a unique identity, and an independence, worthy of great international respect. Working within a less restrictive political and socio-economic environment, contemporary artists are breaking away from their domestic political roots and their internationally designated pigeon-holes.

However, contemporary art is faced with the dilemmas of not only how art should be created and perceived, but also how it can be made accessible and sustainable. New privately run art galleries are mushrooming in many Chinese cities, and major art institutions and cultural centres are also under construction. At the grass roots, artists are designing restaurants, experimenting with architectural projects, staging performances, publishing monographs, and opening new media centres in a wide variety of locales across China.

This rapid expansion of the ways in which Chinese contemporary art can be viewed has resulted in a dynamic and diverse avant-garde art scene - and one reaching out to an ever-widening audience. No longer the domain of a select few, China's contemporary art scene is readily accessible to all and is rapidly becoming an integral part of an explosive cultural scene.

Yue Minjun

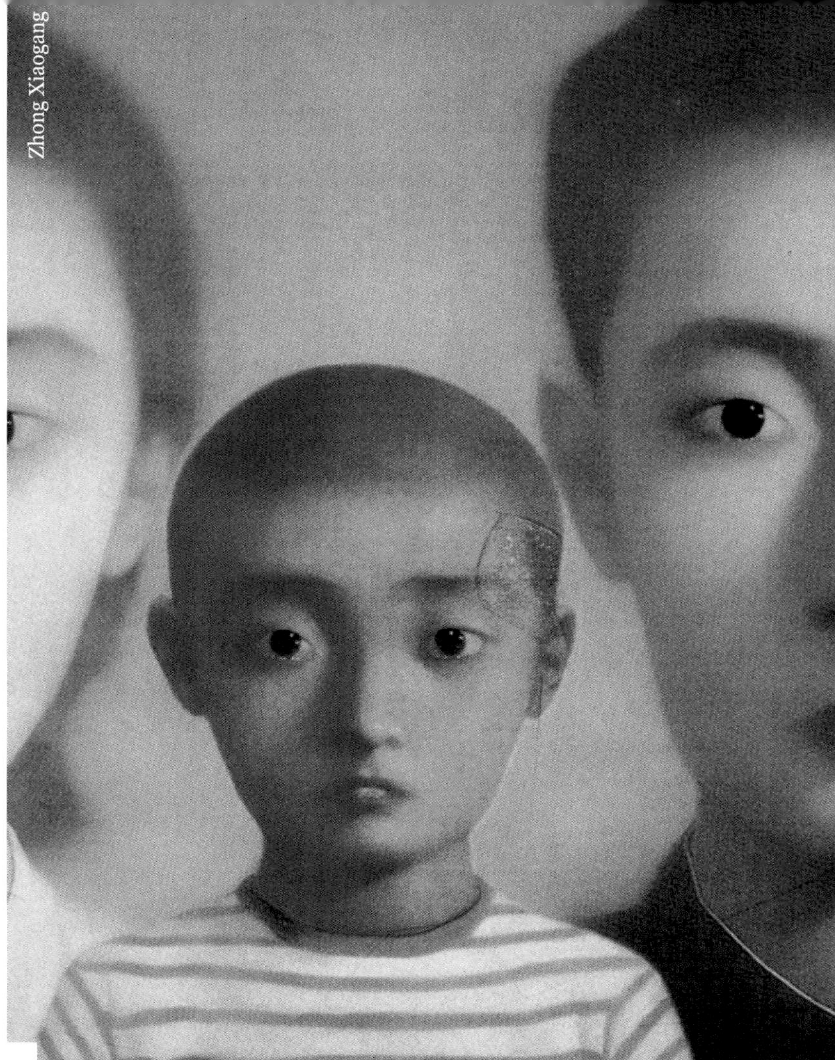

Zhong Xiaogang

Tsuitinyun

Zeng Hao

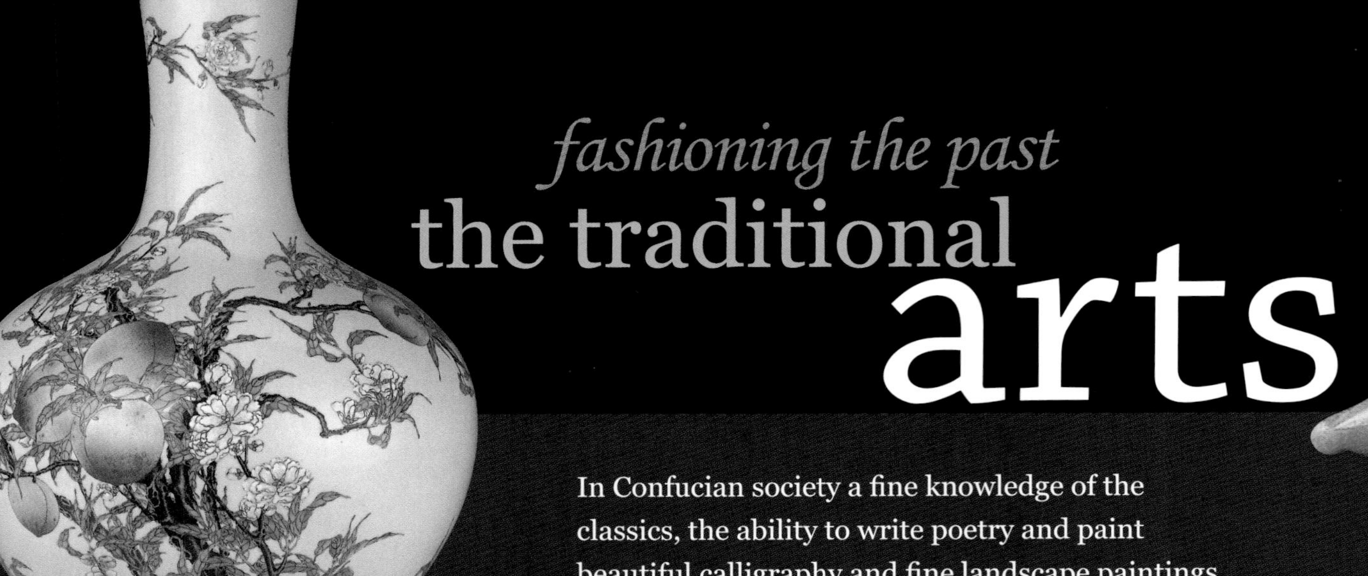

fashioning the past

the traditional arts

In Confucian society a fine knowledge of the classics, the ability to write poetry and paint beautiful calligraphy and fine landscape paintings were the aspirations of the literati and the fantasy of those born into more humble lives

More value is placed on jade than gold in Chinese culture. Some 7000 years ago craftsmen manufactured the first ritual objects out of the exquisite and exceptionally hard stone. The importance of jade not only derives from its intrinsic value, but also from associations with human virtues as it embodies qualities of beauty, hardness, durability and rareness. The ancient Chinese also believed that jade was a divine link between mortals and gods with an ability to repel evil spirits. Burial suits were carved of jade as a statement of permanence and preservation, whilst jade discs and sceptres were used in sacrificial ceremonies.

Depending on the amount of iron it contains; jade can be green, indigo, kingfisher blue, yellow, cinnabar red, blood red, black or white. Jadeite is a harder stone, generally appearing as a dark translucent or brilliant green. Originating in the Yellow River basin in Neolithic times, Chinese ceramics are another collectable art form. Porcelain is a Chinese creation and the secret of its making was not mastered in the West until the 18th century, 1,700 years after the Chinese invented it, with the most beautiful and valuable examples made in the Ming dynasty. Other prized ceramics are genuine Tang dynasty horses - rarely found outside the auction rooms. However, fine, inexpensive pieces of blue-and-white porcelain can be found in shops and markets throughout China.

Good quality Chinese antique furniture is classified by the wood used and period made - style has not changed considerably over the centuries. Confusingly, wood names are based on what a piece of timber looks like, rather than the tree it comes from. Wood originating in Hainan Island, called huanghuali, was used extensively throughout China in the Ming and early Qing dynasties. The wood was revered for its hardness and durability.

Similarly nanmu, a soft wood, was highly prized for its fine grain, its resistance to warping and sweet fragrance. The wood was also extensively used in imperial architecture. Serious collectors of classical furniture tend to prefer aesthetically pleasing simple designs in preference to more elaborate creations.

Kai-Yin Lo's collection at the Asian Civilisations Museum in Singapore is a case in point. She asserts that 'Classical furniture was made for the social elite and the prosperous classes, entailing prescribed refinement in construction, finishing and decoration, using expensive hardwoods often imported from Southeast Asia, and conforming to aristocratic standards of elegance and craftsmanship. Vernacular furniture, while observing the outlines of traditional forms and styles, was not subject to the strict creeds of literati taste, and therefore could afford greater flamboyance, vigour and a freedom that led to variations on classic lines or adherence to earlier forms.'

In the 17th century, snuff bottles were produced in quantity in China - representing Chinese art in miniature. As well as ivory and bamboo carving they embrace painting, calligraphy, enamelling, ceramics, glassware and many other crafts. Glass bottles that are painted on the inside are a much-prized variety of this art form.

Chinese paintings, traditional and modern are popular purchases for visitors. Traditional painting evolved from the written script over 2,000 years ago. In essence, lines dominate over colour, and imagination overrides technical detail. Landscapes are the most prevalent subjects and paintings of idyllic lofty mountain scenes are just as common as wallpaper.

Other popular and highly colourful art forms include woodblock prints, 'naive' paintings and minority handicrafts. Woodblock prints were widely used in the Tang dynasty when pictures of door gods were hung to ward off evil on the occasion of Chinese New Year. Naive, or farmers paintings, are a modern invention, developed in the 1950s and 1960s to record scenes of China's socialist modernisation and to promote mass culture. Countryside and folk legend subjects depicted in bold gouache colours are still produced.

An extravagant diversity of minority arts and crafts enlivens the China market-place. Bright appliqué work from Shaanxi, stunning cross-stitch embroideries form Yunnan, blue batiks from Guangxi, Buddhist thankas from Tibet and colorific Kazak carpets from Xinjiang are but a few expressions of China's ethnic vitality and richness.

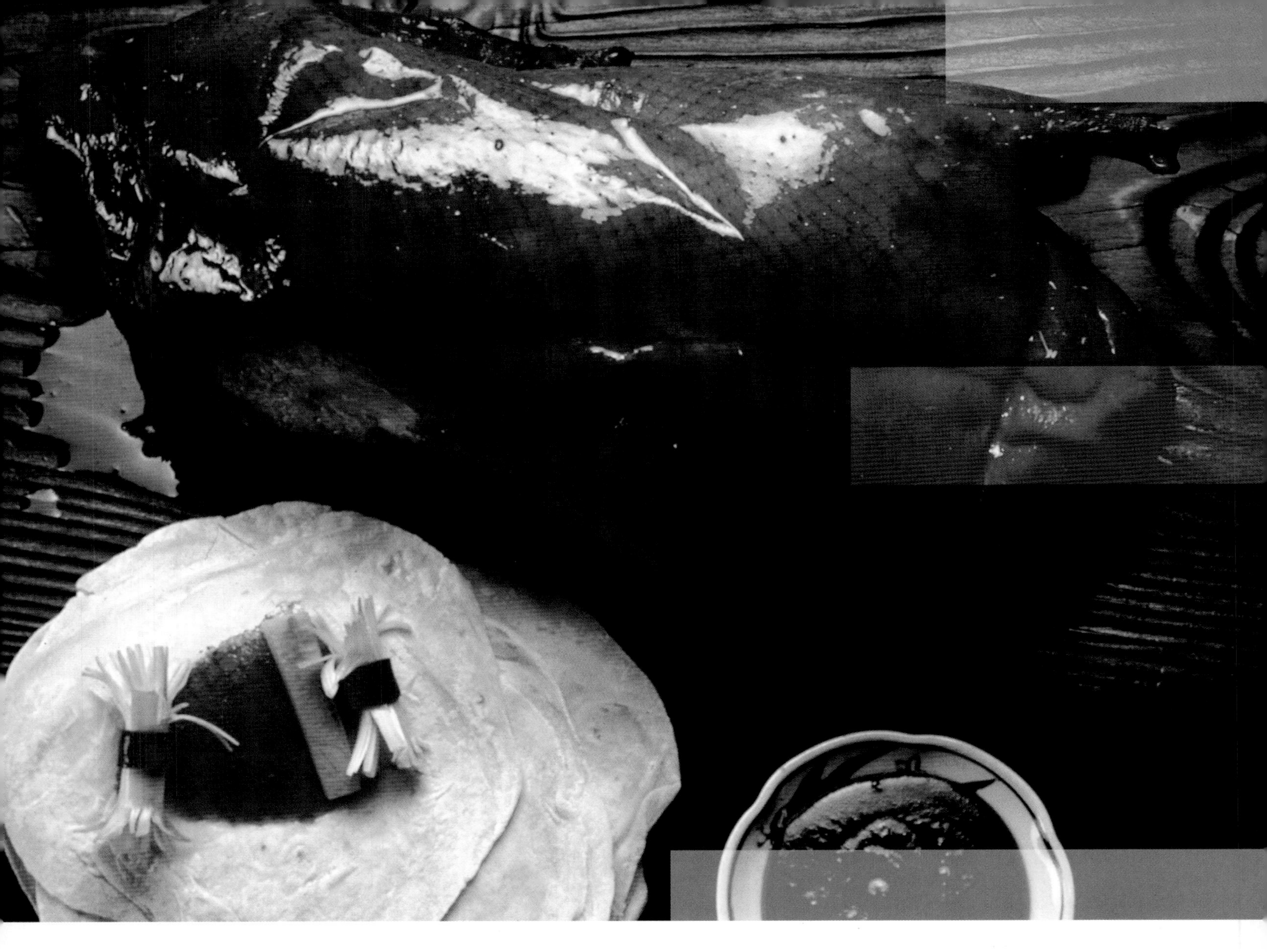

culinary colours

Food has always taken prime place in the lives of the Chinese and no more so than at festival times and times of celebration. During the Chinese New Year 'jiaozi,' meat and vegetable dumplings are consumed by the ton; 'zongzi,' pyramid-shaped cases of bamboo or reed leaves stuffed with glutinous rice are eaten during the Dragon Boat Festival, whilst 'moon cakes' are an indispensable element of Mid-Autumn festivities. Traditionally families would gather to share a large moon cake - putting a piece aside for absent members.

A basic division can be made between the diets to the north and south of the Yangtze River. Northerners eat more grains and wheat, whilst southerners eat more rice. It is convivially asserted that the southern diet produces people smaller in stature, but smarter in wit. Another basic division can be drawn around the four points of the compass - Beijing and Shandong to the north, Guangzhou to the south, Shanghai and Fujian to the east and Sichuan to the west. In reality many diverse regional cuisines have evolved and married to produce an astounding range of practices, styles and dishes.

CANTONESE CUISINE

Cast aside thoughts of the Cantonese food that one encounters in restaurants in foreign countries; food in Guangdong province in southeast China and Hong Kong bears little resemblance - sweet and sour sauces will generally only appear on tourist menus. Authentic Cantonese cuisine is known for subtle, refined sauces and seasonings that set off only the freshest quality ingredients, where mild flavouring most commonly consists of soy and oyster sauces, spring onions and ginger.

Nothing is more popular than seafood and live specimens, displayed in restaurant fish tanks, are especially sought after. If you are offered the fish cheek, regard this as an honour, this is a prized cut. Whole fish, subtly flavoured with ginger and spring onions, are steamed and glazed with hot oil and soy sauce, to accent their fresh flavour. When popular stir-fried dishes are well executed, they are said to have wok hai, literally 'air of the wok.' Soups, usually clear broths that have simmered for hours, are an essential part of a good meal and are often chosen for seasonal health enhancing qualities.

There is a well-known saying in China that the Cantonese eat just about everything with four legs, except tables and chairs, and everything that flies, except airplanes. Dog, snake and lizards are distinguished winter fare. Goose web and chicken's feet are favourites as are honey-glazed roast pigeon. All manner of dried seafood from sea slugs to scallops and shark's fin are gourmet delicacies with price tags to match. At a dim sum breakfast, brunch or lunch expect to enjoy a selection of small dumplings, buns and spring rolls, cakes and tarts, some steamed in little bamboo baskets, some fried.

SHANGHAI CUISINE

As Shanghai has long been regarded a cosmopolitan and sophisticated city, its cuisine has influenced the whole Yangtze River delta area. Shanghainese food is traditionally rich and oily, sweet and luscious. Velvety meat or fish dishes braised with soy sauce, sugar and a touch of vinegar are a speciality. The Shanghainese menu includes a number of 'drunken dishes' where food is marinated or cooked in Shaoxing wine - made from fermented glutinous rice.

A meal often starts with a selection of cold appetisers - at banquets these will be elaborately presented. Drunken chicken or duck's tongues will usually be there; so too will be jellyfish, shredded and tossed in a little sesame oil, as well as various pressed meats and spiced smoked fish. Mock goose or chicken, bean curd sheets rolled and braised to resemble poultry, are another favourite.

Eel is also a favourite, as are tiny crunchy freshwater shrimps - which may be plainly stir-fried or flavoured with tea. Freshwater fish is favoured and whole carp, fried or steamed, garnished with a sweet and sour sauce is also popular. In autumn and winter, dazha xie or 'hairy crabs' are a delicacy enjoyed for their rich roe. For earthy Shanghai favourites try the local dumplings - shengjian and Nanxiang xiaolong bao with a glass of warm fresh soy bean milk.

SICHUAN CUISINE

Sichuan cuisine is renowned for its fiery intensity. Numbing red Sichuan peppercorns and potent chillies flavour most dishes, and garlic and ginger are liberally thrown into the pot. Crispy rice cakes that crackle and pop are served with a rich, spicy sauce and hot and sour soup is exactly as its name suggests.

Freshwater fish is a favourite in the landlocked province. Often the whole fish is fried or steamed and smothered in a chilli sauce spiked with vinegar and hot bean paste. One of Sichuan's most exquisite dishes is smoked duck, first marinated in spices, including aniseed, cinnamon and pepper, then steamed and then smoked over camphor wood chips and tea. Sichuan's signature pork dish, pork with chilli sauce, also requires a double cooking process. The meat is steamed, sliced into slivers and then fried until almost crisp with a sauce of hot and sweet bean pastes.

Hot-pot provides sociable dining. The diner is served raw slices of meat, fish and vegetables that are self-cooked in a bubbling pork-based broth laced with chilli peppers that simmers away at your table.

BEIJING CUISINE

All of China has historically looked to Beijing for its lavish and refined cuisine. Beijing cooking is metropolitan in that it embraces flavours from throughout the kingdom, including Mongolia, Sichuan, the Yangtze River valley as well as from the Imperial kitchens of the Forbidden City. The Empress Dowager Ci Xi was renowned for having the best kitchen in China and insisted on one hundred dishes being served at each meal - enamouring the idea that Imperial food is for the eye as much as for the palette. The dainty confections and elaborate banquets from the Imperial Place can still be tasted today, and many of Beijing's top chefs are descendants of those working in the former Imperial kitchens. Top of the list for most visitors today is the exalted Beijing duck, baked in clay ovens over juniper and revered for its crispy, fragrant skin. It is served wrapped in small pancakes, with scallions and a luscious plum sauce coating.

Lunch is a simple affair for most Beijingers. Large bowls of noodles, flavoured with sesame oil or paste, and a dressing of meat and fresh coriander are consumed in quantity. Tasty dumplings, jiaozi and baozi, that come with an infinite blend of fillings are also a popular local favourite and are served boiled, steamed or fried. The influence of the Mongols is found in the abundance of lamb and wheat based dishes on offer. A perennial favourite, especially during the winter months, is shuang yang rou or mutton hot-pot. Finely sliced slithers of meat are quickly cooked in a simmering broth and dipped into a rich sesame-based sauce and the remaining soup is filled with noodles to finish the meal.

Other popular dishes in the capital turn originate from Sichuan. Chilli minced pork and beancurd (mapo bean doufu), as well as spiced chicken with peanuts (gongbao chicken) and fish-flavoured pork should all be sampled in Beijing as opposed to Sichuan itself. And for street food there are huge markets selling everything from meat filled bread patties, (lao bing), to baked sweet potatoes and spicy kebabs.

CHINESE WINE

A SIP OF HISTORY

In China, the practice of making and drinking wine goes back deep into the mists of time. It can be traced back at least 4000 years. But the definition needs a little clarification. The Chinese (pinyin) word that translates to 'wine' in English is 'jiu' but this covers all alcoholic beverages. There are two main types of 'wine': Chinese yellow liquor brewed from grain ('huangjiu') and distilled liquor ('baiju') made principally from rice. These libations remain extremely popular today, having been used through the centuries at feasts, festivals and for toasting relatives and forebears - and proving particularly effective as an inspiration for writers of classical prose and poetry. And for healing purposes, they developed snake wine - a 'medicinal concoction' that is brewed using snake bile.

CULTIVATING TASTES

The pleasures associated with drinking grape wines in China can be traced back to the Western Han dynasty over 2,000 years ago. The present day Xinjiang, in the west, was the centre of the wine industry until the end of the 19th century. Grape wines were not introduced into central China until the Tang dynasty when the Tai Emperor transplanted vines from Turfan to his imperial garden. However, with the introduction of Western vines, machinery and oak casks the focus moved east to Shandong. The ground-breaking Changyu Winery was set up at Yantai in 1892 and is still in business today.

China's modern wine making industry, with a drive to meet international production standards, was uncorked with the nod of reform in the early 1980s. The Sino-French Dynasty Winery Corporation was established in 1980 and others including the Changyu and Great Wall Wineries followed suit in developing palatable Western-style wines. French and Italian involvement with the wine industry has ensured a culpable supply of drinkable wines. The Huadong Chardonnay is regarded as one the finest wines - past fine vintages including the years of 1993 and 1996. The winery near Qingdao uses French vines and was initiated by Michael Perry in 1984. Palatably effervescent method champenoise, including the Imperial Court label, is also produced in the same region.

Foreign involvement with the industry is becoming widespread with successful recent ventures including the Grace Vineyards in Shanxi and the Sella & Mosca Winery in Qingdao. Some of China's most palatable and best value table wines are produced in the age-old centre of Xinjiang. With French assistance the Lou Lan Winery in Turfan has cultivated particularly good Cabernet and Sauvignon vintages. Traditional sweet red wines, with the best being characteristic of a Port or Madeira, are also widely available.

GRACED

A creeping revolution is taking place in Shanxi province, south of Beijing. Someone in China is making outstanding fine quality wine. The extravagant Grace Vineyard, which opened in 1997, is totally committed to the production of classic French-style wines. Hong Kong-based businessman C. K. Chan invested US$ seven million in building an authentic French-style chateau and importing specialist wine-making equipment. Their first vintage appeared in 2001. The vineyard is now producing 500,000 bottles of wine a year, ranging in quality from table wines to special-label reserve wines - Chardonnay, Dry Red, Cabernet Sauvignon, Cabernet Franc and Merlot. Their wines are now featured in top European restaurants and hotels as well as many closer to home including The Peninsula in Hong Kong and The Peninsula Palace in Beijing.

designs for the body

Today's China loves fine living. One rapidly emerging sign of China's burgeoning lust for luxury and indulgence is found in the growing frequency of grand openings for spas across the land. From north to south, east to west, some of the finest international spas have set up shop in China. And in a surprising turn, China is even exporting her own home-grown spa brand.

It's little surprise that luxury spas are finding a happy home here as the Chinese have long appreciated the connection between mind, body and health. In fact, the Chinese recognized the regenerative properties of massage over two thousand years ago, and have built it into their canon of traditional medicine practices.

So the difference between then and now isn't really in the idea but in the presentation. Massage 'then' was more like going for a relaxing check-up at the doctors. Massage 'now' is an entire experience where space and design play as much part as the treatment itself. Certainly, China still has plenty of examples of the old-fashioned utilitarian approach. Walk any direction in a Chinese city and you'll quickly find a reflexology (foot massage) centre. They're usually recognisable by the bright fluorescent lights and cigarette-smoking customers lounged in front of a loud TV. These don't have a whit of meditative ambiance though they work for a good, inexpensive, powerful treatment.

Not long ago the rather jarring reflexology shop was the only option. That's all changed. Now the world is looking to China as home to some of the most elegant full-service spa's on the planet.

CHINA'S BEST SPAS

DRAGONFLY

When Hong Kong-native Georgie Yam opened a Dragonfly spa in Oslo, Norway he also launched mainland China's first international spa brand. Yam started his 'boutique retreat' concept in Shanghai three years ago. Since then Dragonfly has expanded to one international and 11 domestic locations.

Despite the spreading of its wings Dragonfly Yam's basic design philosophy emphasises cosiness and intimacy. To that end he has located in historic homes, shopping centres, and housing compounds rather than five-star hotels. This way Dragonfly maintains a close connection to daily life and keeps prices in the realm of 'affordable indulgence.'

The concept is built on the idea of offering an urban retreat. With several street-front shops, clients merely need to step off the pavement to escape the daily fray. Once inside, receptionists offer tea from pottery cups while clients sink into the couch.

Each location starts from a minimalist base of dark wood, stone, and warm neutral hues of beige and brown. Then Yam builds on it, giving the retreats their own 'spirit' by using varied decorative elements drawn from China and Southeast Asia. Yam loves vintage pieces and each location makes use of old flowerpots for sinks. In the flagship retreat on Xinle Road in Shanghai's former French Concession, a large Chinese urn has been dressed up by a local contemporary artist. The top floor VIP room features century-old doors from Shanxi province. Each location also has a distinct water feature.

In Beijing Dragonfly's ramshackle courtyard structure, set in a small lane only a stones throw from the Forbidden City, the spirit of the old city blends with the essence of all that's decadent in the new world of spas. A lacquered tree adorned with hundreds of teardrop crystals glitters under the soft light of dozens of candles gently flickering around the room; a breeze catches swathes of chiffon that ripple like ocean waves.

Yam says his boldest design element is the manipulation of light. Dragonfly is indulgently dark. At Dragonfly in Shanghai a thick velvet curtain separates the reception and treatment areas. Behind the curtain, chatter, ringing phones, and traffic noise hushes. Flickering tea lights, soft recessed lighting, and a few select spotlights softly illuminate the foyer, but once inside the treatment rooms the light dims even more. Staff are prepared for the groping clutch of the momentarily blind and frequently have to wake a customer post-treatment.

Website: http://www.dragonfly.net.cn

LOTOS SPA

In Buddhist tradition, the lotus flower represents long life, health, and purity of mind and body - an apt symbol for a luxury spa.

Opened in September 2005, the Lotos Spa resides on the second floor of a modern high-rise apartment building in Shanghai near Xintiandi, the city's hippest retail and dining development. With hip comes traffic and right outside the building is the typical urban chaos.

But once past the water fountain from Thailand and up the copper-lined staircase, the space functions almost like a vault. An attendant skims out with a pot of tea, leaving clients to sip and unwind on the couch for a few minutes before their treatment. Using bubbling water, a flute-like soundtrack, warm lighting and lush foliage in the reception area, the designers have created utter tranquillity in a space that shares walls with a kid-filled swimming pool and a gym.

The long, narrow reception area gives way to a warren of treatment rooms - the focus of the Lotos design. Each room is unique and themed to a natural element or season: wind, stone, leaf, flower, star, spring, sun, moon, bamboo, and cloud. The lotus motif figures prominently of course, appearing in artwork and lamp shades. The decorative accents are an Asian blend favouring China and Bali. Purple, red, and orange accents harmonize in silk and velvet with wood and stone.

Spring, the spa's largest room, features a Jacuzzi tub for flower or essential oil baths. Wind is the VIP suite and expressly designed for couples with two massage beds and a separate shower room with rainforest showers.

Decorative details extend all the way to the rooms' ceilings. The Cloud room is draped in a wave-like canopy. The Stone room feels like the interior of a home with a timber ceiling and brick walls. Lamps, artwork, and arm chairs give the rooms a snug, private apartment-like feeling. Spa managers encourage clients to double their fun by booking their favourite treatment and their favourite room.

Address: 2F, West Tower. Somerset Grand Shanghai, 8 Jinan Road, Shanghai (86 21) 3308 0088

Sanya

MANDARA SPA

Sanya, mainland China's only tropical beach getaway, lounges at the country's southernmost tip. It's not as well known yet as its Southeast Asian competitors but boasts all the same soft sand and five-star luxuries - including a top international spa, Mandara.

Mandara Spa is a well-established international brand with locations in five-star hotels and resorts across the globe. At its heart is Asian culture and design but it differentiates itself from the pack by individualising each spa's décor and treatment menus. Central to the Mandara concept is including treatment traditions indigenous to each location.

At the Mandara Spa at the Sheraton Sanya Resort, tropical fruits feature in specialized treatments like the Papaya and Honey Facial, Coconut Milk and Flower Bath, and the Tropical Island Scrub.

The décor, designed by Bangkok's Bensley Design Studios, mixes stone, wood, and ceramic from Bali, Thailand, and China but the layout is strictly beach inspired. Taking a cue from the vast ocean views, everything about the spa is spacious. The experience starts at the entrance where two wooden doors stand open on either side of an oversized glass door. Inside, the 11 treatment rooms range from 50 to 70 square metres and feature oversized terrazzo bathtubs, steam showers, private changing areas, and day beds. Colours are light and granite sinks, cream-colored canvas canopies, bleached marble tiles, and antiqued aluminium light fixtures complete the look.

Address: Sheraton Sanya Resort, Yalong Bay, Sanya, Hainan (86 898) 8855 8855

The raw yet achingly beautiful mountain terrain of China's Yunnan province seems more appropriate to yak herders than luxury spas. But perched 3,200 metres up in a region so striking it has recently been dubbed 'Shangri-La' is a boutique hotel and spa deserving of comparison to James Hilton's Lost Horizons.

Purists alarmed by the encroachment of corporate-conceived luxury in the midst of such mythical beauty needn't be. Central to the Banyan Tree concept is capturing the essence of the place and their design company, Architrave Design and Planning, has artfully blended the entire Ringha facility into the natural landscape. The Banyan Tree Spa and hotel building consists of traditional farm lodges purchased from local villagers and reconstructed, requiring no new-cut timber - and walls were constructed of concrete hollow block and mud plaster to cut down on topsoil use.

The interiors also reflect the landscape and cultural location. The mountain air has a nip so warm elements feature strongly in the décor and treatments. Hot stone massage, warm ginger scrubs, tea baths, or an Indonesian boreh spice warming wrap in one of the five treatment rooms are complemented by Tibetan arts and crafts, tapestries, lots of rich wood, warm light, woven rugs, and red, orange, and brown hues. Afterwards, steam in the private shower or bath.

Address: Hong Po Village, Jian Tang Town, Yunnan Proviince (88 887) 828 8822

Ringha
BANYAN TREE

The Spa at Shangri-La
CHI

In keeping with the Shangri-La legend from which the hotel takes it name, Chi, The Spa captures a sense of the mystical in its interiors. From the flickering candle light and gossamer curtains in the reception area to the Himalayan art and accessories in the treatment rooms, Chi sighs with inner peace.

Chi, Shangri-La's new spa concept, opened in Bangkok in 2004 and in Shanghai in September 2005. The 11 treatment rooms are billed as the largest in Shanghai. The 'spa suites' occupy 66 square metres and feature their own sitting room, changing area, steam room, shower, and infinity-edged Jacuzzis. Tibetan metalwork accessories, woven carpets, and antiques contrast with the minimalist lines, warm beige tones, carved wood screens, and dashes of jewel-toned colour. The wafts of the fragrant oils and herbs mixed with scented candles complete the design's overall sensory effect.

The spa's serene, meditative design fuses with 'ancient healing traditions, philosophies and rituals from China and the Himalayas' foster inner and outer well-being.

Address: Pudong Shangri-La Hotel, Shanghai (86 21) 5877 1503

Beijing
ZEN SPA

Visitors might feel somewhat sceptical on entering the Zenspa complex - located on the outskirts of Beijing, beside a canal and down a dirty little alley - however once inside the amazing courtyard structure, all doubts will quickly melt away. The brainchild of a highly experienced Singaporean aromatherapy guru, Zenspa oozes class and sophistication. Like the treatment rooms, the waiting area is tastefully decked out in refurbished Chinese and Thai antiques with splashes of vibrant colour added courtesy of throw pillows and silky curtains. Soothing music drifts through candle lit corridors, and slippered staff in colourful kimonos dispense sweet tea and fruit. A series of private treatment rooms spoke off a main courtyard - a serene, white-pebbled area adorned with trickling water features. The treatments are definitely some of the more unusual that you'll find around China and include a range of divine baths, such as the Cleopatra, a fresh milk bath, or the Royal Thai with rose petals. Alternatively, soften your skin and release your inner Qi with a rose petal and gold leaf body scrub, followed by a green tea, yogurt or seaweed body wrap. Then relieve deep tissue aches and pains with the amazing, two hour, hot and cold stone therapy that will leave your limbs as limp as jelly. Even the canal outside smells much sweeter as you wander away from Zenspa.

Address: House 1, 8A Xiaowuji Road, Chaoyang District, Beijing (010) 8731 2530

THE CHINA CHARTER

China's topography has been compared to a huge staircase descending from west to east. The Tibet-Qinghai plateau, or roof of the world, averages more than 4,000 metres above sea-level. Melting snows and ice from the Himalayas are the source for the mighty Yangtze and Yellow Rivers. The second step is made up of the Inner Mongolia and Yunnan-Guizhou plateaux as well as the Tarim, Sichuan and Junggar basins.

To the north of the country plains around the capital become desert, ice-crowned peaks crowd Tibet to the east, palm-peppered white sand beaches populate the south, whilst to the east fertile undulating plains dissolve into the sea.

The densely populated plains of the Yangtze River and of northern and eastern China are areas of agricultural plenitude. The Yellow River, the birthplace of Chinese civilisation, partners the Yangtze, China's longest river, in a trail west to east. The incredible Grand Canal running from Beijing in the north to Hangzhou in the south once linked all the major rivers. With limited arable land the Chinese use every inch, squeezing rice terraces and hillside orchards and tea plantations between wheat fields and golden carpets of corn and canola seed.

The breadth of China's natural landscape is home to a wealth of wildlife, from cranes to tigers, elephants to pandas. Tropical flora and fauna thrive in the Yunnan rainforests whilst coniferous forests dominate in the north and northwest. Thousands of lakes and 18,000 kilometres of coastline are a major breeding ground for rare birds. Serious efforts are being made to strike a balance between man and nature and over 700 nature reserves have been opened across the country.

The variegated vegetation and turbulent topography bear witness to the wide range of climatic conditions that prevail. Northern winters can be extremely cold, dipping below -40°C. Beijing experiences crisp, dry winters with average temperatures around -5°C. During the summer temperatures can soar to around 40°C and are frequently accompanied by high humidity and torrential downpours. The northwest endures very dry conditions and temperatures can verge on 50°C in the summer and drop below -10°C in the coldest months. On the elevated Tibet-Qinghai plateau all the four seasons can be experienced in just one day!

Moving south the Yangtze River valley, including Shanghai, has semi-tropical conditions. Summers are long, hot and sticky whilst the winters are cold, yet comparatively short. The sub-tropical south experiences stultifying summers lasting from April to September and surprisingly cool with winters. The southwest can have pleasant conditions throughout the year and Kunming, capital of Yunnan province, is known as the city of Eternal Spring.

Despite its vastness the whole of China operates completely within one time zone - that is Beijing time - eight hours ahead of GMT and thirteen hours ahead of EST. However in practice the furthermost western Xinjiang Region operates a dual time system that is three hours behind Beijing. Time is just one example of the strong national governmental control that emanates from Beijing. At the apex of the governmental structure is the National People's Congress (NPC) which includes deputies elected by every region of China. The NPC meets annually during its 5 year elected term. Decisions are implemented through the permanent NPC Standing Committee. The NPC elects the head of state, currently President Hu Jintao and the head of the national government, or State Council, currently Premier Wen Jiabao. This basic model of government operates all the way down to the local level and is echoed in the nation's Party structure. The National Party Congress elects a Central Committee, the permanent executive, as well as the highly influential Central Committee Politburo headed by the party secretary general, currently Jia Qinglin.

"China is the world's third largest country, after Russia and Canada, with an area of almost 10 million square kilometres. Spanning some 5,200 kilometres from east to west and 5,500 kilometres from north to south it borders fifteen countries and territories"

Times Past

Flicking through the annals of time, China stands out as having sustained the longest continuous history of development of any civilisation in the world. It's a history that is fabulously intricate, seeped in sorrow, daggered by despots and elevated by aesthetic ardour. A unique feature of China's heritage is the pride and provenance of a people, who believed that their emperor was the son of heaven and that their land the centre of the universe. The Chinese still refer to their country as the Middle Kingdom

Around 7,000 years ago, Neolithic Chinese built settlements in the fertile Yellow and Wei River valleys and lived in well-ordered and protected farming communities. Whilst the four millennia before Christ were dogged with raging wars; important skills, including flood control, irrigation and silk and ceramic production were mastered. Around the time of the first verifiable dynasty, the Xia, writing was invented and the earliest cities were built. In the Zhou dynasty, when China was still a number of separate states, Confucianism and Daoism was born and literature, art and philosophy bloomed.

Around 220 BC a great leader emerged with the vision to unite the states. The first emperor of the Qin dynasty, Qin Shi Huang, presided over a short-lived, but epochal period of Chinese history. He linked defensive structures together to create the first Great Wall and built a palace in what was to become Chang'an - near today's Xi'an - where he also built a massive mausoleum, guarded with pits filled with thousands of life-like terracotta soldiers and horses. During the Han dynasty, Chang'an became a great capital and the crossroads of the Silk Road, the trade route for merchants from Europe, India and the Middle East. Buddhism was imported to China from India at this time, and a civil service based on Confucian principles was created, underpinned by the invention of paper.

This period of peaceful prosperity came to an end when the Han generals battled for power, dividing the empire once again. For more than 350 years, warring dynasties replaced each other in rapid succession, until the Sui dynasty was established. The ensuing Tang dynasty was China's Golden Age, when gunpowder and printing was invented. With the establishment of the Song dynasty in 960 the arts once again flourished, reaching their epitome in porcelain making and landscape painting. Confucianism was revitalised and the compass was invented. In 1279, the Song succumbed to the Mongol hordes of Kublai Khan who founded the Yuan dynasty. The invaders built a new capital, Dadu, on the site of present-day Beijing - whose splendours Marco Polo describes in his journals.

Less than a century later, Han Chinese rebels founded the Ming dynasty - China's equivalent to the Renaissance, an era of prosperity and territorial expansion when Chinese fleets explored trade routes to Arabia and Africa. Jesuit missionaries were officially honoured for their skills in astronomy, map-making and cannon casting. The Qing dynasty began under the enlightened rule of emperors Kangxi, Yongzheng and Qianlong, who kept a firm hold on the country while extending its boundaries.

AND IN THE END

Modern Chinese history is epitomised by an ugly succession of civil wars and foreign subordination. The Opium War of 1839-42 was a disastrous defeat for China, forcing the surrender of a string of treaty ports, including Shanghai and Tianjin, to foreign powers.

Soon to follow the Taiping Rebellion (1851-1864), a thwarted attempt to overthrow the Qing dynasty, resulted in a death toll upwards of twenty million. The Taipings were eventually defeated by the Qing army aided by foreign weaponry and training. The imperial system continued up until 1911, with the overthrow of the Qing Dynasty and the establishment of the Republic of China by Dr Sun Yat-sen and his Nationalist Party. Dr Sun Yat-sen is still revered today as the founder of modern China, but the powerful northern warlord Yuan Shikai quickly dissolved his influence and a new era of despotism was launched.

The period from the 1920s to the 1940s was stained by civil war between the Nationalists and Communists, foreign humiliation and the atrocities of Japanese encroachment and occupation. When the war ended in 1945, China was economically, emotionally and politically drained.

Modern China came into being on October 1st 1949, bringing stability and unity to a shattered nation. The glory years of the early 1950s ensconced an invigorating vitality as the capitalist machine was dismantled - only to be eroded by the solemn consequences of the Great Leap Forward in 1958. Millions perished as a result of inappropriate social, economic and land reforms. Combined with the split with the Soviet Union, Mao's supremacy was tested and the seeds of the Cultural Revolution were sown. President Nixon's opportune and historic visit in 1972 turned a handle on a door that was to be flung open to the world when Deng Xiaoping took power in 1978.

中国地大物博,山川绚丽多娇,气象万千。其景色之奇,文物之博,为世界各国所罕见,千百年来吸引了无数的诗人、画家、名人、学者、探险家、旅行家和国内外各种游人。他们有一些浪游四海,去饱览大好河山;有些登山涉水,去捕捉各地特有的风貌;有些寻幽访古,去窥测天地之奥秘;有些更寄情于山水,给山山水水以诗的幽香,使之更具魅力,更加令人陶醉。从冰雪皑皑的东北,到亚热带风光的琼崖,从帕米尔高原到锦绣江南,名山、大川、巨湖、林海、岩洞、古建筑……处处都有令人欣喜若狂的胜景。

中国是东方的一个大国,面积约960万平方公里,相当于亚洲面积的四分之一,全世界陆地总面积的十四分之一,差不多和欧洲相等,仅次于俄罗斯和加拿大,要比美国本土大200万平方公里。

幅员辽阔的中国从南到北,两端相距5500多公里,兼有热、温、寒三带的气候类型;从东到西,两端相离5200多公里,跨越四个时区。中国陆界总长20000多公里,有朝鲜、俄罗斯、蒙古、哈萨克斯坦、吉尔吉斯斯坦、塔吉克斯坦、阿富汗、巴基斯坦、印度、尼泊尔、锡金、不丹、缅甸、老挝、越南十五个邻国。中国海岸线长18000多公里,濒临渤海和黄海、东海、南海。全国一级行政局划分为二十三个省、五个自治区、四个直辖市(北京、上海、天津、重庆),下辖二千多个县级行政单位,包括特别行政区香港及澳门。

中国较小省区的浙江,就相当于比利时、荷兰、丹麦三个国家加起来那么大。就是过去号称西欧三大国的德国、法国、西班牙,它们的面积合起来,也不过和新疆维吾尔族自治区相仿。中国疆域南起北纬4°附近的曾母暗沙,北至漠河以北黑龙江主航道的中心线,相距5500公里;西自帕米尔高原,东到黑龙江和乌苏里江的主航道会合处,相距5200公里,时差达四个多小时。当你在中国东北部的乌苏里江畔看到旭日东升的时候,西部的帕米尔高原还是沉沉黑夜;当北国还是大雪弥漫的严寒季节,南方的海南岛已经开始春耕播种了,而最南端的曾母暗沙则因靠近赤道而终年炎热!

中国由于地理环境得天独厚,在地貌上还以“多而奇”为突出。“多”,又有种类多和数量多之分。在种类上,中国有巍巍的群山、浩浩的高原、茫茫的草原、坦荡的平原、浩瀚的沙漠、奔腾的河流、秀丽的湖泊、绵长的海岸、众多的岛屿、叮咚的泉水、飞泻的瀑布、壮丽的冰川、成群的火山、多样的气候、种类繁多的动植物,可谓“包罗万象”。从数量来看,可说是数不胜数。就山地而言,中国亦是一个多山的国家,山地面积几乎占了全国总面积的百分之三十三,丘陵约占全国总面积的百分之十。

中国不仅山地、高原、丘陵、盆地、平原五种地形一应俱全,而且各种地貌类型都发育得相当完美。例如华山和庐山的断层地貌,长江三峡和富春江的流水地貌,桂林山水和路南石林的岩溶地貌,陕北高原的黄土地貌,福建武夷山和粤北金鸡岭的丹霞地貌,湖南青岩山的砂岩峰林地貌,新疆罗布泊东北的雅丹地貌,长白山和台湾的火山地貌,喜马拉雅山和祁连山的冰川地貌,山东青岛和福建厦门的海岸地貌等等。

中国的气候复杂多样。强大的季候风给东部地区带来丰沛的雨水；向西北逐渐过渡为干旱的大陆性气候；西南部世界最高大的青藏高原形成了特殊的高原气候区，以空气稀薄、气温偏低、日照强烈为基本特点。全国从东到西、从南到北，有的地方长夏无冬，有的地方冬长无夏，有的地方四季分明，有的地方四时皆春。

由于地理纬度和海陆分布、海拔高度及地形等的不同，导致光、热、水资源数量及其组合的地区差异，从而形成不同的气候类型。中国由于地域辽阔，地形复杂，气候类型同样呈现"全"的特点，即具有多种多样的气候类型。从积温情况来看，东部地区自南而北有赤道带、热带、亚热带、暖温带、温带和寒带之分。

中国是世界上人口最多的国家。现在总人口已达十三亿，约占全世界人口总数的四分之一。全国人口中，百分之九十四是汉族，还有五十多个少数民族，共占总人口百分之六。在中国实行各民族一律平等的政策。

中国的行政区划分，既继承了历史传统，又经过新的变革。总的来说，大体上分为省、县、乡三级。其中的第一级，包括省、自治区、直辖市；第二级，包括县、自治县、市；第三级，包括乡、民族乡、镇。例外的情况是，在有自治州的地方，行政区划分为省、自治州、县、乡四级。遇到这种情况，省、自治区是第一级，自治州是第二级，县、自治县、市是第三级，乡、民族乡、镇是第四级。

历史悠久的中国，有文字可考的阶段，已近4000年。中国古代的重要发明—指南针、造纸术、火药、活字印刷对世界文明的发展有深远的影响。从种类上看，有雕刻、刺绣、陶瓷、景泰蓝、漆器、编织、地毯、抽纱、印染、料器、绢花、泥塑、玩具、文物复制等十几类。雕刻分为玉雕、牙雕、石雕、木刻、竹刻、果壳刻和泥塑。至于刺绣中的苏绣、湘绣、粤绣、蜀绣亦是中国历史上形成的四大名绣。"瓷都"景德镇的瓷器，达到"白如玉、薄如纸、明如镜、声如磬"的水平。"陶都"宜兴的紫砂陶器在国际上享有很高的声誉，所产的紫砂茶壶，造型独特，色泽浑厚，用它泡茶，色、香、味经久不变，素为中外游人所称道。山东淄博以滑石为主要原料生产的乳白瓷，河南洛阳的唐三彩，广东佛山生产的石湾瓷，潮州生产的枫溪瓷，有"北方瓷都"之称的唐山生产的白骨瓷，醴陵生产的釉下彩瓷等，都是中国各地传统的名牌陶瓷产品。景泰蓝是北京特有的传统工艺品，以紫铜作胎，焊上铜丝花纹，填上釉料，反复烧结而成，产品除瓶、盘、罐、盒外，还有茶具、酒具、灯具等，在国际市场上很受欢迎。漆器中的福州麻布脱胎漆器和木胎漆器、北京和扬州的雕填漆器、螺钿镶嵌和玉石镶嵌都很著名。安徽泾县的宣纸、浙江湖州的湖笔、安徽歙县的徽墨、广东肇庆的端砚，合称为"文房四宝"，以历史悠久、制作技艺精良而誉满中外。

中国还有许多农、畜产品的优良品种、传统的精美手工艺品和风味独特的土、特产品。中国的大熊猫、水杉、织锦、茅台酒、茶叶、北京烤鸭更赢得了全世界的赞誉。

中国的宗教主要有佛教、道教、伊斯兰教等多种，其中以佛教的影响最为深远。在佛教中有佛、菩萨、罗汉、护法神、力士之分，其中以佛的地位最高，菩萨其次。在佛教寺庙中，"大雄宝殿"是其主殿，"大雄"为佛的德号，是对释迦牟尼佛的尊称。大雄宝殿中居中的、踞于莲花宝座上的即为佛教创始人释迦牟尼佛，其左为药师佛，其右为阿弥陀佛。在菩萨中，中国以文殊、普贤、观音、地藏四大菩萨为尊，并都有其道场。相传文殊菩萨的道场在山西五台山，普贤菩萨的道场在四川峨眉山，观音菩萨的道场在浙江普陀山，地藏菩萨的道场在安徽九华山。上述四山为中国佛教四大圣山。

中国历史源远流长，有深厚的文化。自然界的神秘造就了中国人对鬼神的敬重，相信祈福、求子、求平安或富贵荣华。古人所创的儒、道、墨、法等教，加上外来的佛教、基督教及伊斯兰教，丰富了宗教哲学。至于外来宗教，应首推佛教。佛教于中国社会上和儒道两教鼎足而立。佛教从印度传入，一直发展，在中国的文化、艺术等方面有重大的影响。

中国现有七成人口的主要语言是普通话。普通话是一套采用罗马字组成的拼音系统，亦是中国的官方语言。另外，各地仍使用本地的方言。中国文字属方块字，总数约几万个，而常用的则有几千，现时中国广泛采用的是简体字。

THE CHINESE DYNASTIES

Xia (夏): c. 2200 - 1750 BC
Shang (商): c. 1750 - 1066 BC
Zhou (周): c. 1066 - 221 BC
Spring & Autumn Period (春秋): 770 - 476 BC
Warring States Period (战国): 475 - 221 BC
Qin (秦): 221 - 206 BC
Han (汉): 206 BC - 220 AD
Three Kingdoms Period (三国): 220 - 280
Jin (晋): 265 - 420
Northern & Southern Dynasties (南北朝): 420 - 581
Sui (隋): 581 - 618
Tang (唐): 618 - 907
Five Dynasties (五代十国): 907 - 960
Song (宋): 960 - 1279
Yuan (元): 1279 - 1368
Ming (明): 1368 - 1644
Qing (清): 1644 - 1911
Republic of China (中华民国): 1911 - 1949
People's Republic of China (中华人民共和国): 1949 -

IMPORTANT DATES IN MODERN CHINESE HISTORY

First Opium War	1839 - 42
Treaty of Nanking- Hong Kong ceded	1842
Taiping Rebellion	1851 - 64
Second Opium War	1856 - 60
The Sino-Japanese War	1894 - 95
The Boxer Uprising	1900
Overthrow of the Qing Dynasty	1911
Founding of the Chinese Communist Party	1921
Death of Sun Yat-sen	1925
Japanese occupation of Manchuria	1931
The Long March	1934 - 35
The Xi'an Incident	1936
The Rape of Nanking	1937
The Anti-Japanese War	1937 - 45
Proclamation of the People's Republic of China	1949
Korean War	1950 - 53
The Great Leap Forward	1958 - 60
The Cultural Revolution	1966 - 76
President Nixon visits Beijing	1972
Death of Mao Zedong	1976
Open Door Policy initiated	1978
Jiang Zemin elected President	1993
Death of Deng Xiaoping	1997
Return of Hong Kong	1997
Return of Macau	1999
China enters the WTO	2001
Hu Jintao elected President	2002
China puts a man in space	2003

THE CHINA COMPASS

THE ADMINISTRATIVE DIVISIONS

MUNICIPALITIES	POPULATION (millions - in 2000)	
Beijing	13.8	
Chongqing	30.9	
Shanghai	16.7	
Tianjin	10.0	
SPECIAL ADMINISTRATIVE REGIONS		
Hong Kong	6.7	
Macau	0.45	
PROVINCES	POPULATION	PROVINCIAL CAPITAL
Anhui	60.0	Hefei
Fujian	34.7	Fuzhou
Gansu	25.6	Lanzhou
Guangdong	86.4	Guangzhou
Guizhou	35.3	Guiyang
Hainan	7.9	Haikou
Hebei	67.4	Shijiazhuang
Heilongjiang	36.9	Harbin
Henan	92.6	Zhengzhou
Hubei	60.3	Wuhan
Hunan	64.4	Changsha
Jiangsu	74.4	Nanjing
Jiangxi	41.4	Nanchang
Jilin	27.3	Changchun
Liaoning	42.4	Shenyang
Qinghai	5.2	Xining
Shaanxi	36.1	Xi'an
Shandong	90.8	Jinan
Shanxi	33.0	Taiyuan
Sichuan	83.3	Chengdu
Taiwan	22.4	Taibei
Yunnan	42.9	Kunming
Zhejiang	46.8	Hangzhou
AUTONOMOUS REGIONS		
Guangxi Zhuang	44.9	Nanning
Inner Mongolia	23.8	Hohhot
Ningxia Hui	5.6	Yinchuan
Tibet	2.6	Lhasa
Xinjiang	19.3	Urumqi

All of China operates on Beijing Time - GMT +08:00

PUBLIC HOLIDAYS AND FESTIVALS

The Chinese Lunar Calendar is based on the cycles of the moon, and is constructed in a different fashion from that of the Western solar calendar. The beginning of the year falls somewhere between late January and early February. The Western calendar has been used since 1911, but the lunar calendar is still used for festive occasions. The Spring Festival is the most important and offers a week-long public holiday - the same duration as the Labour Day and National Day holidays.

PUBLIC HOLIDAYS	
New Year's Day	January 1
Spring Festival	1st day of Lunar Calendar:
(Chinese New Year)	January or February
International Labour Day	May 1
National Day	October 1

Major Festivals	
The Lantern Festival	15th day of 1st Lunar month: March
Children's Day	June 1
Dragon Boat Festival	5th day of 5th Lunar month: June
Mid-Autumn Festival	15th day of 8th Lunar month: Sept.

SELECTED WORLD HERITAGE SITES

1. The Great Wall
2. Mount Tai (Taishan)
3. Mausoleum of 1st Qin Emperor (Terracotta
4. army)
5. Chengde
6. Qufu - home of Confucius
7. Potala Palace and Jokhang Temple - Lhasa
8. Lushan National Park
9. Lijiang
10. Pingyao
11. Classical Suzhou Gardens
12. Yungang Grottoes
13. Mount Emei (Emeishan)
14. Peking Man Site

There are over thirty World Heritage sites in China. For full details go to www.unesco.org.

Beijing

From the glorious imperial architecture of the Forbidden City to the space-age design of the new National Theatre, China's capital is a city of striking cultural and visual contrasts

Twenty-first century Beijing has huge ambition. Clinging to an imperial past that continues to be the main spectacle for visitors, the capital is metamorphosing as a modern metropolis. It is a city of stark, and often, surreal contrasts. Beijing is simultaneously smart ly cosmopolitan and charmingly provincial, cutting-edge and gently timeless. Old pavilions, pagodas and the odd foreign church tower are dwarfed in stature by new high-rise temples, paying homage to commercialism and the needs of modern life.

With preparations well underway for the 2008 Olympics, over US$21 billion has been earmarked to establish Beijing as a leading world metropolis. Most of its fourteen million population, and especially the eight million that live in the urban area, will be affected in some way; many will be relocated and many more will have their routines interrupted as the face of the city undergoes major surgery.

Monumental new city landmarks are appearing as a statement of Beijing's hereditary importance. To the west of the city, the China Millennium Monument exudes a patriotic expression of architecture tinged with an art deco form - a grand plan displaying the glory of the past and the future aspirations of the capital. The monument is an artistic mélange of symbols pertaining to all aspects of China's long history of civilisation and a grand showplace for nationalistic spectacles.

Ambitious transportation, telecommunications and civil engineering projects are changing the face of the city. New ring roads have already been completed to ease traffic congestion and yet still more are under construction. At the same time, the city plans to more than double the extent of its metro system before the Games arrive. Sections of the city canal network have already been cleaned up and opened up for tourist pleasure cruises. Part of a light railway system, that will extend over 250 kilometres in the urban area by 2008, has been completed. A new high-speed rail link to Shanghai is to be constructed and Beijing's Capital airport is to be upgraded and an extra runway added. Some 14,000 environmentally friendly public buses are set to be discharged on to the city's wide avenues, flanked by new space-age commercial buildings. The envisioned digital city is to be greener than green, whilst the protection and conservation of cultural and historical sites is assured.

北京

21世纪的北京雄心勃勃。作为数朝古都，她依然是游客青睐之宝地，同时，她又是不断成长的现代特大都市。她优雅的国际风范和迷人的地域特征超越了时空的限制。

2008奥林匹克运动会的准备工作正在紧锣密鼓地进行着，已经划拨超过210亿美元的资金旨在把北京建成具有世界领先水平的大都市。

一些纪念碑式的城市地面标志正在出现，显示出北京在传承历史方面的自觉。在城西，中国千禧年纪念碑用艺术手法来表达强烈的爱国情感——壮观的计划展示出首都过去的光荣与对未来的热望。借助多种艺术形式，千禧年纪念碑反映了中国悠久文化与历史的各个方面，也集中体现了爱国主义的情怀。

首都宝物

北京这座城市的历史可以追溯到13世纪的忽必烈时代。城市布局经过精心构思和宏伟的系统规划，宽阔的长方形街区布置成棋盘型，奠定了这个城市今天的格局。

首都保留着往昔的许多神秘和浪漫，其街道名字就能唤起历史感。在北京的中心是紫禁城，是明清两代的皇宫。如今它是中国文明的象征之一，是宏伟的宫殿、庭院和花园的集大成者。

故宫的建造始于1406年。传说有100多万民工参与了辛苦的建造。到1420年，明王宫仍未完工。清王朝1644年建立后，对故宫进行了扩建和改建。今日之故宫占地72公顷，有800多座建筑物。周围环绕着10米高墙和护城河。600年后的今天，紫禁城依然被视为北京的中心。

天坛座落在宽阔平整的大花园中央，是老年人每

You would be glad to know that at the newly refurbished guest rooms and suites of the Hilton Beijing, every small detail has been conceived with one goal in mind: to make you feel at home, whether you're in Beijing for fun or business.

In the re-design of our new rooms, particular attention has been dedicated to the needs of the modern business traveler, ensuring a great combination of in-room facilities to make your stay more comfortable and productive. Executive rooms and suites have been fitted with espresso machines, home office systems, LCD screens in the bathroom and Bose music combos at your bedside table. Amidst all this, the Hilton's renowned personalized service is unchanged.

When you're next in Beijing, check – in to your space.

Hilton Beijing, 1 Dong Fang Road, North Dong Sanhuan Road, Chaoyang, Beijing 100027, China Tel: +86 (0)10 5865 5000 Fax: +86 (0)10 5865 5800 E-mail: beijing@hilton.com

Hilton Reservations Worldwide in China: 10 800 650 8091 / 10 800 265 8091

hilton.com

Capital Treasures

The origins of the modern city of Beijing can be traced back to the times of the Kublai Khan in the 13th century. He founded the Yuan dynasty and renamed the city as Dadu, or great capital.

But the city was better known in the West as Cambaluc - Marco Polo's transliteration of the Mongol name Khanbalig, or City of the Grand Khan. When the Mongols completed their conquest of the Southern Song in 1279 AD, Dadu became the capital of the whole of China for the first time and was grandly conceived and methodically planned, with broad rectangular blocks laid out in the checkerboard pattern that still characterises the city.

The capital retains plenty of Old World mystery and romance, with street names that conjure scenes from the history it has witnessed. At the heart of Beijing is the Forbidden City, first built as the palace of the Ming dynasty. Today, it stands as a symbol of Chinese civilisation, a complex of magnificent palaces, courtyards and gardens.

Many of Beijing's most important buildings are on a north-south meridian running from the Drum and Bell Towers in the north, through the Forbidden City to Mao Zedong's Mausoleum and the elaborate Temple of Heaven in the south. The Drum and Bell Towers date back to 1272 and originally signalled dawn and dusk, as well as daytime hours.

No less than twenty-four Ming and Qing monarchs ruled the Celestial Empire from within the vermilion walls of the Forbidden City. Pu Yi, the fabled last emperor, left the palace in 1924. Now nearly 600 years old, this ancient bastion of mandarin authority has become a vast and splendid museum that should top the itinerary of any visitor to Beijing. The grand pavilions and spacious courtyards of the Palace Museum were the setting for Bernardo Bertolucci's Oscar-winning film The Last Emperor, shot largely within its walls. But even his masterful cinematography fails to quite capture the magnificence and enormity of the palace.

Construction of the palace began in 1406. Untold thousands of labourers, some legends claim as many as a million, toiled to build it. The Ming imperial palace was not completed until 1420. It was then expanded under the Qing Dynasty, which came to power in 1644, covering an area of 72 hectares, with over 800 buildings. Today a 10-metre high wall and a moat encircle the palace. Even after six centuries, the Forbidden City is still regarded as the real centre of Beijing.

Just to the south, the vast expanse of Tiananmen Square is the ultimate symbol of New China.
>>>

日锻炼和练习戏剧的好地方。在1420年建成的时候，它可是皇帝祈求丰收的圣地，气势恢宏的三层大理石基座上，三重飞檐圆润碧绿，镀金的顶部流光溢彩。

在城西的中央地带，点缀着好些湖泊，统称为什刹海。什刹海在紫禁城往西，其中的北海和中南海是往昔朝臣们夏日游乐之处。在中南海里有一块围墙环绕的神秘地方，那就是中共中央和国务院所在地。该地区俗称为“中南海”。

大多数来北京的游客最盼望的还是登长城。长城有两千多年的历史，现存的主体建于14和15世纪。秦始皇始建的长城只是夯实的土墙，已经不复存在。城外约65公里处重修后的八达岭是游客们去得最多的地方。附近的居庸关最近也已开放。再往东走，穆天峪和司马台最为壮观，与河北交界处的长城更是险峻蜿蜒。

北京郊区的十三陵附近丘陵苍翠，气象万千。穿过两侧排列着柳树、石人、石雕动物的甬道，就是十三陵。明代十六位帝王有十三位葬于此，其中的宝物在长陵精致的木制展厅中供游人观赏。

繁华的商业

百货商店和国际购物中心如雨后春笋般兴起，满足着富裕起来的人们的购物需求。两大购物街王府井和西单的店铺最为集中，像八佰伴和百盛这样的跨国商号随处可见。宣武门的庄胜崇光百货商店的面积有80,000平方米，居北京之首，生意非常兴隆。

前门座落在热闹的胡同和四合院之间，是非常具有地方特色的购物点。大栅栏街是北京最具地方风情的购物街。20世纪初，西方人称之为“丝街”。欧式建筑与丝绸、手工艺品、茶叶和食品商店相映成趣。有名的店铺有：创立于1893年的瑞蚨祥绸布店、创立于1893年的内联升鞋店、1530年创立的六必居酱菜店和1669创立的同仁堂药店。

附近的琉璃厂文化街有200多年的历史，其独特的艺术品、古玩店和书店，都泛着北京的悠悠古韵。

美味餐馆和娱乐中心

1949年以前，北京就有上万家餐馆，是无可争议的中国餐饮文化之都。如今，随着新的饮食文化的兴起，您走着每隔几分钟就有不错的饭店。西式快餐店、亚洲快餐店，包括日式面条、韩国烧烤、少数民族饭店在商业中心随处可见。快餐文化恰好迎合了快节奏、高收入的年轻一代的需要。在西单和王府井的人行道上，也有露天的餐馆，提供中餐和西餐点心。

北京烤鸭店却保持着不变的风格，依然令顾客流连忘返。前门的全聚德烤鸭店是众多食客争相品尝美味佳肴的地方。另一种四季皆宜的食品是涮羊肉。夹起滑嫩的羊肉片，放入煮沸的汤中片刻即熟，然后蘸上芝麻酱。

北京近年来最引人注目的餐饮成就是出现了不少提供亚洲各国风味的高档餐馆。四合院，设在一座被修缮的古典建筑中，俯瞰紫禁城的宫墙，提供融合东西方风味的美食和雪茄。装潢考究的紫云轩有中国当代最好的美食。

北京是中国现代音乐的摇篮。从1986年起就在国外演出的Wham乐团和中国摇滚乐先驱崔健，都来自北京。叛逆性的地下音乐在一些小酒吧和俱乐部里仍然存在。嘈杂的中式打击乐和呐喊、大胆的装饰、简陋的陈设混合着传统的卡拉OK，千奇百怪。时尚的'The Club'俱乐部播放着最时髦的电子舞曲，Great Wall of China却是一个可以整夜狂吼的地方。其他的有名气的酒吧还有：橙，威克斯，Kiss SuperCity和FM酒吧俱乐部。

东城有两大酒吧区。朝阳公园区的饭店酒吧新装艳抹，如迪斯尼乐园一样，其中有独特的英国人经营的鹅和鸭酒吧以及Schillers 3。近来，工人体育馆附近也涌现出不少时尚的电子酒吧和俱乐部。风景如画的后海岸旁，有最时髦的酒吧。北城大山子的Factory 798已经成为北京时尚艺术的领地。

When you need to stay a little bit longer...

北京棕榈泉万豪行政公寓

Building No.11 & 8, No.8 Chaoyang Park South Road,
Chaoyang District, Beijing, P.R.C. 100026
中国北京市朝阳区朝阳公园南路8号，11号楼及8号楼 邮编：100026

Marriott, A Name You Can Trust

Tel: (86 10) 8595 7777

Fax: (86 10) 8595 7666

YOU ARE OUR FIRST PRIORITY.

An elegantly designed luxury hotel is now ready to take care of your every need. High profile business visit, group meetings, official delegations, or simply a weekend retreat with your loved one.

Your spacious room... equipped with a 2-line phone, high-speed internet connection, well equipped bathroom and special amenities will make your stay a memorable one... you'll want to come back for more...

Going above and beyond.
IT'S A MARRIOTT WAY.SM

Beijing Marriott Hotel West
No. 98 Xishanhuan North Road,
Haidian District, 100037 Beijing,
P.R. China
Tel: (8610) 6872 6699
Fax: (8610) 6872 7302
E-mail: bc@bjmarriott.com

© 2005 Marriott International, Inc.

中苑宾馆
CENTRAL GARDEN HOTEL

The famous 4-star Central Garden Hotel is conveniently located in the northwest of downtown Beijing, within walking distance to Beijing Exhibition Center、National Library、the famous Zhongguancun High-tech Electric Street、government bodies、a great numbers of universities, and 15 minutes to the Summer Palace,45 minutes from Beijing International Airport by car .

Amidst 50 acres of traditional Chinese garden grounds, the hotel has one tower、three villas、and the recreation club. It comprises 415 elegantly appointed guestrooms and suites、one 760 square meters function room、and other 12 different size meeting rooms, which have been host to some of the most premier events attended by VIPs and the heads of state around the world.

Fittingly Mao's proclamation of the People's Republic of China was made overlooking the square from where eons of imperial edicts had been handed down. Expanded in 1958 and conjoined by the Great Hall of the People and the Museum of Chinese History, the square is also the resting place for the Great Helmsman. Mao's Mausoleum was built over a 10-month period following his death in 1976.

Tiananmen has witnessed momentous political demonstrations, including the May 4th Movement of 1919, which led to the founding of the Communist Party and the April 5th Movement of 1976 which led to the downfall of the Gang of Four. To the south of the square the two gate towers of Qianmen (Front Gate) were derived of function when the adjoining city wall was demolished in the 1950s.

The trail of the city wall is now a major artery for traffic, occupied by the Second Ring Road above, and an underground loop below. Already remnants of the sturdy city wall are resurfacing and being restored as unforgiving reminders of Beijing's imperial past. A few gate and watchtowers remain, such as at Dongbianmen, which now houses the impressive Red Gate Art Gallery. In this area, tower blocks have been razed and gardens planted around the wall exposing a new face of civic amenity.

The Temple of Heaven, nestling in a massive manicured park, is where elders assemble to perform ritual exercises and impromptu opera. Originally built in 1420 for the emperor to pray for good harvests, all the present buildings are of the later Qing dynasty. The main building, the Hall of Prayer for Good Harvests, is regarded as the epitome of sacred Chinese architecture and has been adopted as a popular symbol of Beijing. Arising from a marvellous three-tiered terrace marble base the circular blue triple-roofed construction is topped in gold.

Beijing is home to countless historical monuments, both within the confines of the former city wall, and beyond into the picturesque mountainous countryside.

Within the city, other notable sights include the Lama Temple and Beihai Park. The Lama Temple is an isle of Tibetan Buddhist tranquillity in the heart of Beijing. Originally the home of the Emperor Yongzheng - it was converted into a lamasery for Mongol and Tibetan priests in 1744. The trees and the shadows they cast on the tiles echo Buddhist truths about the ephemeral nature of existence and the saffron walls are brilliant beneath blue skies. The authentic artwork inside the halls is breathtaking. Amidst its gold-roofed temples and Tibetan thanka tapestries sits an extraordinary 26-metre high standing Buddha carved from a single piece of sandalwood.

In the west central part of the city, there are a series of lakes collectively known as the Shichahai - 'The Seas of the Various Buddhist Temples.' The lakes were constructed during the Ming Dynasty and are fed by canals bringing water from the Western Hills. Legend has it that the Mongols, never having seen lakes so large, called them 'seas,' and the name stuck. The lakes directly to the west of the Forbidden City - the North, Middle and South Seas, were once the summer pleasure-gardens of courtiers. In the walled sanctity around the Middle and South Seas, Zhongnanhai, are to be found the headquarters of the Communist Party Central Committee and the State Council.

The North Sea, or Beihai, is now open to the public as a park. Originally built as a palace for Kublai Khan in the 13th century, it is laid out around a beautiful lake and hosts an array of architectural achievements from over the centuries. The palace collapsed in the 16th century after an earthquake, and in 1651 was replaced by a white Dagoba. To the north of the park are found magnificent gardens, wooden halls and the largest remaining nine-dragon screen in China. Beihai has become a popular place to promenade, relax, eat and take boat rides.

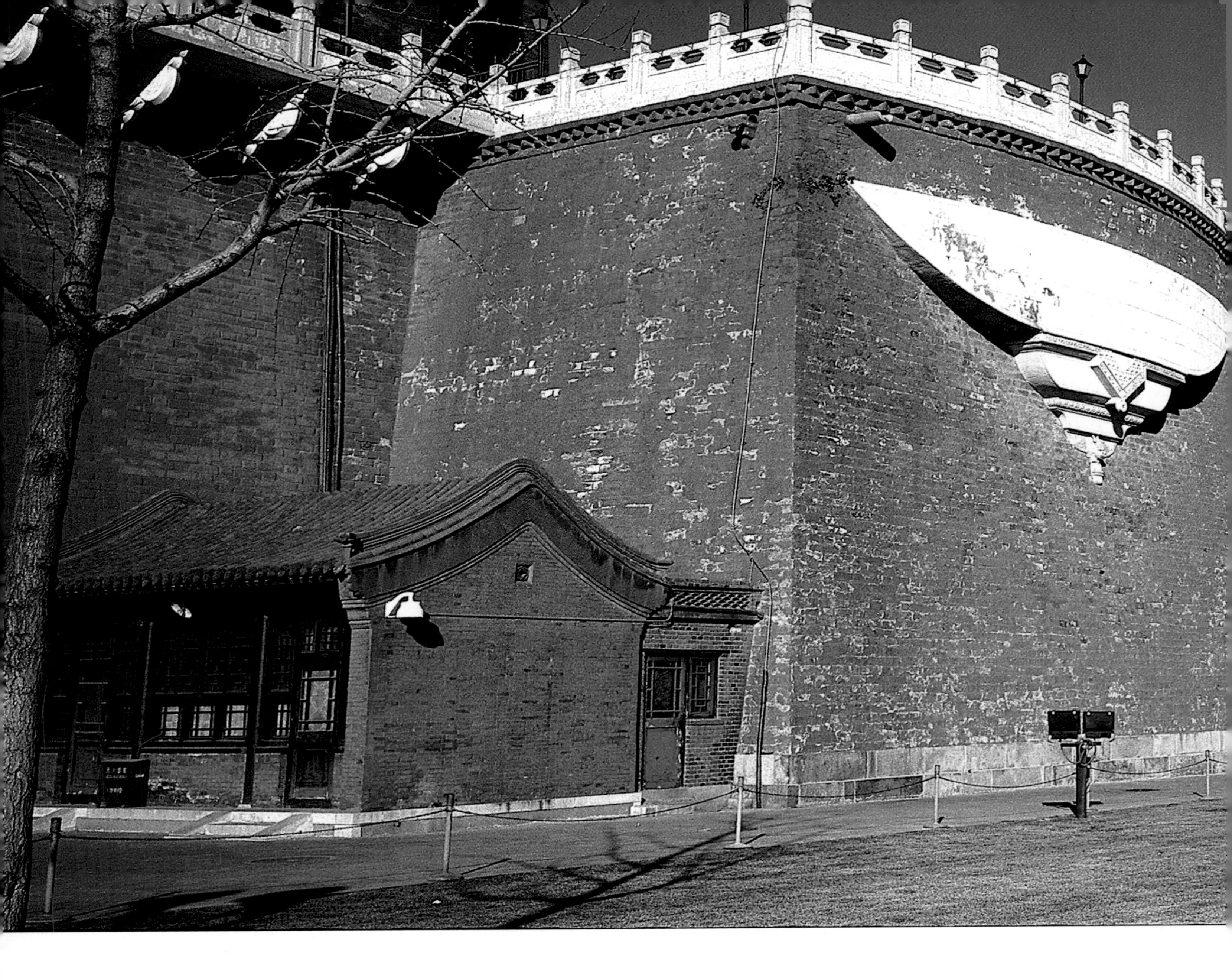

The Beijing Municipal area extends well beyond the city, occupying a land area roughly the size of Kuwait or Belgium, and is penetrated by many historical treasures. The sprawling Summer Palace, a beautiful retreat in the northwest suburbs, is the largest and most splendid of all imperial gardens. Emperor Qianlong laid them out around the shimmering Kunming Lake in 1750 for his mother's 60th birthday. Favoured by the Dowager Empress Cixi, the palace was rebuilt during the late 19th and early 20th centuries. The complex includes temples, courtyard residences, an opera theatre, graceful bridges as well as the revered Long Corridor, richly decorated with imaginary and historical scenes.

The highlight for most visitors to Beijing is, of course, the Great Wall. With a history of over 2,000 years, the most significant construction took place in the 14th and 15th centuries. The original wall, built by Qin Shi Huang, was in fact little more than a rammed earthen wall and none of it survives. The great masonry wall with its parapets and signal towers was built during the Ming Dynasty (1368-1644) and many sections have been reconstructed since 1949. Most of the Wall is about 8-metres high and 6-metres wide at the top. It includes about 25,000 towers, spaced two arrow-shots apart so that the guards could defend its entire length, and extends, though not continuously, from the Yellow Sea to the Gobi Desert.

Polished with recent restoration, Badaling, some 65 kilometres outside the city, is the most accessible and most visited section. Nearby, the Juyongguan section is the most recently opened. The most impressive sections of the wall are to be found further east at Mutianyu and Simatai. Just across the border with neighbouring Hebei province rests a steep and snake-like belt of the wall at Jinshanling.

Bulbous earth mounds, marking the resting places of emperors, notate the melodic Beijing countryside. The Ming Tomb area is entered through a lyrical willow-lined avenue of stone animals and statues of government officials. Thirteen of the sixteen Ming emperors are entombed beyond.

Mazes of Markets and Malls

Beijing offers an almost infinite variety of shopping experiences. Gone are the days when quality items could only be found in the Friendship Store. The Friendship Stores, set up in the 1950s for Soviet and East European patrons, remained closed to ordinary Chinese up until the early 1990s. The original Friendship Store in Jianguomenwai, although a little pricey and with customers thin on the ground, remains a convenient one-stop shop for purchases and souvenirs. Anything from musical instruments, books, fabrics, garments, Chinese medicine to foreign newspapers and silk carpets are stashed inside.

Department stores and international shopping malls catering to the enriched generation are mushrooming around the city. Whilst the two main shopping streets of Wangfujing and Xidan offer the highest concentration of large stores and malls, international names like Yaohan and Parkson are appearing citywide. Future ambitions are realised in the

Beijing Oriental Plaza, just minutes away from Tiananmen Square, and Asia's largest indoor shopping complex, the Golden Resources Shopping Mall in the west of town. Beijing's prestigious hotels including the China World, the Kempinski and the Peninsula Palace offer fine shopping opportunities for luxury goods, apparel and curios.

Set amidst an area crowded with old lanes and dilapidated courtyard houses, the Qianmen area is the most atmospheric and interesting shopping destination. Dashilanr is the city's most colourfully ambient shopping street, and is one of the 300 areas targeted by the government to be restored to its original glory before the Olympic Games. Known as 'Silk Street' by foreigners in the early 1900s, many colonial facades front emporia flouting silk, handicrafts, tea and foodstuffs amongst other enticements.

Antique and clothes markets abound in the capital. The long established and famed Silk Market was uprooted from its location in 2004 and is now part of a huge new, multi-story market. For those in search of antiques or curios there is no need to look further than the amazing Panjiayuan market to the east of the Third Ring Road. Busiest at weekends almost every imaginable Chinese antique, collectable and souvenir can be found there. It's a fun place to visit and haggle over a vase that could have been made last week or a hundred years ago. The nearby Beijing Curio City houses a vast array of arts and crafts items including jade and furniture. The Hongqiao, or Pearl Market, just east of the Temple of Heaven, is another great place for curios, as well as pearls. The quality and price of the precious seeds ascend with each flight of steps inside.

Ten Thousand Gourmet Palaces & Entertainment Halls

In the days before 1949 Beijing was the undisputed food capital of China - the city of ten thousand restaurants. Just 15 years ago few restaurants were left and most closed by 5.30 in the afternoon. However, in the days since, a new culinary revolution has swept across the capital and, just like the old days, you never have to walk more than a few minutes to find somewhere to feast. Foreign fast-food outlets are commonplace targets for a swelling army of appetite conscious customers. Asian fast food outlets, including Japanese noodle and Korean BBQ restaurants and multi-ethnic food courts in shopping centres, have also proliferated. Fast food, on-the-go, is complementing the change of lifestyle and rising income levels of an ever growing corps of young urbanites. On the major shopping streets of Xidan and Wangfujing, the widened pavements have surrendered space to open-air umbrella festooned eateries supplying both Western and Chinese snacks.

Beijing's hearty traditional fare is also enjoying a monumental revival. Increasingly popular 'old Beijing' themed restaurants with staff garbed in Ming dynasty costume, clutching copper kettles with exaggerated spouts, vociferously chant greetings to stunned arrivals. Meaty fresh noodles with

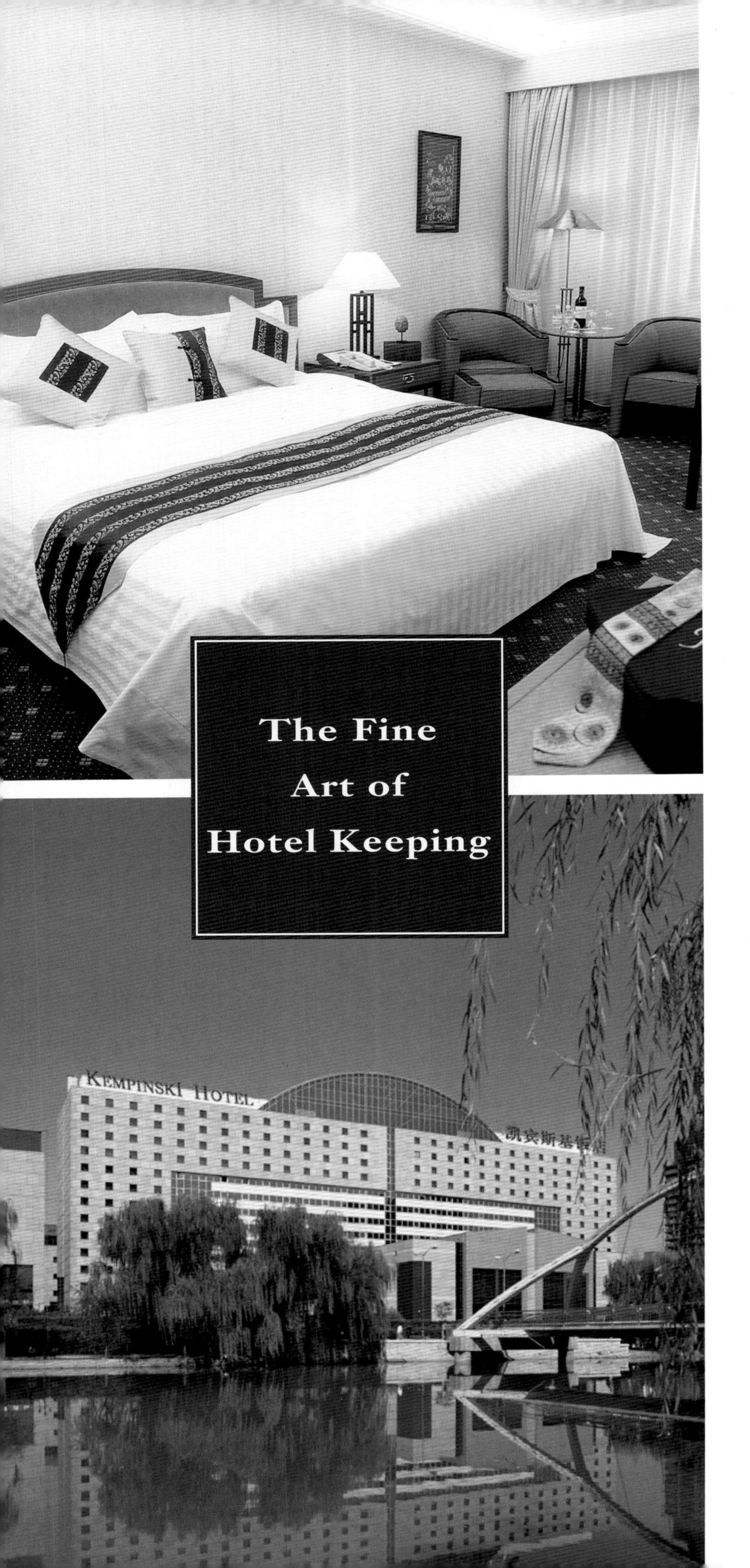

Our aim is always
to raise the expectations
of our most
valuable guests.
And then to meet them.

Kempinski Hotel
Beijing Lufthansa Center
CHINA
凯 宾 斯 基 饭 店
北京燕莎中心有限公司

No. 50, Liangmaqiao Road,
Chaoyang District, Beijing 100016 P.R.C.
Tel: (86-10) 6465 3388
Fax: (86-10) 6465 3366
E- mail: reservations.khblc@kempinski.com
Website: www.kempinski-beijing.com
Toll Free: Northern China: 10800 650 0362
Southern China: 10800 265 0363

A member of The Leading Hotels of the World®
global hotel alliance

Kempinski
HOTELIERS SINCE 1897

Loong Palace Hotel & Resort is the first international premium hotel in Changping District. The hotel is situated in the rapidly developed northern area of Beijing, conveniently located just 25 minutes drive from the Capital International Airport and within easy access to many well-known sightseeing spots, such as Great Wall, Summer Palace and Ming Tombs. The hotel is close to the hi-tech district of Zhongguancun, China's Silicon Valley, also within easy reach to the city center and key shopping areas by the city light rail.

Loong Palace Hotel & Resort has 593 luxurious furnished guest rooms and suites, with five restaurants, providing guests an array of international cuisine including Cantonese, Sichuan, Italian and Japanese.

Meeting facilities include a Grand Ballroom which can hold 1200pax and another 14 well-furnished function rooms, served by an efficient and competent Conference Services Department which meeting planners will appreciate.There are extensive recreational facilities, so guests can fully relax and enjoy themselves after a long working day.

Loong Palace Hotel & Resort
Add: Huilongguan, Chanpging District,
Beijing 102208, P. R. China
Tel: 8610-8079 9988
Fax: 8610-8079 8866
E-mail: loongpalace@loongpalace.com
Website: www.loongpalacehotel.com

luscious and intensely flavourful sauces, as well as stuffed dumplings, or jiaozi, are the local addictions. To the west of Wangfujing, behind the Beijing Hotel, a charming old food street has been re-created. Nearby, the astoundingly atmospheric night food market parades an incomparable display of affable snacks and esoteric delicacies including insects and sparrows on sticks.

Confronted with almost limitless choice, constantly changing and evolving tastes and fashions, it is no surprise that restaurants come and go at a frightening pace. However, Beijing duck restaurants have attained immutability and no visitor should leave without gorging on a duck banquet. The original Quan Ju De restaurant at Qianmen is where most visitors head for their first taste of this succulent delicacy. Another perennial favourite, especially during the winter months, is mutton hot-pot. One of Beijing's most impressive culinary achievements in recent years has been the establishment of up-market restaurants serving pan-Asian food. The CourtYard Gallery and Restaurant, located in a beautifully restored traditional house overlooking the walls of the Forbidden City serves Asian influenced western food and cigars - and the tastefully decorated Green T. House offers the best of China's contemporary cuisine.

Beijing is the cradle of China's contemporary music scene. The city hosted the first ever-foreign live concert by Wham in 1986 and cultivated Cui Jian, the progenitor of the Chinese rock scene. The rebellious underground tradition lives on in small bars and clubs. Beijing has a volatile club scene. Contingently, a more genteel Latin-wave is sweeping the capital as Salsa supplants the syncopated movement of ballroom dancing. Until the early 1990s, the Beijing jazz scene was largely confined to overseas bands playing to expatriate and tourist audiences. That all changed in 1993, when the Goethe Institute sponsored the Beijing International Jazz Festival - attracting thousands of local people. The city now supports a small number of jazz clubs - with the Browns, CD Jazz Café and The Big Easy cutting the groove.

A great hotspot for nightlife, especially in summer, is around the bustling shores of the Hou Hai (Back Lake) district - Nuage is for people watching, the Left Bank is the place for intimate encounters and the Hou Hai Café cooks up some of the coolest sounds around. To the east of town an old warehouse area in Dashanzi, known as the 798 Art District, has become the trendiest art enclave in Beijing, and is the site of the Dashanzi International Art Festival which attracts over 100,000 visitors every year. The warehouse area hosts dozens of galleries, studios, exhibition spaces, design companies, restaurants, bars and a trailblazing spot - the Yan Club.

More traditional forms of entertainment are flourishing in the capital. The annual Beijing Music Festival attracts an impressive ensemble of international orchestras and musicians, and last year added some of the biggest international rock performers in the world to its play list. The home-grown Beijing Opera lives on, though performances are now largely supported by visiting tourists.

THE BEIJING OLYMPIC GAMES

"The Olympics can change a person's life," said Deng Yaping, former Olympic table tennis champion and member of the Beijing 2008 Olympic Games Bid Committee. They're certainly changing the lives of the millions of people who live in and around Beijing. Since the capital won the bid to host the Games in 2008, Beijing has undergone massive changes. The dizzying developments in preparation for the Olympics are expected to run some RMB131 billion (about US$16 billion), and everywhere signs of spending are evident. Beijing real estate is the scene for some of the most ambitious urban planning ever seen in China, with dozens of incredible stadiums and buildings under construction, designed by top architects in preparation for hosting sporting events and athletes come 2008. Clocks at major intersections throughout the city countdown the number of days until the Games start, vendors are already selling t-shirts, caps and other paraphernalia, and volunteers have been recruited to manage the estimated 550 million tourists that will flock to the city for those couple of weeks in August. 2008

ESSENTIAL BEIJING >>>>>>>>>

Imperial Times Spend a day at Forbidden City and Tiananmen Square, popping in to visit Mao in his Mausoleum and climbing Jingshan Hill for a great view of the town. Climb the Great Wall at Mutianyu.
Starving? Feast on Beijing Duck at the Quan Ju De Restaurant, or snack on skewers and pancakes at the night food stalls in Wangfujing. After a big night out, head to the hotpot and baby lobster restaurants that line Ghost Street – open 24-hours. Alternatively, treat yourself to a slap up meal a t the CourtYard with views of the Forbidden City.
Party time Club-hop along the West Gate of the Workers Stadium – dance to international DJs and drink Chivas in opulent surrounds.
All you ever wanted Panjiayuan, Liulichang and the Pearl Market for antiques and jewellery, the Silk Market and Yashow for fashion items, the Qianmen shopping district for interest and the Peninsula Palace Hotel for pride.
At ease Take a boat ride on the lake at the Summer Place or Beihai Park. Stroll Houhai Lake and its adjoining hutongs and take refreshments in the neighbourhood. Join in the dawn morning exercises practised in the Temple of Heaven Park.
A dose of culture Admire modern Chinese art in the dozens of galleries and warehouses that comprise the 798 Dashanzi Art District, pausing for a drink in one of the chic cafes.
That's entertainment Watch local punk, rock and folk bands in Sanlitun bars. Admire the balancing skills of Chinese acrobats at the Chaoyang Theatre. Relive Chinese history through tales sung at the Peking Opera.

Beijing Huguang Guildhall
Peking Opera. *3 Hufangqiao. Tel: 6351 8284*

CD Café Jazz Club
Beijing's premier jazz venue run by local saxophonist Liu Yuan. The cream of Beijing's jazz bands play live on Sundays. *Dongsanhuan Beilu, west gate of Agriculture Exhibition Hall. Tel: 6501 8288*

Chaoyang Theatre
36 Dongsanhuan Bei Lu. Tel: 6507 2421

The Courtyard
Ranked on the Conde Nast Traveler's Hot List of world restaurants, The Courtyard is simply fantastic. The upstairs cigar room affords a fine view over the Forbidden City wall. *95 Donghuamen Dajie. Tel: 6526 8883*

Fangshan Restaurant
Nicely located inside Beihai Park, this restaurant offers one of Beijing's most unique dining experiences with 14 and 20 course banquets. *Beihai Park (east gate entrance). Tel: 6401 1879/89, 6404 2573*

The Loft
The coolest, most modern Western-style bar in Beijing. There is also a beautiful garden and a New Media Art Space was added to The Loft's ensemble. Excellent food, service and music. *4 Workers Stadium North Road. Tel: 6501 7501*

No Name Bar
With prime lakeside views, great background music, and the most laid back staff in the city, it's not hard to understand why this is one of the most popular Beijing bars. *A3 Qianhai East Bank. Tel: 6401 8541*

Qianmen Quan Ju De Roast Duck Restaurant
Although there are numerous branches of the restaurant around, the original one in Qianmen is the place to feast on bronzed ducks, pancakes, sesame buns and all the trimmings. *32 Qianmen Dajie. Tel: 6511 2418, 6701 1379*

Red Gate Gallery at the Watchtower
Dongbianmen Watchtower. Tel: 6525 1005

Redmoon
An elegant cocktail bar with a contemporary décor offering an impressive selection of drinks accompanied by modern music on traditional Chinese instruments. *Grand Hyatt Beijing, 1 Dong Chang'an Jie. Tel: 8518 1234*

THE CAPITAL'S TOP SPOTS

LeQuai

The CourtYard

When legendary Chinese-American lawyer Handel Lee purchased a dream traditional courtyard house right next to the east gate of the Forbidden City, he gave little thought of turning it into one of China's finest restaurants. Since its opening, The CourtYard, with its unsurpassed fusion cuisine and impeccable wine list, has been described as 'one of the world's most exciting restaurants' by Condé Nast Traveler. *95 Donghuamen Dajie, Dongcheng District, Tel (010) 6526 8881/3*

The Courtyard

Green T. House

JinR, the charmingly child-like owner, designer and creative master-chef behind Green T. House, is also a highly accomplished musician. With no detail left unattended, her interior design and cuisine incorporate natural, simple and elegant elements to create a tantalizing array of beauty that is not only stunning to the senses, but also soothing to the soul. Artfully created menus guide the passage through an inspirational tea-infused cuisine. Long dining tables are set end-to-end to create a communal dining space that everyone squeezes onto as if part of one huge family - and a very privileged one at that. *6 Gongti Xi Lu, Chaoyang District, Tel (010) 6552 8310/11*

My Humble House

Internationally acclaimed chefs, including Sam Leong, have devised a short, sharp and frankly beautiful menu, showcasing "Modern Chinese" cuisine at My Humble House - the third outlet sporting the successful Humble brand from Singapore's Tung Lok Group. Lines of poetry are woven into descriptions of dishes that team culinary imports such as foie gras and truffles with age-old Chinese flavours. Presentation is not unlike the general ambience of the place - smart, stripped back and elegant. *Podium, Oriental Plaza, Dongcheng District, Tel (010) 8518 8811*

Red Moon

Serving up some of the best Japanese cuisine in Beijing, Red Moon stretches expense accounts with innovative cocktails and Cuban cigars. Japanese design group, Super Potato, have fashioned an elegant dining room with earthy woods and soft lines. The open kitchen is a lively place to sit and watch the experts carve up deep-water delicacies for your pleasure. Recline in the comfy sofas after a meal and understand why the Grand Hyatt enjoys its reputation for high quality dining. *Grand Hyatt, 1 Dong Chan'an Jie, Dongcheng District, Tel (010) 8518 1234*

Green T. House

Made in China

Another Beijing institution located within the Grand Hyatt, Made in China serves old Beijing and North-eastern (Dongbei) cuisine in an ultra-chic setting. Super Potato have worked their magic here again - the dark wooden panels give way to an open kitchen complete with traditional kilns for duck-roasting. And make no mistake; the Peking Duck here may be the best you'll ever have. *Grand Hyatt, 1 Dong Chang'an Jie, Dongcheng District, Tel (010) 8518 1234*

Made in China

Nuage

Located on the northern bank of Qianhai, owner Zhu Cheng Xiang has created a quirky venue that caters to everyone. Nuage's restaurant dishes up delicate Vietnamese cuisine in a quaint wooden dining room complete with rickshaws. A gorgeous rooftop patio affords views of the Drum & Bell Towers and is one of the best spots in town to hit on a balmy summer evening. Then there's the basement-bar providing after-dinner tipples, DJs and live music for Beijing's new colonialists. *22 Qianhai Lke East Bank, Tel (010) 6401 9581*

Red Capital Club

From the chair that Madam Mao used to sink into, to an antique telephone playing a recording of the Chairman himself, Red Capital Club has cornered the market for revolutionary kitsch. The creation of prominent American writer and old China hand, Laurence J. Brahm, the kitsch comes together in this small courtyard restaurant with style and charm. Dishes are prepared according to old Party leaders' tastes, whilst beverages include "Lin Biao's Crash" or the "Black Cat, White Cat." Before your meal, you can cruise around town in the Club's limousine, and then settle into the romantic Red Capital Residence. Look out for the new Red Capital spa complex or take a country break at the Red Capital Ranch. *66 Dongsi Jiutiao, Dongcheng District, Tel (010) 8401 6152*

Red Capital Club

Le Quai

In landlocked Beijing, water aspects are obviously at a premium - hence, the owners of Le Quai were quick to sweep on the vacant block adjacent to the Worker's Stadium lake and provide east-siders with a place to sip cocktails with a water view. Owned by a consortium including Weng Weng - one of Beijing's original DJs - Le Quai offers an interesting clash of old and new. The glass entrance opens up to an interior of carved wooden beams and floorboards resembling an old, loft-style house in Anhui Province. The menu offers a smattering of continental dishes among the Cantonese and Sichuan staples. *Opposite Stand 12, Worker's Stadium, Chaoyang District, Tel (010) 6551 1636*

My Humble House

House by the Park

Green T. House Living

The second Beijing venture for JinR, Green T. House Living is a restaurant, but much more. Located on the way to the airport, from the outside, Living is somewhat akin to a huge, white sarcophagus. Inside, the design is stunning but minimal, with Feng Shui principals used to optimise the flow of energy between the dining area and the glass-encased Tearoom, Retreat and Bathhouse. The retreat has exclusive accommodation and decadent spa treatments, whilst the teahouse offers a cosy haven to read books and participate in Chinese culture classes. *318 Cuige Zhuang Xiang Hege Zhuangcun, Tel 13601137132*

Green T.House Living

House by the Park

Sister restaurant to My Humble House, House by the Park is the brainchild of the Tung Lok Group, but points for the stunning décor go to Japanese design firm Studio Myu. Simple and modish, the restaurant is criss-crossed with water features and employs quirky flourishes including dozens of different designer lamps, and stunning sperm-shaped cutlery. A beautiful 'Work of Art' menu uses watercolours to describe dishes in categories such as 'a breath, a whisper, a bloom' (entrees) or 'a sea of love, an ocean of eternity' (seafood). A feast for all the senses. *Clubhouse Level 2, Block 19, China Central Place, 89 Jianguo Lu, Chaoyang District, Tel (010) 6530 7770*

Area

The owners of Area – artist Yan Dong and Japanese fashion designer Nami – have created an intimate venue where arty types can revel in austere, but stylish surrounds. The focus here is on swanky décor, down tempo music and upscale drinking. Plans for a sculpture garden and art gallery are underway, as is the development of a large outdoor park, making Area one of only a handful of classy, inner-city venues to provide its patrons with bona-fide outdoor partying. *Behind Pascucci Restaurant, Lido Park, East of Xiao Yun Qiao, Fang Yuan Xi Lu, Chaoyang District, Tel (010) 6437 6158*

Area

Bed

Having somehow avoided the wrecking ball that has claimed so much of the neighbourhood, Bed is still one of the more difficult bars to locate in Beijing - but losing your way in the hutongs is a small price to pay. Owned by Cho Chonggee, proprietor of Sambal - a popular Malaysian restaurant only a stone's throw away - this chic cocktail bar is tucked away in an alley north of the Bell Tower. The interior of Bed revolves around, you guessed it, beds. Great mixed drinks, live music in summer, dim lighting and tapas make it the perfect spot to get up close and personal. *17 Zhangwang Hutong, Xicheng District, Tel (010) 8400 1554*

Bed

Coco Banana

Beijing's newest superclub has the backing of experienced owners, responsible for hugely popular club Banana and the Spicy Room. Located in the thriving Gongti West Gate area, Coco creatively employs copious quantities of LED lighting and neon, as well as a gauche, illuminated ceiling. Perhaps the best feature - notwithstanding the cowhide couches for which 88 bovines donated their skins - are the private rooms surrounding the main bar area. Decked out *a la* Studio 54, and resplendent with beds, deluxe furnishings and large-screen TVs, this is the place to check out mega DJs when they tour Beijing. *8 Gongti Xi Lu, Chaoyang District, Tel (010) 8599 9999*

The heart of Beijing

Right in the heart of
the metropolis and
close to the city's cultural
charms, experience an
intimate haven of warm
hospitality in the stylish
Park Plaza Beijing Wangfujing.

97 Jinbao Street, Dongcheng District, Beijing, 100005 P.R.C. Tel : +86-10-8522 1999

Toll-Free number:10-800-610-8886 (North China) · 10-800-261-8888 (South China)

www.parkplaza.com/beijingcn

TALK INFORMS

BE BETTER INFORMED

WITH **BEIJING TALK**

EVERY MONTH

Published since 1987, Beijing Talk is part of the "Talk" network of city-living magazines in China.
Please send subscription, editorial, advertising enquiries to media@ismaychina.com

BEIJING BUBBLE
The National Grand Theatre

Who says there's no property bubble in Beijing? Doubters need look no further than the massive bulge emerging out of a hole in the ground only a stone's throw from Tiananmen. This glass and titanium structure, dubbed the 'Egg Shell,' is Beijing's new National Grand Theatre.

Paul Andreu, the French architect responsible, does not take kindly to being described as an airport architect. Fair enough - it's a long time since he came out of the hangar, gradually shedding his image as a waiting lounge specialist with projects such as the Osaka Maritime Museum. Yet his luggage carousel days came back to haunt him in May 2004 when the roof he designed for Paris's Charles de Gaulle airport collapsed. 'I can't explain what happened. I just don't understand it,' Andreu reassured reporters at the time.

So, while a night at the opera normally involves dusting off one's best threads, hard hats may be the accessory of choice for patrons wary of the architect's safety record when the curtain lifts on the National Grand Theatre. Lifejackets may also make an appearance - the building, constructed in the middle of a lake, is connected to the shore by a 60-metre long transparent underwater passage.

The nation's new centre piece for the performing arts has been a long time coming. Once the project was approved by the State Council in April 1998, China held its first open international architecture competition to choose the designer, with Andreu emerging victorious. After a number of modifications to the original blueprints, the project formally entered the construction phase in 2001.

The building, sited to the west of the Great Hall of the People on Chang'an Jie, is dominated by a titanium shell in the shape of a super ellipsoid, with a maximum span of 213 metres and a height of 46 metres. The shell is divided in two by a curved glass covering, 100 metres wide at the base.

The centre houses three performance auditoriums - a 2,416-seat opera house, a 2,017-seat concert hall and a 1,040-seat theatre. If you can't afford the ticket to a performance, you'll still have access to art and exhibition spaces open to a 'wide public.' Streets, plazas, shopping areas and restaurants open to the general public are also designed to lend the building an air of open forum. Nevertheless, the complex, which has cost well over US$300 million, may struggle to shake off an elitist tag.

Light and transparency are two of the key design themes. By day, light penetrates the glass roof and flows into the building. By night, the movements within can be seen from outside. The opera house, at the centre of the building, also allows ample opportunity for voyeurism – covered by a gilt metal mesh, its walls becomes translucent when light from the inside allowing onlookers to observe those inside.

More orthodox views are provided from the lounge on the highest level under the roof, where spectators will be able to appreciate the surrounding cityscape from a hitherto unseen perspective.

Critics say the structure is out of step with surrounding buildings, and in particular that its curved lines do not sit well with the four-square form of the adjacent Great Hall of the People. Andreu's view is that most great buildings are controversial in the construction phase, and that modern architecture should be as bold as the surrounding buildings were in their day. He has described the project as 'his life's work' and feels that it was out of the question to build an obscure, less prominent building of lesser importance. His ambition is to give Beijing a new district of spectacles and dreams - open to one and all.

The theatre is scheduled to open in 2007.

Tianjin

Tianjin, the former 'Paris of The North,' flourishes as Beijing's port and northern China's major gateway for international trade and shipping

Just seventy-five minutes away from Beijing by train, Tianjin, China's fourth largest city with 10 million inhabitants, is considered an outstanding example of the country's successful development policies. Since being rebuilt, following a devastating earthquake in 1976, the city has boomed to become the biggest northern port. Its facilities are designed to accommodate today's massive container vessels, as well as hundreds of visiting ocean-going liners. In addition, Tianjin is a manufacturing centre in its own right and claims to have produced China's first wristwatch, first bicycle and first TV set and more recently China's first microprocessor chip.

Because of its strategic location on the Bohai Bay, Tianjin has a long history of providing a gateway to the north, and a tradesman's entrance to the imperial capital. It first came to prominence in the 14th century at the beginning of the Ming dynasty. At that time the city's name, meaning 'the place where the emperor crossed the river,' was bestowed on it by Emperor Zhudi, and from then on it continued to operate as a centre for trade at the intersection of sea and inland navigation routes. Tianjin was considered to be one of China's most important military fortresses in the Yuan Dynasty (1271-1368) due to its particular geographic location as access point to Beijing, the national capital. Tianjin was further expanded to become the second largest business and communications center in the country. By the end of the 19th century, it had grown into a bustling centre for international commerce.

By the 19th century its importance was obvious to the West and, at the conclusion of the second Opium War in 1859, the French and British were allowed to establish concessions in the city. Later, additional concessions were given to Japan, Germany, Russia, Austria, Italy and Belgium. As a result of these settlements, Tianjin inherited a mixture of architectural styles as well as improved shipping facilities.

The foreign presence stimulated trade and industry targeting the export market, especially textiles, and the city gained a worldwide reputation for its handmade carpets. Wealth and fame brought a diversity of visitors, many of whom stayed at the Astor Hotel - built in 1863, now the New World Astor.

Tianjin's European legacy makes the city a worthwhile stop-off for tourists. Numerous colonial buildings have survived war and earthquake, notably those on the west bank of the Hai River, clustering around the main thoroughfares, Heping Road and Jiefengbei Road. As the former Victoria Road and Rue de France, the Jiefengbei Road, housed many banks, financial institutions and parks in a splendid colonial setting. Many remain. Apart from the Astor Hotel, another British establishment, the Imperial Hotel built in the 1920s also survives. Nearby the former Italian Concession has been renovated, restoring some of its former glory.

The Hai River esplanades, with their Parisian railings and bridgework, are good places to observe local activities such as fishing, early morning shadow boxing, opera, and airing caged birds. Tianjin's traditional arts and crafts can be purchased at the Ancient Culture Street along the Hai River, close to the city centre. The street incorporates a renovated 14th century temple to the local goddess of fishermen and contains a folk museum. While exploring the street, try the famous Tianjin steamed dumplings called goubuli baozi. The name means 'dogs won't touch them,' but despite their name, they are delicious.

Tianjin offers a gourmet playground of pleasures. Not to be missed is the Erduoyan Fried Cake Shop - a century-old institution specialising in delicious rice flour cakes. Food Street off Nanmenwei Dajie is a cheerful, bustling two-storey covered alley with over 100 restaurants and food shops - each delivering their own distinctive flavours. A branch of the famous Beijing Quan Ju De Roast Duck Restaurant is found on Heping Road. Nearby Chuansu specialises in spicy and mouth-numbing Sichuan food. The Goubuli Stuffed Dumpling Restaurant is famous for dough buns, whilst the Haihe River Palace, built in classical Chinese style on a pontoon, serves up-market Cantonese cuisine.

In the cultural area around the Drum Tower, the local craft of *ni ren* or 'clay men' figurine production still thrives. Tianjin is also famous for its vividly hand-painted New Year posters and kites. Tianjin is historically important for the production of fine hand-knotted carpets. They are woven in an almost unlimited variety of colours, patterns and sizes. The selection of designs defies the imagination, and many draw their inspiration from modern international art forms, however, the most popular still incorporate classic designs using traditional motifs.

To the north of the city, the Buddhist Temple of Singular Happiness, founded in the 7th century, is famous for its 11-headed statue of Guanyin (Goddess of Mercy). Further to the north a magnificent section of the Great Wall can be found at Huangyaguan. It was originally built in 557 and rebuilt during the Ming Dynasty and today is the host to an arduous annual international marathon. The eastern gate of the temple is the earliest of its kind to survive. To the west of the city the ancient town of Guzhen, the Home of New Year Pictures, offers numerous demonstrations and exhibitions of local crafts as well as canal boat rides.

Often called the Shanghai of the North, Tianjin is in a strong position to compete for overseas business with its old rival Shanghai. It has increasingly become a place to spend time as well as investment, with first-class international hotels, restaurants and recreational facilities, including a championship golf club. A modern subway system is evolving and Tianjin has excellent transportation facilities including a large international airport and convenient highway and railway links.

天津

天津市简称津，与北京市、上海市、重庆市同为中国四大直辖市，是中国工、商、外贸综合发展的对外开放的重要城市，有“北方巴黎”之美誉。天津市位于华北平原的东北部，渤海湾西岸，海河五大支流的汇合处，京哈、京沪铁路的交叉点，是中国北部地区重要的交通枢纽和北部沿海重要经济中心。全市面积1.13万平方公里，人口八百万。城市建成区面积283平方公里，市区非农业人口五百五十万。有汉、回、朝鲜、满、蒙古等民族。

天津是一座历史悠久的文化名城，是首都北京的门户，明永乐二年(1404年)置天津衙，因而得名。近几年，各方面取得了更为显著的发展，现已成为中国一个门类齐全、配套完备的综合性工业基地和重要的对外贸易通商口岸。工业尤以海洋化工、石油化工为著名，纺织工业在全国也占有重要地位。天津新港已成为目前最大的人工港，也是中国北方最大的贸易港。

天津主要名胜有盘山风景区、独乐寺、白塔等。近年来，又以发展“当代旅游”为主要特色，开辟了一些新的旅游活动中心，有古文化街、食品街、博物馆等。而天津著名特产有小站稻、天津鸭梨、长芦盐、“风船”牌手工地毯(被誉为最高贵的地毯)、杨柳青木板年画、泥人张彩塑、风筝、大漆镶嵌家具等。传统风味中的狗不理包子、桂发祥麻花和耳朵眼炸糕被誉为“津门食品三绝”，白记水饺、知味斋爆肚也是很有名的风味食品。

Northeast China

CHANGCHUN • DALIAN • HARBIN • JILIN • SHENYANG

The three provinces which comprise China's northeast are now commonly referred to as Dong Bei. Despite having been on the outer edges of the Chinese empire until recent times, today the region is an integral and important part of modern China. Its natural resources are essential to the country's plans for modernisation

Kempinski Hotel Shenyang
CHINA
沈阳凯宾斯基饭店

The newest Boutique hotel offering the most magnificent views overlooking the skyline of Shenyang and the finest dining experience provided by our professional and dedicated team.

109 Qing Nian Street • Shen He District • Shenyang P.R.C. 110014
Tel: (86-24) 2298 8988 • Fax: (86-24) 2298 8888
E-mail: reservations.shenyang@kempinski.com
Website: www.kempinski-shenyang.com
Toll-free: 1 0800 650 0362

大连

大连位于辽东半岛南端，东濒黄海，西临渤海，是中国重要的对外贸易口岸之一。由于气候温和，景色宜人，也是中国北方旅游和疗养的胜地。大连古称青州，公元前108年汉武帝时开辟了从山东半岛到辽东半岛的海上航线，促进了大连地区的经济和文化发展，19世纪末叶，清朝政府辟旅顺口为北洋海军基地，大连逐步发展为城市。大连是闻名世界的北方不冻港，水深港阔，设备先进，港口吞吐量为全中国第二位。大连亦是中国的体育名城，被国家体委确定为全国足球运动重点城市，有"足球之城"、"田径之乡"的美誉。

大连工业以机械制造、石油化工、轻工纺织为主，还有冶金、造船、电子等工业。此外，大连又是中国最大的苹果产区之一，有"苹果之乡"之称，其产量约占全国的四分之一。

大连这座海滨城市，夏天绿荫浓密，不觉燥热；冬天微微飘雪，不感寒冷。这里有整洁的街道、明快的建筑，特别是金黄色的海滩。不管走到哪里，都给人以幽雅和宁静的感觉。它是中国著名的避暑和疗养胜地。大连的海滨，是最迷的人。在黑石礁海滨，人们可以看到由石灰岩构成的石芽。它和钟乳石不同，一簇簇、一丛丛直接长在礁石面上。奇特的礁石和蔚蓝的海水相互映衬，使这里的景色别具一格。

此外，大连还是中国北方主要渔业生产基地，水产资源丰富，是中国对虾、海参、干贝等珍贵水产品的重要产地。大连风景名胜较多，主要有星海公园、老虎滩公园、海水浴场、老铁山、蛇岛等。

Dalian

Dalian is a city that has had ties with the Russians - brought about by their search for a deep, sheltered ice-free port in the 1890s. Today, the city retains its maritime tradition and is the third largest port in China and a trading gateway for the north.

Despite intense industrial activity, Dalian is considered by many to be one of the most beautiful, cleanest and smartest cities in China. One of the city's major attractions is Zhongshan Square - formerly known as Stalin Square and originally known as Nicholas Circle. This is ringed with turn-of-the-century Russian banks, art deco finance houses, the former British Consulate and a 1930s Japanese-built hotel. Stately tree-lined avenues radiate from the square's landscaped gardens.

The beach closest to town is located at the end of Zhongshan Road. It curves around a deep bay, which is lined with a mix of Edwardian hotels and modern fast-food restaurants. It is also the site of Sun Asia Ocean World, a US$12 million joint venture

between Hong Kong and New Zealand. Another popular attraction is the superb Golden Pebble Beach Golf Course, which offers a 36-hole facility designed by Peter Thompson. Dalian's other attractions include the Botanical Gardens, Laodong Park and the Museum of History.

Partly to service the growing tourist industry, there are regular air services to Dalian from Hong Kong, Tokyo, Osaka, Russia and all major Chinese cities. There are also passenger ships from Japan and Korea. International hotels include Shangri-La, Gloria Plaza, Holiday Inn, Furama, Kempinski and the Hilton.

Changchun

Changchun, meaning 'everlasting spring,' was so named because of its verdant parkland setting. And it may have remained green had it not been for the Japanese conquest of northeast China in 1931. The site was then renamed Manchukuo, the capital of Japan's overseas empire, and they made every attempt to make it a grand city worthy of its position. Results were commendable, and Changchun boasts vast squares joined by tree-lined avenues, overlooked by palatial stone buildings that sport Gothic towers and pagoda-style roofs. Many former Japanese buildings fringe the Cultural Square. Undoubtedly the most famous is the Puppet Palace. Here, for 14 years, Henry Puyi, the last emperor of China was installed as the 'puppet' emperor of Manchukuo. The two-storey house, with a central courtyard, is very modest compared to contemporary standards for Japanese government offices. Puyi, his empress and concubine, lived in small, shabbily genteel quarters, and even the throne room and banquet hall are quite spartan. The rest of the rooms, once offices, are now devoted to a museum with most exhibits depicting Japanese atrocities in China during the war and occupation. The complex caters primarily for domestic tourists and there are few explanations in English.

Not that overseas visitors in Changchun spend much time sight-seeing - they invariably have business to conduct. The city remains highly dependent on manufacturing and heavy industry with the automobile sector being the major employer. The largest project is the Sino-German joint venture between the local First Automobile Works - producer of trucks and Red Flag limousines - and Volkswagen.

长春

吉林省省会长春位于松辽平原中部，长大、长哈、长圆、长白四条铁路的交汇处。是新兴的工业城市和东北交通枢纽之一，以"汽车城"、"电影城"和盛产光学仪器闻名全国，其他还拥有食品、电子、医药、建材等大骨干行业，市内街道整齐，绿树成荫，又有"森林之城"的美誉。城市建成区面积一百零五平方公里。长春土特产除"关东三宝"外，还有哈什蚂油、通化葡萄酒、杜鹃花雕、根雕、长春君子兰等。而主要的旅游景点有南湖公园、净月潭、新立城水库、伪满洲国皇宫、电影城及汽车城等。

哈尔滨

黑龙江省省会哈尔滨是一个美丽的城市，亦是一个有特殊风格的城市。城市高层建筑多为俄式建筑，墙面大多粉刷成乳黄色，并饰有多种图案，有的在屋顶上还以耸立的尖塔或圆塔作为装饰，其中尤以"喇嘛台"最为典型。秀丽的松花江更以波光潋艳的流水，从哈尔滨市区蜿蜒流过，把这个北国城市妆扮得更加璀璨闪光。哈尔滨主要名胜有斯大林公园、太阳岛公园、儿童公园、文庙以及极乐寺等。此外，哈尔滨冬季冰上活动丰富多彩，冰灯游园活动尤为突出，素有"冰城"之称。

Harbin

Harbin, formerly known as the 'town of fishing nets' by its Manchu population, is a city of modern creation and now boasts over four million inhabitants. As the capital of Heilongjiang, China's most northerly province, its development was closely linked to that of the Far Eastern Railway in the 1890s. Harbin became an important Russian base during their 1904-1905 war with Japan, when the railway was joined to the Trans-Siberian Railroad. Russian influence was further enhanced when, in 1917, half a million fled south to Harbin.

As a consequence, it is understandable that Harbin retains a strong Russian heritage. The city has broad avenues edged with neo-classical mansions, and is dotted with heroic monuments and parks. In winter, the Songhua River becomes an ice rink and sleighing thoroughfare. In addition, there is a winter park alongside the river, which becomes partially covered with thick ice. Here hardy Harbin families take rides in pony carts, practice ballroom dancing, and spin tops.

Most people visit Harbin in winter, some to ski or hunt wildlife, but the majority come to see the magnificent annual ice sculpture festival. The winter is long in Harbin, lasting six months, with temperatures dropping well below -30. Then Russian cuisine helps to stave off the cold, with meat and potato dishes laced with garlic, often washed down with a tot of vodka. Many Russian food outlets prosper, including one in the dining room of the Moderne Hotel, with its French Renaissance-inspired architecture.

In contrast, the pleasant summer temperatures attract many to Sun Island in the Songhua River. Its numerous sanatoriums and hotels spill on to an inviting natural beach.

Europeans as well as Russians formerly inhabited Harbin and numerous renovations have taken place in an effort to preserve the heritage of the 'Moscow of the Orient.' The city has around thirty churches, the finest being the Byzantine, St. Sophia Cathedral, which was completed in 1931. Some churches are being given a new lease of life as a shelter for the trading activities of Russians who commute from Nakhodka to trade leather goods, silver tea services, and Red Army watches for Dong Bei fur pelts, Shanghai silk and dried foodstuffs.

The city has been officially declared 'the first inland open port for foreign trade,' and this has allowed much of Harbin's imports and exports to be transported in containers by regular freight train to the port of Dalian. Tourism is also on the increase. Many internationally managed hotels have been established, including the New World, Gloria International, Singapore, Flamingo and Holiday Inn.

Shenyang

The city gained prominence in the Qing dynasty, and in its guise as Mukden it became the capital of Manchuria. It was the Qing's secondary capital mainly because of the importance of the northeast region to the lucrative ginseng trade. As the present capital of Liaoning province, it is the fifth largest city in China.

Today, visitors to this industrial city can visit the Manchu Imperial Palace, a complex of some 70 buildings that was completed in 1636. The palace is beautifully maintained, and displayed within its pavilions are 10,000 antique treasures, including the birch-bark bow of Emperor Shunzhi and a throne with arm-rests made of deer antlers. The main courtyard is lined with The Banner Pavilions, once used by tribal chiefs, whose weapons are on show.

The Manchu imperial tombs are a short distance from the city. Fuling, the Eastern Tomb of Nurhachi is set in a forest of ancient pines, and approached through a dragon-dominated gate leading to a Spirit Way of stone animals and mandarins. Beyond are pavilions with red-tiled roofs, monumental gates, watchtowers that lead to a simple, circular tomb. The Northern Imperial Tomb of Abahai, Nurhachi's son and founder of China's Qing dynasty, is located in Bei Ling Park. Visitors enter through a classic white stone arch, guarded by four imperial lions, cross a courtyard to the Vermilion Gate and on to the Spirit Way which leads to a cluster of ornate pavilions and the Tomb Mound. The mausoleum remains in a good state of repair and exhibits a marked military style. Indeed, Shenyang's historical treasures rival anything to be found throughout the country.

The modern city is vibrant and productive. It has a population of over seven million, and is the largest city and transportation hub in the northeast. Shenyang is a major financial and trading centre, and automobile manufacture has become a key industry with overseas partners including General Motors.

The city boasts many first-class hotels, such as Shangri-La's Traders, the New World and Gloria Plaza. There is a nine-hole golf course built by Korean investors at Fuling, and the city is developing as a shopping destination, with new department stores, including the Zhongxing and Eastern Asia Shopping Plaza. Indicative of the mood of the city, some of its streets have been paved with coloured tiles and made pedestrian areas. These provide adjacent stores with a stage for open-air fashion shows and musical entertainment in the evenings.

Jilin

Jilin confusingly shares the same name with that of the province, which it used to be the capital of until 1954. It is a modest city, making no claim to greatness, nor having a rich history, and yet many visitors feel it that it is a particularly pleasant little place. During winter the city offers enjoyable, inexpensive seasonal entertainment. In January the city puts on its own version of an ice festival, and there are three adjacent skiing and sledding parks for the energetic to choose from.

The authorities have been keen to beautify the city and as a result, a new promenade along the Songhua River was completed in 1998. In winter this provides a pleasant diversion. The trees lining the banks become thick with frost as a result of condensation from the city's Fengman hydroelectric plant on Songhua Lake, east of town. The phenomenon has achieved national recognition and provides the city with an additional tourist attraction. Apart from power generation, Jilin's other main industry is chemical production.

In summer, the city has a number of excellent and beautiful parks to ramble in, and the local countryside is pleasant and scenic. A popular destination for visitors is Beishan Park, west of town, which is crisscrossed by pathways and is the site of numerous temples. The most famous of them is the Jade Emperor's Temple.

沈阳

辽宁省省会沈阳曾为清朝故都，称过盛京和奉天。它位于辽河平原中部，京沈、哈大、沈丹、沈吉铁路交汇点，是东北地区最大的城市和交通枢纽，也是中国最大重工业城市之一，机械制造、有色金属加工、无机化工、橡胶、农机、制药、食品工业在中国占有重要地位。沈阳特产有玉器、羽毛画、贝雕画、柞蚕丝绸等，风味菜有熊掌、麒面(驼鹿的鼻子)、飞龙、榛鸡、熏肉大饼、老边饺。沈阳旅游业发达，国际级饭店如国贸、新世界及凯莱均提供高档的住宿服务。而名胜景点则首推沈阳故宫及东北三陵(福陵、昭陵、永陵)。

始建于1625年的沈阳故宫位于沈阳旧城中心是女真族(满族前身)杰出的领袖清太祖努尔哈赤及其继承人皇太极的宫殿，共有建筑七十多所，房屋三百余间，占地六万多平方米，是中国现存仅次于北京故宫的最完整的皇宫建筑群。全宫分为三大部份。中路，四大建筑均位于同一轴线上：大清门为故宫正门，是文武群臣候朝叩首之处；崇政殿(俗称金銮殿)为故宫中心建筑，是皇太极日常处理军政要务、会见外国使臣的场所；凤凰楼雄伟壮丽，是皇帝小憩及举行宴会之地。清宁宫独成一组城堡式建筑群，是帝后寝食之所。东路以大政殿为中心，是皇帝举行大典和议政之所。西路的文溯阁，是皇帝巡盛京时读书、看戏之所，阁内所藏《四库全书》是全国七阁中保存最为完整的一部。整个皇宫楼阁耸立，殿宇轩昂，雕梁画栋，富丽堂皇，体现了中国古代建筑艺术的优秀传统和独特风格，反映了满、汉、蒙古各族文化融合在建筑上的辉煌成就。现经大规模候修整，辟为沈阳故宫博物馆。

Northwest China

THE SILK ROAD • XI'AN

One of the country's most visually and culturally rich regions incorporates some of the most breathtaking landscapes

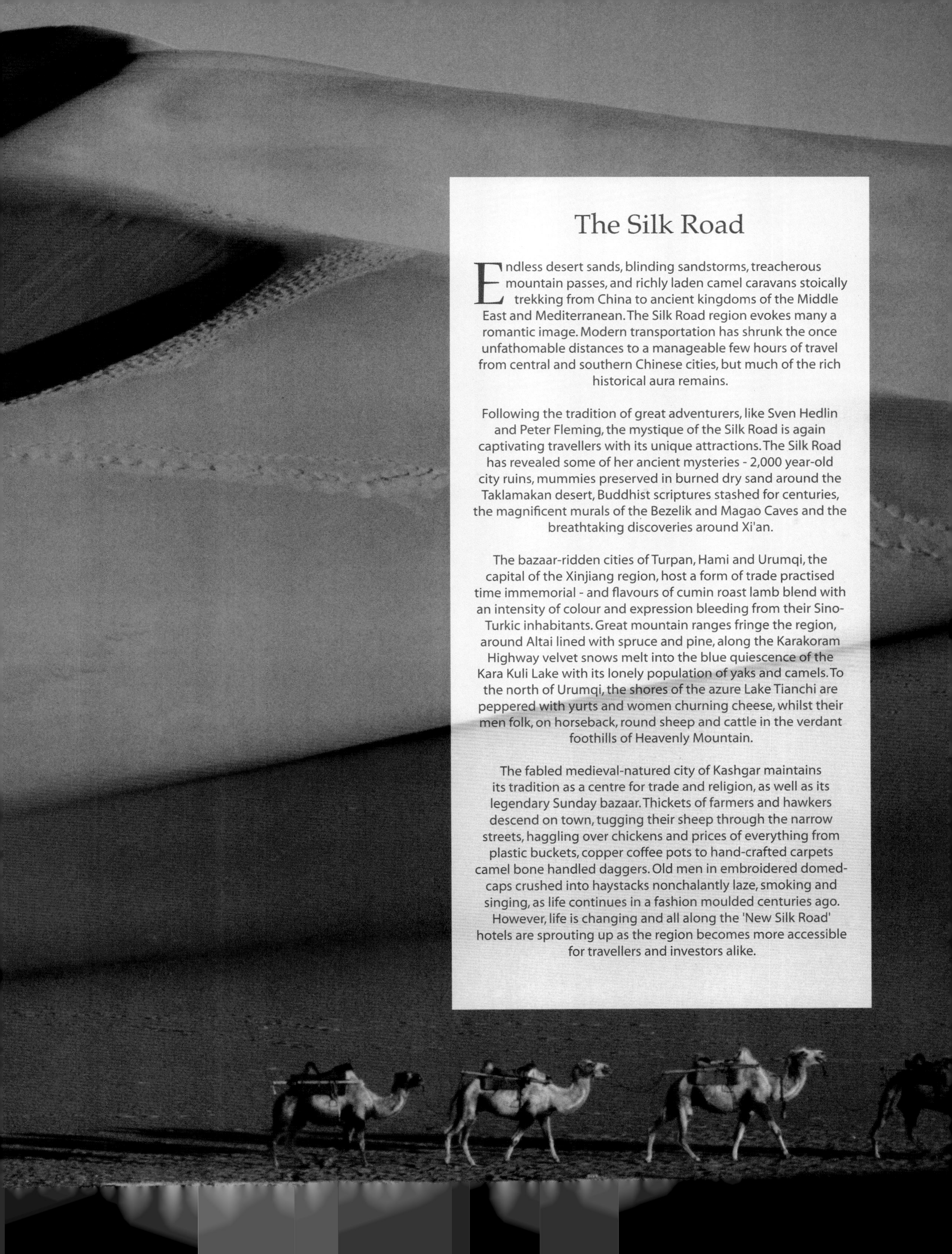

The Silk Road

Endless desert sands, blinding sandstorms, treacherous mountain passes, and richly laden camel caravans stoically trekking from China to ancient kingdoms of the Middle East and Mediterranean. The Silk Road region evokes many a romantic image. Modern transportation has shrunk the once unfathomable distances to a manageable few hours of travel from central and southern Chinese cities, but much of the rich historical aura remains.

Following the tradition of great adventurers, like Sven Hedlin and Peter Fleming, the mystique of the Silk Road is again captivating travellers with its unique attractions. The Silk Road has revealed some of her ancient mysteries - 2,000 year-old city ruins, mummies preserved in burned dry sand around the Taklamakan desert, Buddhist scriptures stashed for centuries, the magnificent murals of the Bezelik and Magao Caves and the breathtaking discoveries around Xi'an.

The bazaar-ridden cities of Turpan, Hami and Urumqi, the capital of the Xinjiang region, host a form of trade practised time immemorial - and flavours of cumin roast lamb blend with an intensity of colour and expression bleeding from their Sino-Turkic inhabitants. Great mountain ranges fringe the region, around Altai lined with spruce and pine, along the Karakoram Highway velvet snows melt into the blue quiescence of the Kara Kuli Lake with its lonely population of yaks and camels. To the north of Urumqi, the shores of the azure Lake Tianchi are peppered with yurts and women churning cheese, whilst their men folk, on horseback, round sheep and cattle in the verdant foothills of Heavenly Mountain.

The fabled medieval-natured city of Kashgar maintains its tradition as a centre for trade and religion, as well as its legendary Sunday bazaar. Thickets of farmers and hawkers descend on town, tugging their sheep through the narrow streets, haggling over chickens and prices of everything from plastic buckets, copper coffee pots to hand-crafted carpets camel bone handled daggers. Old men in embroidered domed-caps crushed into haystacks nonchalantly laze, smoking and singing, as life continues in a fashion moulded centuries ago. However, life is changing and all along the 'New Silk Road' hotels are sprouting up as the region becomes more accessible for travellers and investors alike.

AN HISTORIC Earth-moving Experience

Despite the city's wealth of historical treasures the Terracotta Warriors Museum is the prime reason why visitors come to Xi'an - if not their main motive in coming to China.

Modern folklore goes that a group of farmers stumbled upon the greatest archaeological discovery of modern times whilst digging a well in 1974. The subterranean cache guarded the tomb of the first Emperor of China, Qin Shihuang. Some 750,000 slaves toiled for 37 years and still failed to complete the project. The entire site is believed to contain nearly 8.000 terracotta warriors and horses at various stages of excavation. It consists of three main halls, or pits, and an exhibition room. Pit One, the largest, once contained around 6,000 figures and over 1,000 have now been restored. Pit Two is the most recently opened and whilst there are fewer recovered figures, the archaeological work underway is fascinating to watch. A small command chamber is found in Pit Three.

The figures are all male and average around 1.8 metres in height. They represent the whole range of Qin society with a variety of classes, cultures and ages depicted in the differing costumes, statures facial features and adornments. No two are alike. The figures were brightly painted, though now traces of colour can only be found on a few.

The burial tomb of the emperor, which lies 1.5 kilometres away, still conceals many secrets and great treasures as it remains unexcavated. However treasures from several nearby attendant pits have been unearthed. The most startling find was two bronze chariots located close to the emperor's burial place. The two-wheeled chariots each with four horses are highly elaborate, each with over 3,000 separate components not only in bronze but also gold and silver. The chariots are half-size reproductions of originals which they emperor used for inspection tours of his kingdom. To commemorate the 50th anniversary of the People's Republic they were given their own exhibition hall in 1999 where you will also find many fine examples of other bronze-wear and stone armour found near the tomb. UNESCO declared the area a World Heritage Site in 1987.

Xi'an

As the starting point of the Silk Road, Chang'an, the Xi'an of 1,300 years ago was the largest, most cosmopolitan and most powerful city on Earth. Amongst its two million inhabitants were Arabs, Jews, Indians and Turks and its sphere of influence spread across Asia to the Middle East. Today, Xi'an is regaining its strategic and historical importance as a new Silk Road unfolds.

Xi'an is not only the capital of Shaanxi province, but also the economic and political hub of the entire northwest region. Ignorant of the high-rise modern world, many millennia of mysteries are concealed in the subterranean cache below. The area is perhaps the world's most expansive archaeological treasure trove and its riches are reappearing as layers of concealment are swept away. In 1953, construction workers unearthed the remains of one of China's earliest civilised relics - a Neolithic village at Banpo, a few kilometres east of Xi'an, dating from around 4,500 BC. In 1974, a group of farmers digging a well stumbled upon the greatest archaeological find of modern times - exposing the awesome valour of the Terracotta Army for the world to behold.

Yet another amazing discovery was made when the airport highway was being dug in 1990 - that of the Han Yang Tomb. It is estimated that the site contains around 40,000 burial objects including small, magnificently crafted clay figurines that were clothed in silk and had wooden arms. A sizeable and remarkable menagerie of pottery animals has also been unearthed, alongside a host other figures and everyday objects. These are on display in a purpose-built museum. The tomb was built for Emperor Liu Qi and his Empress and was completed in 146 BC during the Western Han dynasty - a glorious age of Chinese history. It will take many years before the full grandeur of this find will be on show to the public.

Many superb remnants of the past can also be found in the Shaanxi History Museum in the southeast of the city. Completed in 1991, and considered to be China's first modern museum it has over 350,000 exhibits, including astounding ancient bronzes, pottery figures and mural paintings.

Buddhism reached China through the Silk Road and Xi'an attracted numerous scholars, monks and artists. As early as the second century, the King of India sent the gift of a finger bone of Buddha and the Famen Temple

西安

以秦始皇陵墓出土的兵马俑而闻名世界的西安是陕西省的省会，位于沃野千里的关中平原中部，渭河之南，陇海铁路线上，是中国西北最大的工商业城市，教研基地和交通枢纽。工业以机械、高压输电设备、纺织为主。

西安古称长安，是中国历史文化名城之一。自西周迁都澧、镐以来已有三千多年的历史，文物古迹荟萃，历史文化系统极为完整丰富，是一个举世闻名的中国历史“自然博物馆”。先后有西周、秦、西汉、新莽、西晋、前赵、前秦、后秦、西魏、西周、隋、唐等十二个王朝和唐末黄巢、明末李自成两个农民政权在这里建都，历时一千二百多年之久，是中国七大古都中建都较早、历时最长的都城。从西汉时期开始，这里是“丝绸之路”的起点，盛唐时期成为当时世界上唯一拥有百万人口的大城市。西安以其悠久的历史和灿烂的文化，与埃及的开罗、希腊的雅典、意大利的罗马并称为世界四大文明古都，成为国际性旅游胜地。旅游景点以古城建筑和古遗迹为主，除了有被称为“世界八大奇迹”的秦皇兵马俑外，著名游胜地有大雁塔、小雁塔、西安碑林、半坡遗址、阿房宫遗址、骊山风景名胜区、华清池、清真寺、与教寺塔、西安文庙和卧龙寺等。

此外，西安著名特产有仿唐三彩、西安香包、刺绣、扎染、西凤酒、黄桂稠酒、临潼三宝(火晶柿、石榴、大红枣)、西安辣椒干、驴肉干、长安板栗、水晶饼、鲜花饼等。

was built west of the city to house it. Two magnificent Tang dynasty blue brick pagodas still dominate the skyline. The Big Wild Goose Pagoda housed Sanskrit scriptures transported from India by a Chinese monk called Xuanzang. His adventures have been re-told throughout history in the form of 'Journey to the West' or 'The Monkey King.' The Small Wild Goose Pagoda is set amidst a charming temple complex.

The city centre, marked by the 16th century Bell Tower, hosts a fascinating blend of new and old. The adjacent square and underground shopping mall, sporting every major international designer label, are sealed by the Drum Tower - the entrance to the atmospheric and engaging Muslim quarter. Xi'an also boasts an intact 14-kilometre Ming dynasty city wall.

There are some 60,000 Hui Muslims in the city and carrying on their trading tradition, a huge tourist market envelops the peace and dignity of the Great Mosque. The mosque, with its superb Sino-Arabic architecture was set up in 742 AD, though most of the surviving structures are of the last 400 years. The air in the surrounding streets is thick with the smell of homely cooking and spices - kebabs, lamb pasties and persimmon cakes are just part of a capacious fare on offer.

Central and Western China

THE YANGTZE RIVER • CHENGDU • CHONGQING • WUHAN

Distending 6,300 kilometres eastward from the fragile wilderness of Tibet to the metropolitan mass of Shanghai, the Yangtze river is the longest in China, and the third longest river in the world. The Chinese simply refer to it as the Long River or Changjiang

The Yangtze

The Yangtze cuts a grievous open wound through the heart of China, and is regarded by the Chinese as marking the division of their country into the north and south - both geographically and culturally. Chairman Mao's famous swim across the river symbolised the unity of a nation that has often been tormented by its tantrums and dispassion. The mighty river gushes through eight provinces before bellowing its sullen, silt-laden waters into the East China Sea.

The Yangtze's strategic position has made it important to the historical development of China, and today the river is influencing modernisation schemes for the regions through which it flows. The most ambitious of these is the Three Gorges Dam, which is under construction at Sandouping, 40 kilometres upstream from Yichang, in Hubei province. When completed in 2008, this will be the world's largest hydroelectric facility - producing the equivalent power of 10 nuclear plants, to supply Shanghai and the Lower Yangtze cities. Controversy has surrounded the Three Gorges Dam project since its inception in 1992. Plans to control the might of the ruthless waterway and stop its carnage date back to the 1920s. Apart from flood-alleviation and power generation, the dam will also ensure much safer navigation of the muddy and melancholy mater.

Once completed the water level of the 640-kilometre long Three Gorges Reservoir will reach between 145 to 175 metres, changing the mountain scenery for eternity. In November 2002 the diversion channel through which cruise and other river traffic once flowed was blocked in preparation for an initial rise in water levels to 135 metres that took place in June 2003, coincident with the opening of 4 of the 5 stages of the permanent ship lock. As part of this momentous transfiguration well over one million people have been relocated during the last decade.

Along the 200-kilometre section of the gorges, the peaks climb from 800-1,100 metres above sea-level and there has arguably not been an adverse visual effect as some foretold. New vistas and new scenic areas have already been opened up and numerous ugly factories satisfyingly submerged. The dam site itself, already a stop on most cruise itineraries, is destined to become a major tourist attraction and international tourist facilities have opened nearby. The mind-boggling monumental structure crests at 185 metres and will breach the Yangtze with a barrier over 2,300 metres long.

Chongqing and Wuhan are regarded as 'furnace' cities with boiling summertime temperatures. Spring and autumn are the best times for taking a river cruise. However, with the tall mountains and gorges through which the river winds, precipitation is very high and the peaks are usually shrouded in cloud and mist, although a light haze can enhance the beauty of the scenery.

The Three Gorges are the focus of any journey up or down the river between Chongqing and Wuhan or Yichang. The fascination of the gorges is not simply their awe-inspiring geological dimensions, but in the history that surrounds them. During the Han dynasty, over 2,000 years ago, generals fought battles for territorial control and in the later Three Kingdoms period, alliances were forged by some of the greatest heroes in Chinese history.

The journey through the gorges is also an awe-inspiring adventure of epic proportions. The Qutang Xia Gorge is the shortest but grandest - with perpendicular cliffs towering over 1,400 metres above the severely constricted river. The violent beauty of the mountains mellows as Wu Gorge comes into sight. Its velvety soft and verdant mountains present a much larger and mellow landscape, with an almost coastal appearance. The real blockbuster is the last gorge - the Xiling - the might of its waters and its craggy, fissured mountains extend for over 70-kilometres before dissolving into an undulating land bearing farming communities.

长江

长江在中国的心脏刻下了一道深深的印迹，中国人把长江看作中国南方和北方地理以及文化意义上的分界线。毛主席著名的长江畅游标志着中国，这个曾经饱受内战和军阀折磨的国家最终统一。这条大江流经六个省，然后咆哮着将泥沙淤积的江水注入东海。

长江的战略位置使得它在中国的发展进程中显得十分重要。现在，这条江正影响着它所覆盖的流域现代化的进程。长江最为著名的工程就是湖北宜昌上游40公里正在建设的三峡工程。到2009年工程完工时，它将成为世界上最大的水利工程，具备十个核电站的输电能力，可涵盖上海及其他长江下游的城市。自从三峡工程1992年被提上议事日程以来，围绕着它的争论就从未停止过。从20世纪20年代起，人们就计划能够控制这条大江汹涌的水流，停止它对居民造成的危害。到了20世纪50年代，又有新的方案出台。长江，这千百年来的生命之源，同时也是威胁之源。在1870年的洪水中，超过100万的人被失去了生命，而1931年和1935年发生的洪水更夺走了大约30万人的生命。除了防洪和发电的功能之外，三峡大坝同时确保了在这泥沙淤积、喜怒无常的大江中航行的安全。

到工程完工之日，长达640公里的三峡水库的水位将达到145到175米，永远改变当地的地理景观。2002年11月，水路航道关闭，为水平面在2003年6月上涨到135米做准备，同时竣工的还有五道船闸。为了实现这一巨大工程，超过100万的人在过去十年中迁移了住处。

在绵延200公里的峡谷中，最高峰高出水平面800到1100米，而且，预计中的危急状况并未出

现。新的景观和景点已经开放，众多的污染性工厂永久地沉入了水底。大坝已经成为众多游客新的目的地，它必将吸引更多目光，国际旅游设施也已开放。这座不朽的建筑高达185米，将长江打开了一个长达2300米的缺口。

重庆和武汉因其炎热高温的气候被称为火炉城市，所以乘船旅行的最佳季节是春秋两季。但是，由于长江流经的区域山高谷深，这里降雨量很大，时常云雾缭绕，轻微的模糊更增加了三峡的美感。

如果要在重庆、武汉或宜昌之间做水上旅行，三峡是不容错过的景点。它最大的魅力并不在于令人惊叹的多样地形，而是在于山水间呈现的沧桑感。在两千多年前的汉朝，将军们在这里为疆域征战；在三国时期，中国历史上最受人尊敬的英雄人物们在这里抵抗。

同时，三峡的旅程是瑰丽壮美的。瞿塘峡最短，但却最为壮丽，高达1400米的险峰直耸云天。随后，巫峡那汹涌雄伟的山脉映入眼帘。它连绵的山峰使整个景色显得极为大气，如同沿海般开阔。真正令人叹为观止的是最后的西陵峡，这里江水澎湃，山峰陡峭，鬼斧神工的景色绵延70公里，连接着中游肥沃的农业土地。

在1900年蒸汽船出现之前，水路交通是通过纤夫实现的。船只在悬崖绝壁间穿行，这些纤夫拉着绳索，将船向前逆流移动。现在，游客们可以在配备一流设施的轮船上欣赏三峡美景了。

Before steamboats were introduced in 1900, teams of men called trackers powered river traffic. From narrow tracks carved out of the face of cliffs, these men tugged on ropes to haul the boats upriver, often against the flow of violent rapids. Today visitors can spectate at the marvels of the gorges from modern cruise boats equipped with the conveniences of first-class hotels.

Chengdu

Chengdu, the capital of Sichuan province, is a surprisingly modern and sophisticated city and home to over 10 million people. The brightly illuminated city centre, hosting a huge statue of Chairman Mao, holds a cosmopolitan flavour and luxury apartments have been constructed at speed. Despite its enormity, the city takes life at an easy pace. Tea-houses are always full, and market stalls are always overflowing with local farm produce. The city centre has wide boulevards with pavements shaded by overhanging trees. Although the real grandeur of ancient Chengdu has vanished, even today remnants of it can be found along the Jin River. Here two-storey frame houses, painted deep red, overhang a tangled web of interesting lanes.

Traditionally home to some of the best craftsmen in China, Chengdu has many small curio shops. Here it is possible to find antiques or recently crafted pieces; particularly those produced by local goldsmiths, silversmiths and silk spinners.

The relaxed atmosphere of the city lends itself to dining out and provides an ideal backdrop for savouring Sichuan's distinctive cuisine, rich and spiced with hot chillies. Furthermore Chengdu's tea-house tradition is the most intact in the whole of China. New avenues for relaxation have recently been established along the banks of the Funan River. As part of an award-winning project to harness the downtown river, thousands of residents have been relocated and walkways and gardens now line the waterfront.

In the rural western suburbs stands Du Fu's Thatched Cottage. From 759 to 763, the poet spent four of his most productive years here, during which he wrote more than 200 poems. The original cottage was destroyed and the present buildings, from 1500 and 1811, contain various relics and editions of Du Fu's work. There is also a charming tea-house in its beautiful garden.

The Wenshu Buddhist Temple is located south of the railway station. It is dedicated to the God of Wisdom and is the headquarters of the Chan (Zen) Buddhist sect, having about 100 seminarians in residence at any one time. The temple houses many sacred relics and a large collection of sutras. The Provincial Museum has a spectacular collection of bronzes, stone bas-reliefs and tomb figurines, whereas an astounding display of ethnological exhibits can be found at the Sichuan University Museum.

Since Sichuan is home to the giant panda, Chengdu is the perfect place to view this charming, endangered animal. The local zoo

成都

成都是四川省省会，位于成都平原中部，是一座历史悠久的名城。周朝末年，当时的蜀诸侯将国都由郫县迁此，取《史记・本纪第一五帝》中：一年而所居成聚，二年成邑，三年成都意，名其为“成都”。成都市又名锦官城、蓉城，位于富饶的成都平原中心，是中国历史名城之一。成都一直是西南地区的政治、经济、文化中心。名胜古迹荟萃，为成都旅游区的主要特点。最为著名的名胜古迹有杜甫草堂、武侯祠、望江楼公园、王建墓、青羊宫、文殊院和三苏祠等。

重庆

重庆简称渝，古有渝州、恭州之称，是古代巴国的都城，位于长江和嘉陵江交汇处。古时从四川到中原，大多经重庆出三峡。抗日战争时期，重庆是当时国民政府的陪都。重庆城建于两江所夹半岛的山丘之上。城市街道上下迂回相通，房屋大多建于山坡，层次繁多，形成独特的山城风格，是名闻海内外的美丽而又古老的山城。重庆城常年迷雾笼罩，也有“雾都”之称。除山城风貌，重庆旅游区还有革命旧址红岩村，南、北温泉，缙云山等风景名胜。

武汉

武汉位于鄂中长江与汉水交汇处，地处长江中下游分界点，素有“九省通衢”之称。全市由武昌、汉口、汉阳三部分组成，昔称“武汉三镇”。湖北省省会武汉市，是中国重要的水陆交通枢纽和工业基地，气候温暖湿润，物产丰富，历史上一直是军事重镇和商贸名城，旅游资源十分丰富。市内三山、龟山、蛇山和洪山，是武汉名胜古迹的集中处。武汉长江大桥飞架龟、蛇二山之间，湖光山色，气象万千。景点以黄鹤楼、东湖最负盛名，汉阳区的归元禅寺、古琴台、晴川阁、石榴花塔等景点也颇受游人青睐。

takes pride in giving some of the animals an enclosed, if captive, haven, and not only adults but also baby pandas can usually be glimpsed in the compound. Visits can also be made to the Chengdu Giant Panda Breeding and Research Centre, 12 kilometres away from the city.

South of the city at Leshan, the largest Buddha image carved out of a cliff in China sits in perpetuity over looking the charming town. The 1,300-year-old sacred image radiates 71 metres up the cliff face. It draws numerous visitors and has recently been restored to its former glory. Another major attraction in the area is the sacred Mount Emei. Rising to 3,000 metres the lofty peak symbolizes Puxian, the Bodhisattva of Universal Kindness. The mountain is a great place for hikers - presenting rock, pine and bamboo clad trails opening onto secluded monastical retreats.

Chengdu has traditionally been a base for heavy industry; food processing and aircraft manufacture, but is now carving a name for itself in the fields of high-tech and electronics. Its recently opened Nanjiao Airport, to the north of the city, has numerous international links - including direct flights to Korea. The city offers a wealth of fine accommodation, including the Crowne Plaza, the Jinjiang and Sheraton Lido hotels.

Chongqing

The 'Mountain City' of Chongqing clings to the cliffs above the confluence of the Yangzte and a major tributary, the Jialing River. The bustling city rises far above docks that are held firm in the swirling river currents by cables, anchored into the rocky shore. Cable cars glide across the river to the opposite bank, and giant bridges carry continuous lines of trucks loaded with the city's vast industrial output.

The city, which has been a major transport hub since earliest times, has developed into the largest industrial area in southwest China and the manufacturing centre of Sichuan Province. It is China's most recently established municipality. In 1997 it was endowed with the status deemed necessary to fast-forward development. With a total population of around 31 million, Chongqing can now fairly claim to be the world's largest metropolitan region, although around 20 million residents still rely on farming for their livelihoods. It is the centrepiece of the government's 'Go West' strategy and up to US$20 billion is to be pumped into the city each year over the next decade.

As a consequence of its newfound status and the new realities contingent with the construction of the Three Gorges Dam, the city is undergoing immense reconstruction. Impressive modern high-rise apartments line the rivers with their presence exaggerated by their mountain elevation. Two bridges across the Yangtze have been completed, numerous pollutant factories have been moved out, the use of coal and leaded fuel has been banned and a new light rail line has been constructed. Ambitious road building schemes are underway to reduce travelling times within the municipal area that occupies a territory three times the size of Belgium.

Despite the massive scale of the grand design, the city retains an earthy appeal. On summer evenings, residents stroll about in the hope of catching a refreshing breeze, and there are street food markets, colourful flower markets, sidewalk restaurant stalls, herbalists and calligraphers. The city's northern riverfront has recently been given a new lease of life with a promenade packed with bars and eateries offering a wealth of dining and entertainment possibilities.

Within the city limits are a number of museums, including one devoted to General Joseph Stilwell, Commander-in-Chief of the US forces, who played a major role in overcoming the Japanese forces in Asia during the Second World War. This fascinating museum is housed in the General's former residence inside Eling Park, permitting fantastic views across the city.

Best River View, Best City Location

DISCOVER THE NEW FIVE-STAR
HOWARD JOHNSON
PEARL PLAZA HOTEL
FOR YOUR NEXT TRIP TO WUHAN!

Perched elegantly over the city of Wuhan and the famous Yangtze River, the new 43-story deluxe Howard Johnson Pearl Plaza Wuhan opens its doors offering unique standards of service for the business and leisure traveler.

Located at Hankou District's bustling riverfront, in the heart of the city's government, business and entertainment district, and 40 minutes from the international airport, this upscale international hotel features 393 deluxe rooms, 38 serviced apartments and 12 office units.

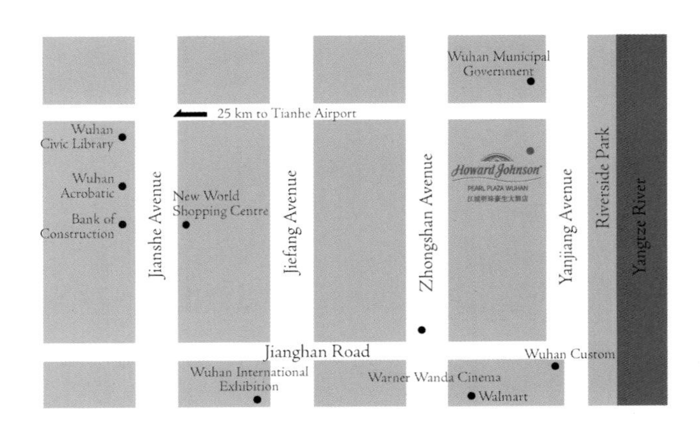

THE HOWARD JOHNSON CLUB

The Howard Johnson Club rooms and suites have been meticulously designed to offer the utmost level of comfort and convenience for the seasoned business traveler.

Occupying levels 27 to 30 of the hotel, the Howard Johnson Executive Floors feature exclusive benefits and services such as personalized check-in and check-out, access to a private lounge, complimentary executive breakfast and refreshments, early evening cocktails and canapés, high-speed Internet access and a choice of international newspapers and publications.

No.182 Yanjiang Avenue, Hankou District, Wuhan 430014, Hubei Province, P. R. China
Tel: +86 27 8277 6666 • Fax: +86 27 8277 6888 • Tel/Fax: +86 27 5223 3388

For Special Promotional Rates, please contact the Sales and Marketing Department

Tel: +86 27 8277 6666 • Fax: +86 27 8277 6888 • Tel/Fax: +86 27 5223 3388
E-mail: sales@hojowuhan.com • Website: www.hojowuhan.com

Yet, Chongqing's history stretched far beyond the relics of the Second World War. In the fourth century BC, Chongqing was called Yuzhou and was the capital of the Ba state. In the Southern Song Dynasty (1127-1279), Yuzhou was renamed Chongqing, or 'double happiness,' to mark the enthronement of the Emperor Zhaodun, a native of the city. Chongqing was opened to foreign trade in 1890 and its riches of gold, copper, silk, fur and opium were shipped down river to greedy Shanghai.

Outside the city spectacular cave carvings are to be found in Dazu County. One translation of Dazu, is 'Big Foot,' and legend has it that Buddha left a huge footprint in a nearby pond; hence the name. Fifty sites have been found with some 50,000 carvings in 290 niches and grottos. The earliest sculptures date from the Tang dynasty. Another popular day trip is to the Northern Hot Springs, 50 kilometres north of the city, and to the nearby Beipei Natural History Museum with its extensive exhibit of dinosaur fossils.

To cater for the influx of visitors, several first-class hotels have opened, a major new cruise ship dock has been created and the enlarged international airport is served by frequent flights from Hong Kong, Bangkok, Nagoya, Seoul and Munich, as well as all major Chinese cities.

Wuhan

Wuhan is set in the vast Jianghan Plain, a region that is said to be more water than land. Levees are needed to protect the city from seasonal flooding. Along the waterfront, the jumbled old neighbourhoods and alleyways are now being replaced by shopping malls. Even the city's graceful early 20th century houses are being replaced by multi-storey buildings. Nevertheless, it is still possible to catch a bicycle pedicab to visit some of the remaining street markets, whilst the most fascinating sectors of the old city can only explored on foot.

Apart from being the capital of Hubei Province, Wuhan is the seventh largest city in China, with a population of over 8.3 million, and it is the nation's largest inland port. The city is also set to move up the world's economic and population league. Wuhan is also a major crossroad on the Beijing-Kowloon railway. Located at the confluence of the Yangtze and the Hanshui rivers, it has long been a centre for traders. The focus changed at the beginning of the 19th century when it became the first city in the interior of the country to be industrialised. It is now considered to be the industrial, commercial, scientific and cultural hub of central China.

Whilst the city lives up to its reputation as one of the 'three furnaces of China' on account

of its soaring summer heat, its cooling rivers cut the city in what is known as 'the three towns of Wuhan.' The Hanshui and Yangtze rivers separate the three plainly different urban areas of Hanyang, Hankou and Wuchang - though they are comprehensively linked by a series of bridges, partnered by a rapid transit rail system.

Hanyang is the smallest of the three, built around one of Wuhan's most famous landmarks, Tortoise Hill, on the northern bank of the Yangtze. West of Tortoise Hill is the beautiful Yuehu Lake with a famous terrace called the Ancient Music Terrace, a popular tea-house with various halls and pagodas.

Hankou is the busiest part of Wuhan and is where the docks and the new railway station are situated. At the end of the 19th century, foreign concessions belonging to Britain, France, Germany, Russia and Japan were located here. Some villas and monumental office buildings the 1920s and 1930s have been renovated to their former glory. One of China's busiest shopping centres is nearby on the renowned Jiangshan Road. A wide variety of entertainment waits - with karaoke halls, dance halls, and theatres hosting world-class acrobats or Han and Chu opera. The People's Parade - a recently renovated 1919 building on Zhongshan Dadao is now the established centre for the arts and culture. The complex also includes an amusement centre, a cinema and a parade of modern shops.

Wuchang, the seat of the Hubei Government, is a modern district with long, broad avenues. This area of the city is almost surrounded by water, of which the East Lake, covering an area of 3,000 hectares, is considered the most scenic. Wuchang's most famous landmark is the Yellow Crane Tower on Snake Hill. The tower has been widely celebrated by poets throughout the ages, and is associated with the legend of a Taoist sage who flew away on a yellow crane to become an Immortal. The Hubei Provincial Museum has a fine collection of artefacts excavated from within the province.

在武汉，华美达天禄酒店位于市中心繁华的商业区，酒店设施齐全，员工服务卓越，是商务差旅，城市观光的绝佳下榻之所。

Ramada Plaza Tian Lu Hotel, Wuhan, ideally located in the business shopping and entertainment center of Wuhan City. The hotel offers fully equipped facilities and unrivalled personalized services. Whether you stay for business or travel, you will be assured of warm hospitality and complete satisfaction.

RAMADA PLAZA WUHAN
武汉华美达天禄酒店

中国武汉市汉口青年路 5 号 邮政编码: 430030
No.5 Youth Road, Hankou, Wuhan, China 430030
电话Tel: (86 27) 8363 0888 传真Fax: (86 27) 8363 0849
网址 Web Site: www.ramadaplaza-tianlu.com / www.ramadainternational.com

Shanghai

Since the early 1990s Shanghai has experienced a frenzy of activity reminiscent of the heady speculative years of the 1930s, when the 'Paris of the 0rient' came of age

BANKING ON THE BUND

The Ginger Griffin

Asia's former 'Golden Mile' of finance, commerce and trade, is now enjoying a renaissance with the opening of new high-end eateries, emporiums and art centres in magnificent historical architectural surroundings. Many buildings still house financial and commercial concerns - whilst others lay dormant awaiting their new beginning.

The word Bund, often mistaken for a German expression, actually derives from the Hindustani word band meaning a promenade. Its row of commanding historical buildings presents an incredible architectural face reflecting the importance of foreign, primarily British, business interests in Shanghai in days of old. An esplanade with lawns stretching along the entire waterfront was first laid out in the 1880s. The Bund's new wide, raised promenade is an essential destination for sightseers - especially at night when the buildings' façades are spectacularly illuminated.

IMPOSING

The brainchild of Sir Victor Sassoon the former Cathay Hotel, which opened in August 1929, symbolised the city's passage to sophistication and modernity in the 1930s. The hotel was practically built around an arsenal of fashionable Lalique lights - including its illuminated bathroom shaving mirrors. Some Lalique wall plaques still survive on the eighth floor. The same floor also houses a Chinese restaurant in the Dragon and Phoenix Hall. It was created in 1933 to show China to rich American tourists who were disappointed with how Western-looking Shanghai appeared to them. Its vivid Chinese design was adopted from door panels in the Forbidden City and the Temple of Heaven in Beijing. Shanghai's most famous art deco icon, at No. 20, is now the north wing of the Peace Hotel. Its legendary jazz band plays nightly.

Bund 18 in the former Chartered Bank Building, built in 1923, was converted into a sophisticated multi-level space for dining, shopping and the arts in 2004. Magnificent Italian marble columns and facings have been preserved on the ground floor. Look no further if you want Cartier or Zegna, or to feast on the finest French cuisine at Sens & Bund, or Chinese Cuisine at Tan Wai Lou. The views from the hot spot seventh floor rooftop Bar Rouge are breathtaking.

The huge clock tower of the Custom House Building at No. 13 which used to play the chimes of Westminster's Big Ben now plays a rather muted CD version of The East is Red. Look out for the loudspeakers above the clock. The Chinese Maritime Customs was managed by the British as far back as the 1850s.

The most opulent building on the Bund can be found at No. 12. The former Hongkong and Shanghai Bank building, with two bronze lions at its entrance, was completed in 1923 and is now occupied by the Pudong Development Bank. The bank was designed to dominate the Bund. Its domed entrance hall displays a collection of superb Italian mosaics depicting the great banking centres of the world, topped off with figures from Greek mythology. The mosaics which were feared lost in the 1950s when the building was occupied by the Shanghai Municipal Government were in fact covered with plaster and paint. They were uncovered virtually intact when the building was restored in 1997.

The rooftop of the former Japanese NKK Shipping Company at No. 5 provides a stylish and sophisticated setting for M on the Bund – the first and most revered international restaurant to be established along the waterfront. The atmospheric Glamour Room at M on the Bund also hosts regular literary, cultural and musical events.

Handel Lee, the Chinese-American entrepreneur, was behind up-market centre for the arts, culture and cuisine at Three on the Bund. The institution incorporates the Shanghai Gallery of Art, fine restaurants including Jean Georges, the Whampoa Club, Laris and New Heights as well as designer outlets and beauty shops. It occupies the former Union Building, built for a British insurance company in 1915.

Shiatzy Chen opened her second outlet in Shanghai at No. 9 on the Bund in 2005 and is proud to fly the flag of exquisite Chinese fashion design in the face of the international designer labels alongside. The latest designer name to arrive on the Bund, Dolce & Gabbana, moved into premises at 6 Bund in 2006.

Peter Hibbard, alias The Ginger Griffin, specialises in tours around the Bund and other historical districts of Shanghai for the most discerning corporate clients. He is author of the Odyssey Guide to Shanghai and his book The Bund Shanghai: China Faces West will be published by Odyssey Publications in March 2007.
www.gingergriffin.com

With its position at the mouth of the Yangtze River, the life giving artery of China, Shanghai grew from being a modest commercial town into Asia's most important and flamboyant city after the British first arrived in 1842. As a treaty port, British nationals enjoyed immunity from Chinese law and a freedom to trade as they desired. Two years later the French and Americans struck similar deals with the Chinese. The American Settlement was amalgamated with the British in 1863 to become the International Settlement - the financial and commercial heart of the city. The French Concession developed into a magnificent residential district. The neutrality and safety of the foreign areas attracted millions of Chinese, far outnumbering their foreign overlords, who had little say in the running of the city.

The city's immutable spirit and soul, has been rekindled by recent government policies and enacted by a Shanghai public with a very distinctive mind set. Since the early 1990s Shanghai has experienced a frenzy of activity reminiscent of the heady speculative years of the 1930s, when the 'Paris of the Orient' came of age. Shanghai is again in the throes of a physical, economic and social revolution, designed to restore the city's former status as the Far Eastern centre of trade, finance and culture. Billions of dollars are being spent on infrastructure projects bent on transforming the outdated fabric of Shanghai.

Numerous spectacular bridges and tunnels traverse the Huangpu River linking the Puxi and Pudong districts. An elevated ring road and an elevated light railway circle the city and a sophisticated metro system is still evolving. Huge green lungs - parks and lakes have been inserted, replacing block upon block of old housing and their long-term residents. The rattle of construction is never far from earshot.

The former main streets of the International Settlement and the French Concession have changed beyond recognition. Coloured and neon lights create avenues of enticement for the wealthier modern Shanghainese, whilst modern skyscrapers arise from the ashes of the past at a hungry speed. Shanghai has been evolving at a pace unmatched by any other city in China, or indeed the world, challenging Hong Kong as the country's international conduit to the future.

Spectacle Of Sights

The early 20th century European buildings of the Bund, emblazoned at night with a vignette of magical illuminations, represent the face of Shanghai that all visitors admire. Nearby in the heart of the city the former British racecourse has been converted into People's Square.

上海

上海座落在中国的生命之河——长江的入海口，1842年根据当时清政府同英国之间的一项条约，英国人如愿获得在上海的法律豁免权和自由贸易权。两年后，法国和美国政府也强迫中国政府签定了相同的协议。1863年，美租界与英租界合并成为一处国际租界，这里也逐渐成为上海的金融和商业中心。与此同时，法租界发展成为华丽的居民区。这些外国租界所特有的中立和安全优势吸引了众多的中国人，上海终于成为一座独特的城市。

超越历史——非同寻常的上海景色

上世纪初期建成的外滩仍是这座城市的精髓所在。到了夜晚，闪烁的灯光更是把它点缀得无比妖娆。这里的建筑通常是银行、贸易大楼和宾馆，它们至今仍然保存着往昔风韵。浦东发展银行的前身是富丽堂皇的香港上海银行大厦，它的穹顶采取了威尼斯式的设计，门口的铜狮栩栩如生。和平饭店的前身是中国饭店，这里仍然是二战前舞蹈的乐园。最近，外滩3号原联合大厦里新设置了高级餐馆、商店和各式文化展览。

从前的赛马场被改造成人民广场，这座现代化的设施是城市的骄傲。在广场上座落着上海博物馆，它建于1995年，内有世界一流的古代艺术品展览。广场上还建造着富丽堂皇的大剧院、上海艺术博物馆、市政府大厦和上海城市规划展示厅。

如果说上海老城映射出上个世纪30年代上海的野心，那么黄浦江对岸的浦东新区则以其现代化的风貌引人注目。浦东占地超过500平方公里，在20世纪90年代初期还是一片农田。现在，这里已经到处是高楼大厦、美丽公园、高档公寓和林荫大道。陆家嘴金融贸易中心是浦东的中心区域，这里被称为亚洲的华尔街。华尔街也是它日后发展的目标。

上海的欧式建筑掩映在高耸的大厦之间。绿树成荫的前法租界能带给人怀旧的情绪。这里的建筑红顶白墙，草地碧绿，幽雅的住所和洛可可房屋不会随岁月老去。许多优美的房屋已被用作政府机关，还有一些成为了私人别墅和旅馆。另外，还有一部分建筑被改装成酒吧和餐厅。

市区还有一个风景如画、游人如织的豫园，这里的茶社湖心亭建于16世纪，18世纪豫园建成，这里曲径通幽、荷花飘香，美丽的假山和曲折的长廊历经岁月不改雍容。

上海西北部有座玉佛寺，建于1911年，至今仍然香火旺盛。在这里保存着精美的两尊来自缅甸的玉佛。上海最古老的建筑是龙华塔和龙华寺，位于城市的西南部。

感觉上海——简单的快乐

南京路一直是中国头号商业街，从前，它以出售各种西方商品而闻名天下。现在这条路被拓宽了，成了步行街，但红火的生意却依然如故。沿着街道向西走，便到了各种现代化的购物中心和商业广场，比如恒隆广场和梅隆镇广场。

现在，淮海路比南京路更具魅力。这里从前是法租界的主要街道，现在已经被重新装修，成为艺术时尚的汇集地，吸引了世界各地的品牌店，使上海可以与米兰、巴黎和伦敦相媲美。

徐家汇将上海新城区和老城区连接在一起，

是居住的理想选择。上海城中心的静安区有全市最好的居住区。而新天地作为时尚天堂和休闲去处，与太平桥相邻，于2002年末开始营业。上海的郊外和浦东地区有许多诱人的去处，比如配备游泳池、高尔夫球场和餐厅的乡村俱乐部。

老式建筑在上海2001年开业的时尚娱乐的大本营新天地同样占据着重要的地位。这里让人想起伦敦的海德公园。整片的石库门被重新翻修，房屋被赋予了新的特点和功能。在北里，老式建筑被设计得新颖时尚，装修豪华富丽，许多餐厅就设在这里。这里提供各地美食，比如法国、美国、德国、英国、巴西、意大利、日本及中国各地的美食，是真正的万国风味世界。豪华的餐厅，如时尚的T8和意大利餐厅，与喧嚣的酒吧和俱乐部相邻，营业直到清晨。新天地的主要投资方在2002年中期完成了现代化的南里的建设，这里除了代表世界各国美味的豪华餐厅，还有时髦商店、零售店铺、饭店和电影院。

也许上海现在的夜生活场面与上世纪30年代相比少了些奢华，但却更显动感，一系列迪斯科舞厅相继开业。现场乐队，包括国外的乐手，层出不穷。面向成年人和青年人的酒吧生意兴隆，综合了传统与时尚。爵士乐，曾一度销声匿迹，现在又重新回到了舞台。最为火热的酒吧是科顿俱乐部和蓝调爵士之家。除此之外，上海一些高级酒店里也能听到优美的爵士音乐。在和平饭店的酒吧里，仍然上演着二战前就很流行的爵士音乐，而演出者都是一些花甲老人。

上海——城市万花筒

随着豪华先进的大剧院的建成开放，上海的文化艺术水平又上升到了新的高度。这是全国最为专业的艺术圣殿，在夜晚，它光芒四射，好似一座冰宫。它的透明墙壁和上翘的屋檐使人恍如隔世。这些光彩夺目的墙壁据说是象征全国范围内的对艺术的开放态度。

但上海作为国际会议和商业中心的迅猛发展不适于其成长为艺术中心蒙上了阴影。为了取代香港成为亚洲展览会之都，上海将于2010年承办世界博览会，这将巩固上海在世界都市中的地位。这个博览会将吸引7000万游客。上海先后于1999年举办了财富论坛，于2001年举办了亚太经合组织会议，现在，它又计划进一步改造展览设施。随着上海将于2004年到2010年承办F1赛车系列锦标赛，世界的目光将再次聚焦上海。上海也像一座迷恋汽车的城市，随着更多的投资涌向上海，这座城市必将继续繁荣。

It's a showcase of modern architecture and civic pride, housing the world-class Shanghai Museum, the spectacular crystalline structure of the Grand Theatre, the Shanghai Art Museum, the City Government building and the Shanghai Urban Planning Exhibition Hall, which houses a huge scale model of how Shanghai will look in 2020.

Contemporaneously mirroring the ambitions of Thirties Shanghai, the Pudong New Area with its fantastically futuristic face shines in the Huangpu River opposite the Bund. The area, covering over 500 square kilometres, was little more than farmland at the turn of the 1990s. Today it is a superbly choreographed spectacle of skyscraper spires, attractive parks, massive housing developments and wide tree-lined boulevards. At its core, the Lujiazui Financial and Trade Zone has been designed to be Asia's Wall Street - an aspiration well within reach.

The dramatic, punctuated, Stock Exchange building is Asia's largest and nearby Shanghai's modern symbol, the Oriental Pearl TV Tower, soars 468 metres in to the sky. Nearby the striking 88-storey Jinmao Building contains the luxurious Grand Hyatt Hotel with its cavernous telescopic atrium. Just next door work is progressing on the Shanghai World Finance Centre, which is destined to become the world's tallest building. On the waterfront, the landmark Shanghai International Conference Centre, flanked by two huge glass globes made its debut by hosting the Global Fortune 500 Forum. Nearby, exclusive high-rise apartments announce a new penchant for decadent waterfront living. The vast Century Park with its manicured topography and huge lake, capable of hosting water sports, sits aside the fabulously ingenious Museum of Science and Technology. Occupying almost 100,000 square metres, the museum's fine interactive displays and cavernous exhibits are a must for children and for those young at heart.

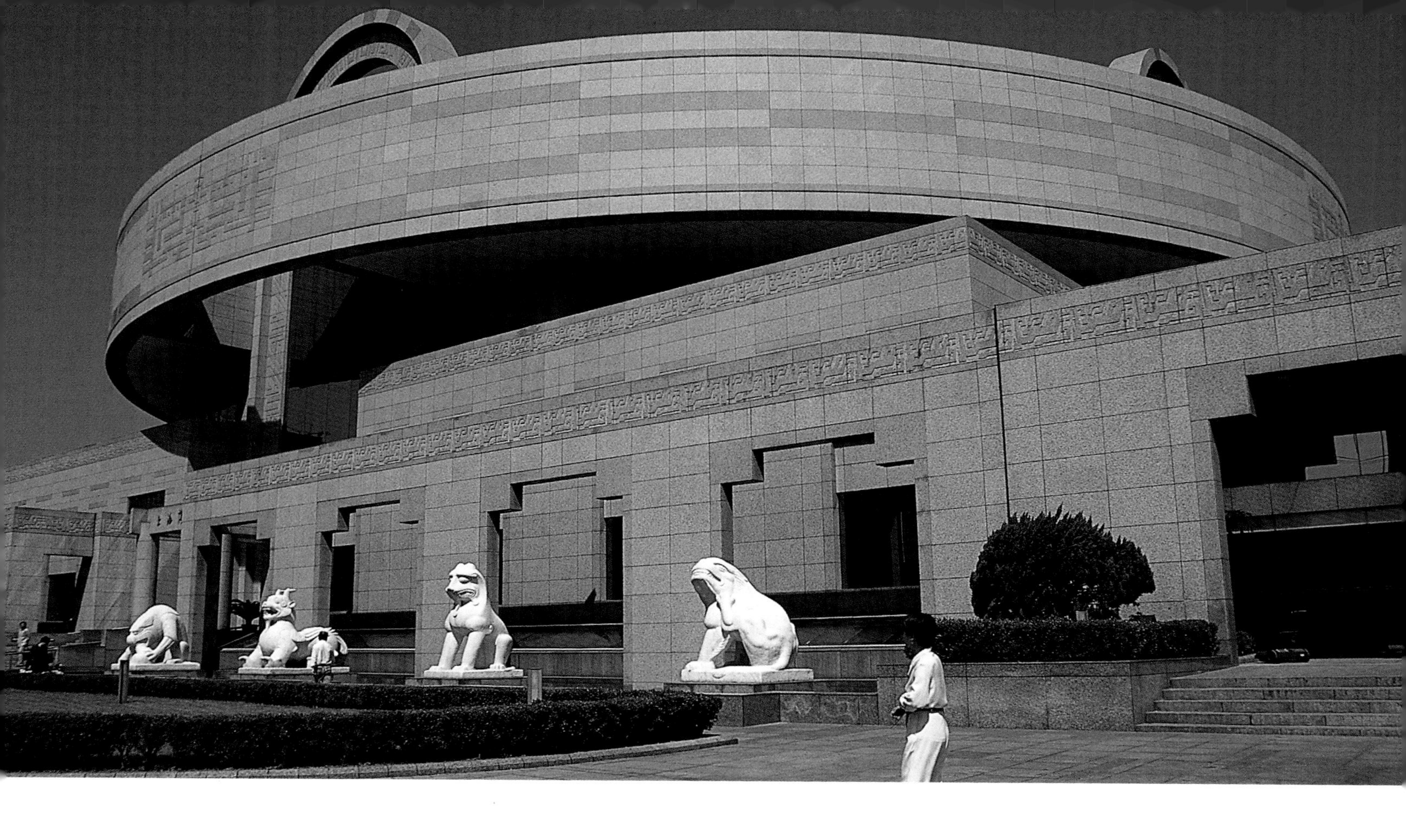

Where Pudong meets the sea its sophisticated international airport is now linked to the city metro system by the Maglev railway capable of speeds up to 430 kilometres an hour. In 2002 all international flights were moved from the overloaded Hongqiao Airport to Pudong with the intent of establishing it as one of Asia's busiest transport hubs by 2010. The present annual capacity of around 20 million is set to rise to an astounding 50 million during this period.

Frequently obscured by high-rise buildings or by impenetrable concrete walls, huge pockets of Shanghai's western heritage have survived. The plane tree-lined avenues of the former French Concession evoke feelings of familiarity and nostalgia. Red-roofed, ivy-clad houses with lawns, gracious art deco apartment blocks and huge rococo mansions impudently defy space and time. Many of the finest buildings are used as government offices and are strictly off-limits. The most accessible estates have been converted into villa hotels, whilst many other architectural gems have found new careers as bars and restaurants.

Shanghai was a fertile breeding ground for revolutionary politics as whilst its foreigner residents enjoyed the good life most of its Chinese population was downtrodden. Abject squalor prevailed behind the fabulous facades of Nanjing Road - Asia's premiere shopping street. Ironically the Chinese Communist Party was founded in 1921 at a dwelling in the former French Concession. The house is now a part of a museum which, even more ironically, now sits amidst the fashionably chic and decidedly up-market Xintiandi entertainment district.

There are a number of other house-museums dedicated to key historical figures including the former residence of Dr. Sun Yat-sen and his wife Song Qingling on Xiangshan Road. The charming wood-panelled house contains many beautiful photographic portraits and a facsimile of his fascinating personal library, amongst other priceless antiques and revolutionary relics. Nearby, Zhou En-lai's former residence on Sinan Road, which served as the office to the underground Communist Party, is also open to the public.

Like a bulbous egg, nestling to the east of the former French Concession, the narrow lanes and traditional architecture of the old town provide a stark contrast to the capaciousness and modernity of Pudong. The old town area is, in fact, a Chinatown in a Chinese city. At the core of a huge bazaar area is the picturesque, but rarely tranquil Yu Garden, embracing China's most famous tea-house. Commonly referred to as the Willow Pattern tea-house, it sits in the middle of an ornamental lake. The governor of Sichuan province built the Yu Garden, or Garden of Leisurely Repose, in the 16th century. Containing over 30 pavilions, ponds full of carp and lotus, grand rockeries and winding corridors the design has survived with impunity. Other elements of traditional Chinese culture are speckled across the city. The Jade Buddha Temple, dating from 1911, is very popular with visitors and houses two fine white Burmese jade Buddhas.

SHANGHAI
Shopping Nirvana

Shanghai is experiencing a massive retail revolution. Ultra-modern stores, mega-malls and hypermarkets have sprung up all over the city - often sat next to local shopping areas that not only offer a striking visual, but also a remarkable commercial contrast. Shopping cities, with integral recreation and amusement facilities and food courts, are very much in vogue. Designer stores are found in abundance, where the price of a simple handbag may be more than most people's annual salary. Ostentatious showrooms proffer modern Western lifestyles in anything from brocaded French period furniture to Bentley cars. With China's entry to the WTO, tariffs are falling for imported goods, though prices are still far higher than in the West for most products.

REMEMBER THE THRILL
OF TRYING SOMETHING NEW?
Embrace that feeling once again at the new Millennium Hongqiao Hotel Shanghai.
Millennium Hotels & Resorts introduces its latest 5-star international hotel and its first in Shanghai. With an impressive glass façade, sophisticated décor and luxurious rooms within a botanical haven of lush greenery, the elegant Millennium Hongqiao Hotel Shanghai brings luxury to a whole new level.
For a truly memorable stay, call our reservations hotline at +86 21 6208 5888 or email: sales@millenniumhongqiao.com
INTRODUCTORY ROOM RATES
From RMB 1,320 per room/night (40% off published rates)
10 Jul – 31 Aug 2006
1 – 31 Dec 2006
From RMB 1,540 per room/night (30% off published rates)
1 Sep – 30 Nov 2006
Terms and conditions apply.
www.millenniumhongqiao.com
MILLENNIUM
HONGQIAO HOTEL
SHANGHAI
上海千禧海鸥大酒店
AFRICA
AMERICAS
ASIA
EUROPE
MIDDLE EAST
NEW ZEALAND
More than 88 hotels in 16 countries worldwide

However away from the international shopping arena, in local stores and in the city's bustling markets there is plenty to interest the visitor. Shanghai remains a shopping nirvana with a wealth of great value gifts and souvenirs, as well the promise of many fun-filled hours.

In the Chinese mind Shanghai and shopping are synonymous. The millions that descend on Shanghai from all around China will all find their way to the Nanjing Road, China's number one shopping street. The road is divided into two sections – West Nanjing Road used to be known as Bubbling Well Road and now houses some of China's classiest shopping malls and office towers, including Plaza 66, Westgate Mall and CITIC Square. Shanghai's largest department store, the New World, also houses Madame Tussaud's Wax Museum, opened in 2006, featuring global icons including David Beckham and Yao Ming. East Nanjing Road, which runs up from the waterfront has largely been pedestrianised and public squares have been installed. It's a great place to stroll, window shop, and rub shoulders with hordes of Chinese purchasing pilgrims.

Central Huaihai Road rivals the Nanjing Road in the style stakes. The former glamour of Avenue Joffre, the main street of the old French Concession, has been restored. >>>

Executives stopping over in Pudong stay at the Novotel Atlantis

Novotel Atlantis Shanghai provides the smart alternative to luxury accommodation, offering the astute traveller comfort, convenience and professional hospitality. If you are looking for a well-located city hotel, Novotel has the answer, providing international standards of service and quality in destinations across the region.

We know you'll enjoy our level of service. After all, we're the business class of hotels.

Novotel Atlantis Shanghai 海神诺富特大酒店
728 Pudong Avenue, Shanghai 200120, P.R.China
Tel: +86 (21) 5036 6666 Fax: +86 (21) 5036 6677
E-mail: mail@novotelatlantis.com

For further information call +86 (21) 5036 6666 or check our website: www.novotel.com
www.accorhotels.com/asia

Accor operates over 400 Novotel hotels & resorts worldwide.

For reservations call, **Australia** 1300 65 65 65, **China** 800 830 2688*, **Hong Kong SAR** 800 93 8768*, **Japan** 00531 61 6353*, **Singapore** 800 616 13 67*. (*toll free)
If calling from countries other than those listed please phone: (61-2) 8584 8666, fax: (61-2) 8584 8699 or e-mail: Accorres.BKK@accor.com

▶ A new perspective on our Hotels and Services

CATS
上海大剧院

The street and many smaller ones running off it are crammed with chic boutiques, interior design shops, eateries and huge stores - it's the place to be seen. The Pudong New Area also packs a punch with a frenzy of commercial activity centred on the Times Square area, with the Yaohan and Takashimya department stores. The Xujiahui area, near the former St. Ignatius Cathedral, has also emerged as a major shopping and commercial district, with an emphasis on high-tech goods as well as fashion.

In complete contrast the more native atmosphere of the Yu Garden bazaar area oozes pleasure-giving opportunities. The old Chinese neighbourhood with its slum housing and narrow courses of closely packed houses has largely disappeared, being supplanted by a compelling maze of alleys, small shops and large emporia cloaked with Ming and Qing style features. It is a colourful attraction in its own right and draws hundreds of thousands of visitors daily. It's also a great area for antique hunting - in the basement of the Huabao Building, in the multi-storey Fuyou Road market on Central Fangbang Road and at the nearby Dongtai Road. Everything from old brass doorknobs to magnificent Qing dynasty and art deco furniture is on offer. To the north of the main bazaar runs Shanghai Old Street - a skilfully renovated 800-metre stretch of wooden-fronted shops, restaurants and tea-houses offering glimpses of life of the old.

SHOWCASE SHANGHAI
City on Parade

Shanghai has been an important hub for arts and entertainment for more than a hundred and fifty years. The city's cultural and arts scene has been elevated with the advent of the dazzling state-of-the-art Grand Theatre - the nations most eloquent statement of its commitment to the arts. This temple to culture glitters like a fantasy ice palace at night, its transparent walls and upswept eaves giving it a sense of 'otherworldliness.' The clear walls are said to symbolise a new artistic openness that is sweeping across the country.

Home to the Shanghai Broadcasting Symphony Orchestra, which hosts foreign musicians and conductors, the Grand Theatre is a sell-out success. The Shanghai Concert Hall, a city landmark dating back to 1930 has been physical transplanted 100 metres from where it formerly stood and still plays host to classical concerts.

Marking the advent of a new age for the city the butterfly-shaped Shanghai Oriental Arts Centre in Pudong staged its first performance on New Year's Eve 2004. As Shanghai's first purpose built performance venue, at a cost US$120 million, it is now home to the Shanghai Symphony Orchestra. Designed by French architect Paul Andreu, who also designed the Grande Arche de la Defense in Paris and the Beijing National Grand Theatre, it houses a 2,000-seat concert hall and a 1,000-seat opera house.

Shanghai is also attempting to establish itself as a major centre for the arts - though set upon a canvas of aggressive commerce and set against the established artistic hegemony of Beijing - its aesthetic credibility is open to debate. An international art fair is held each November and numerous galleries are springing up around the city. Most notable is the modern art gallery opened at Three on the Bund in 2004. The major city art gallery is housed in the former race club to the west of People's Square - which also houses a continental restaurant on its roof.

In an area surrounding the newly cleaned-up Suzhou Creek, increasing numbers of artists and musicians are invading the fast diminishing supply of studios and warehouses. No. 50 Moganshan Road, formerly a large industrial complex, has been reworked into Shanghai's premiere district for artists, galleries and bijou shops. Another artistic community has established itself in Taikang Road - a largely unspoiled 1920s street in the heart of the former French Concession.

Shanghai's stature as an exhibition centre for the arts is over-shadowed by its meteoric rise as an international convention and commercial exhibition centre. Promising to supplant Hong Kong as Asia's exhibition capital, the staging of the World Expo in 2010 will cement the city's eminence in hosting the world. Kick-started by the 1999 Fortune 500 Forum and the 2001 APEC meeting the city plans to massively expand its exhibition facilities. Shanghai already earns roughly half of the whole nation's income from such activity and boasts five major exhibition centres, as well as hundreds of hotels and smaller venues offering convention-related facilities. The international spotlight is also focusing on Shanghai in the sports field with the city hosting the F1 championship racing series between 2004 and 2010. For a city that is obsessed by cars and with raising its visitor count - it's full throttle ahead.

All That Jazz

Certain aspects of the lifestyle that lent Shanghai the sobriquet 'Paris of the East' in the 1930s have been revived in recent years. Nowhere is this more evident than in Shanghai's glittering parade of nightspots. There's all manner of bars and clubs ranging from those suitable for a first date to sleazy watering holes full of Asian businessmen, to state-of-the-art clubs, with major international DJs patronised by the young international

nouveau-riche and all-night karaoke bars. There has been an explosion in the number of private bars and clubs, many of which are foreign-owned or managed.

Shanghai's classy new clubs may lend themselves to sipping flutes of chilled champagne and nibbling hors d'oeuvres, but those who prefer a beer and a bar snack in a more casual environment are also well catered for. The city's three Irish bars are perenially popular - as are the landmarks of the city's bar scene, Sasha's and Face.

Although Shanghai's current nightlife scene may not yet be as ebullient as it was in the Thirties, jazz, lost to the city for a generation, is back. Jazz enthusiasts in Shanghai - foreigners and locals alike - are attempting to make their own musical mark rather than live in the shadow of the past. For this reason, you'll find no shortage of jazz venues in the city. Hot spots include the JZ Bar, the Cotton Club, CJW and the House of Blues and Jazz. Most of the high-end hotels also sport a resident jazz combo, with personnel consisting of Americans, Australians, Canadians and the occasional local player. For a night of jazz which is less dynamic though more evocative of Shanghai's 1930s, try the Peace Hotel, where a group of octogenarians continue to belt out the Dixieland and swing tunes from that bygone era.

Trendy.
Detailed. Personalized.
Contemporary Rooms.
Unforgettable Sofitel MyBed.
Exclusive panoramic Lounge.
Elegant board rooms.
Dedicated service.

Sofitel Hyland Shanghai
海崙賓館

505 Nanjing Road East, Shanghai 200001, P.R.China
Tel +86 (0)21 6351 5888 Fax +86 (0)21 6351 4088
sofitel@hyland-shanghai.com www.sofitel.com

▶ A new perspective on our hotels and services

WORLD EXPO 2010
SHOWCASE SHANGHAI

Preparations for one of the world's greatest ever showcase events have already had a massive impact on the city as swathes of old housing have been demolished and pollutant industries displaced. Apart from the waterfront Expo site itself the site itself, the city's successful 2000 bid has spurned numerous ambitious new developments along its previously unfashionable waterfront. By 2010 the North Bund will have been totally redeveloped as a commercial and residential area featuring a Ferris wheel larger than the London Eye and a brand new international ocean-going passenger terminal. To the north end the city's famous Bund, in the 'Waitanyuan area,' plans are underway to transform an historic area into a world-winning leisure and entertainment district incorporating super-luxury apartments and a brace of boutique hotels – as well as a new Peninsula Hotel.

ESSENTIAL SHANGHAI >>>>>>>>

Culture Buffs Allow at least half a day for a visit to the spectacular Shanghai Museum. Head over to the centre of Shanghai's art scene at 50 Moganshan Road, as well as the Taikang Road Art Street. Catch a performance of Shanghai's own inimitable local opera and an acrobatic show.
Go Chinese Visit the impressive Yu Garden and its ever hectic and colourful neighbouring bazaar area. A Chinese Disneyland.
Past Splendour Stroll the Bund in the daytime to see the splendours contained in the Peace Hotel and the former Hongkong and Shanghai Bank building. Stay on till the evening and take a drink, or dinner, at one its fine establishments and be amazed when the city's illuminations are switched on. Be nosey and walk down the myriad of lanes found off streets in the old parts of town.
Peckish? Sample Shanghai's very own dumpling treats - 'xiao long bao' and 'sheng jian.'
Spending Time Hunt out antiques on Central Fangbang Road and Dongtai Road, shop for fashion items around South Shaanxi Road and in the upmarket malls of Nanjing Road (W) and Central Huahai Road.
Taking it Easy Take a one hour cruise on the Huangpu River. Spend Sundays in Fuxing Park or in the grounds of the Shanghai Zoo. Relax at one of the city's top spas or chill out in the grounds of the Yongfoo Elite.
Trendy Eat and drink in the Xintiandi area, at Bar Rouge in Bund 18, or on Hengshan Road. Dine in a top restaurant perched high above the city.

Art 50
Fusion cuisine at this revolving restaurant amongst modern Chinese art courtesy of ShangHART art gallery. *50/F Novotel Atlantis Hotel, 728 Pudong Avenue. Tel: 5036 6666*

Bar Rouge
The latest hotspot for sophisticated cocktails, soirees and scintillating views. *7/F, 18 Zhongshan No. 1 Road (E). Tel: 6339 1199*

Canton
Spectacular views from the 55th floor of the Jin Mao building complement the spectacular Cantonese cuisine and the sumptuously contemporary Chinese décor. *Grand Hyatt Hotel, 55/F Jin Mao Tower, 88 Century Boulevard, Pudong. Tel: 5049 1234 ext. 8890*

Cloud 9
Simply the highest bar in the world - with 360-degree city views and complementary table-side fortune telling. *Grand Hyatt, 87/F Jin Mao Tower, 88 Century Boulevard, Pudong. Tel: 5049 1111*

Club Jin Mao
The most exclusive Shanghainese restaurant with an exquisite menu from Shanghai's top chefs. *Grand Hyatt Hotel, 86/F Jin Mao Tower, 88 Century Boulevard, Pudong. Tel: 5049 1234 ext. 8688*

Face
A contemporary, sophisticated, spacious and stylish bar housed in a 1930s mansion in a fabulous garden setting. *Ruijin Guesthouse, Building No. 4, 118 Ruijin No. 2 Road. Tel: 6466 4328*

M on the Bund
Sister restaurant to the renowned M at the Fringe in Hong Kong, this classy Continental eatery is generally considered to be the best in town, in no small part for its unbeatable location on the Bund. *7/F, 20 Guangdong Road. Tel: 6350 9988*

Shanghai Centre Theatre (Acrobatics)
1376 Nanjing Road (W) Tel: 6279 8663

Shanghai Museum
210 People's Avenue. Tel: 6372 4030

Shintori Null-2
Occupying a huge hall in minimalist style - this is one of Shanghai's most imposing and inspired venues. And it has fantastically inventive Japanese food to match. *803 Julu Road. Tel: 5404 5252*

Star East Shanghai
Jackie Chan and friends are behind this venture. Bustling, glitzy, smoky and decidedly upbeat. *Unit 1, House 17, North Block, 181 Taicang Road, Xintiandi. Tel: 6311 4991*

T8
Voted as one of the best restaurants in the world by Conde Nast Traveller - creative continental cuisine and superb service. *House 8, North Block, Xintiandi, Lane 181 Taicang Road. Tel: 6355 8999*

The Yongfoo Elite
Simply one of the best environments in the world to entertain and to be entertained. Sheer class. *200 Yongfu Road. Tel: 5466 2727*

Va Bene
One of the hottest Italian restaurants in town, set in an ultra-stylishly restored shikumen house in fashionable Xintiandi. *House 7, North Block, Lane 181, Taicang Road, Xintiandi. Tel: 6311 2211*

Yifu Theatre (The Shanghai Kunju Opera House)
701 Fuzhou Road. Tel: 6351 4668

TALK INFORMS

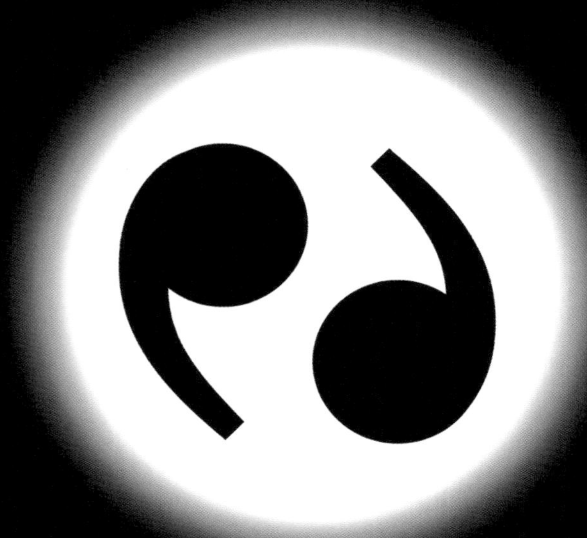

BE BETTER INFORMED

WITH **SHANGHAI TALK**

EVERY MONTH

Published since 1993, Shanghai Talk is part of the "Talk" network of city-living magazines in China.
Please send subscription, editorial, advertising enquiries to media@ismaychina.com

Indulgent Pleasures

On the culinary front, Shanghai offers all that one might expect of an international metropolis and the choice is expanding just as fast as the city itself. Shanghai has thousands of restaurants and local people delight in eating out. The hosting of banquets or taking friends out for dinner is often a grand affair.

Apart from the superlative cuisine available in the top hotels, the main eating areas are in the former French Concession in the western suburbs. Shanghai's plane tree-lined streets conjure up an infinite palette of sensual experiences.

The Shanghainese have a notoriously sweet tooth and the city carries on its European tradition in the form of cake shops - said to number over 1,000. Coffee shops have never fallen from favour and despite the arrival of Starbucks, independent, often eclectic, cafes rule the roost. Numerous old buildings house cake and coffee shops that wouldn't look out of place in London or Venice.

Historic architecture also plays a major role in Shanghai's stylish eating and entertainment area at Xintiandi, which opened in 2001. This is Shanghai's answer to London's Covent Garden. A whole block of traditional stone-framed door 'shikumen' houses have been refurbished and recreated to perfection. In the north block, traditional buildings featuring stylishly modern interior designs, decorations and equipment, play host to a dazzling array of restaurants aside bubbling bars and clubs.

A modern south block opened in 2002 with a series of international restaurants representing the flavours of the world, as well as classy boutiques, accessory shops and a cinema.

Although the Bund has long been the main attraction for sightseers to Shanghai, it has not been a place to indulge in fine culinary delights until recently. The restaurant renaissance on the Bund was led by Michelle Garnaut with the opening of 'M' - and with the advent of Three on the Bund, Bund 18 and latterly 6 Bund, the range of fine dining opportunities has catapulted the area into the realm of sheer indulgence.

TOP OF THE WORLD

Pier One

Blowing a fresh and trendy breeze into the dilapidated alleys of the Moganshan Road art district is Pier One, a collection of four "M"-themed entertainment venues all housed in a wonderfully restored 1930s brewery, with views of perhaps the most pleasant stretch of Suzhou Creek.

The centerpiece of the collection is Mimosa, a supper room set in a stunning lofted space which manages to merge industrial minimalism with genuine elegance. Monsoon and Minx represent the bar and club limbs of the Pier One project: the former features a wonderful sun-room style lounge and classy cocktails, while the latter is a thumping club of international standards with imported sound systems and DJs. And completing the collection is M Suites, a boutique hotel in a city with a distinct lack of this kind of accommodation. *82 Yi Chang Lu, Tel (021) 5155 8310*

Mesa & Manifesto

With its welcoming ambience, stylish decor and quality contemporary cuisine, Mesa & Manifesto has proved a popular addition to the city's dining scene. The restaurant (Mesa) and its adjoining bar (Manifesto) nestle in their own little enclave on Julu Road, surrounded by a school, residential buildings and a few charming noodle houses. As far as owner/manager Charles Cabell IV is concerned, it's just as rewarding eating here as it is dining on the fiftieth story of a hotel or somewhere with Bund views. Here, at least, you get a real sense of daily life. 'This is a cityscape,' says Charles. Judging by the groups of families and friends who flock to the expansive second-floor deck for weekend brunch, many in Shanghai would agree. *748 Julu Lu, Tel (021) 6289 9108*

Mesa & Manifesto

an extremely loyal band of regulars in the early evening, after which it plays host to a more international clientele. One can eat outside behind the huge black doors in the front yard or behind the diamond-panelled windows typical of old Shanghai, knowing that the staff will be more than happy to mull over matters, as well as to provide a very personal food service. *Unit 4, Building 9, Lane 169 Taicang Lu, Tel (021) 6336 4746*

Bund 18

Shanghai's latest design and culinary triumph on the Bund is sizzling with style - from the contemporary Chinese creative themes of the Tan Wai Lou, presided over by master chef Zhi-Hai Tou, to the extravagant richness of the rooftop Bar Rouge. And just downstairs the chic, sensual design of Sens & Bund by Algiers-born Parisian Imaad Rahmouni, a former associate of Phillippe Starck, melts with Michelin 3-star management. The famous Pourcel brothers, Jacques and Laurent, whose legendary 'Le Jardin des Sens' in Montpellier has been an inspiration for other world cities have now added Shanghai to their personal portfolio. *18 Zhongshan Dong Yi Lu - Sens & Bund, Tel (021) 6323 9898; Bar Rouge, Tel (021) 6339 1199; Tan Wai Lou, Tel (021) 6339 1188*

Palladio

The trendsetting Palladio at the Portman-Ritz Carlton in Shanghai is regarded by many to be the finest Italian restaurant in China, if not Asia. Apart from its superlative cuisine and fabulous interior, visitors are invariably touched by a tangible sense of ease and personal service that shines from the commitment and creative brilliance of its multi-award winning team. And it's a touch that really has endeared the Palladio to its Shanghai kin, past royal visitors and the likes of Luciano Pavarotti and Placido Domingo. The contemporary, neo-classically inspired setting of the Palladio is a place where love affairs are started and one where compromises are never made. *Portman Ritz-Carlton, 1376 Nanjing Xi Lu, Tel (021) 6279 8888*

On Fifty Six

On Fifty Six

Few places can boast vertiginous views both outside and inside, but On Fifty Six is such a place. This sterling collection of restaurants occupying the 56th floor of the Jinmao Tower is part of the imposing Grand Hyatt, the world's highest hotel. Once you've pulled yourself away from the windows and the sight of Shanghai stretching forever below, you'll be equally awed by the hotel's unique interior, with a 33-storey atrium tunnelling its way from On Fifty Six to the upper floors.

These lofty heights are matched by the food. The quartet of quality establishments encompasses Italian restaurant Cucina with its wood-fired brick oven for pizzas, Kobachi Japanese specializing in sushi and yakitori, the popular seafood and steakhouse The Grill, and the Atrium Lounge, situated directly beneath the hotel's towering internal chamber. On Fifty Six remains one of Shanghai's most sophisticated and exciting venues. *56F, Grand Hyatt, 88 Shiji Dadao, Tel (021) 5049 1234*

Fabrique

Many new nightclubs in Shanghai tend to play it safe, opening within a stone's throw of one another and settling for derivative interiors and soundtracks. Fabrique sets an independent tone from the start, nestled in its own nook of the city and with a clash of dayglo pink at the entrance and warehouse minimalism inside. Having already met with success in Paris and Tokyo, the people behind the Fabrique concept are finding Shanghai to be a perfect accompaniment to those two stunning cities.

Visitors to Fabrique will discover local and international DJs playing well into the night with two huge video screens displaying original artwork to accompany the music, and a bar serving the city's trendiest concoctions. As well as all of this, before the night surrenders to the dancing throng, Fabrique is a French restaurant of considerable repute. *8-10 Jianguo Zhong Lu, Tel (021) 6415 1600*

M on The Bund

M on The Bund

M had long been a legend by the time of its fifth anniversary in early 2004. The advent of M not only defined new standards of fine dining. It was the first independently managed restaurant to occupy a lofty and dominant position on The Bund, Shanghai's famous waterfront. Proprietor Michelle Garnault, M for short, and the Bund make a perfect partnership. And when it comes to ambience and views, M has no peer. M on the Bund has received more awards and honours than any other independent restaurant in Shanghai and has become the rendezvous for roaming glitterati, statesmen and royalty. And to accommodate, entertain and stimulate even more patrons a new sophisticated, sexy, chill-out space called the Glamour Bar opened in June 2006. *7F, No. 5 The Bund, 20 Guangdong Lu, Tel (021) 6350 9988*

Xinjishi

Xinjishi

The original Jishi restaurant, opened over 10 years ago, was renowned for its home-style Shanghainese cuisine and patronised by the likes of Hong Kong film stars Jackie Chan and Maggie Cheung. But it is not the big names that make the Xintiandi restaurant so special. Its unassuming, simple charm and conviviality confer it with a family-run atmosphere, seldom stumbled upon in China. Its setting in a fabulous 1920s large stone-frame door residence, containing numerous original features, further heightens the sense of being a privileged guest in a private house. The 100-seat restaurant is crowded out with

Paul Pairet conjures up the most extraordinary dining experience at Jade on 36; where the wonderful aromas of fine, freshly cooked, food are hermetically sealed and presented in a cellophane bag or a jar - where succulent scallop shells are clipped with an unassuming clothes peg and where fluffy mousses spring from a sardine tin with its lid rolled back. Sheer genius - rather than gimmickry - this rave restaurant is a real gourmet's delight. Pairet's avant-garde adventures in food are combined with the best floor-to-ceiling view in Shanghai, peering directly down onto the boats of the Huangpu and the beautifully lit buildings of the Bund - all within the extravagant surrounds of design genius Adam D. Tihany. *Jade on 36. 36F Pudong Shangri-La, 33 Fucheng Lu. Tel: (021) 6882 8888*

Three On The Bund

Three On The Bund

The near century-old neoclassical building is now home to a collection of world-class restaurants. Not the least of these is Jean Georges, just the second restaurant in the world to carry the name of renowned chef Jean-Georges Vongerichten. Here you'll find an expansive and elegant space filled with the aromas of modern French cuisine, prepared in inimitable style with the freshest of local and imported ingredients.

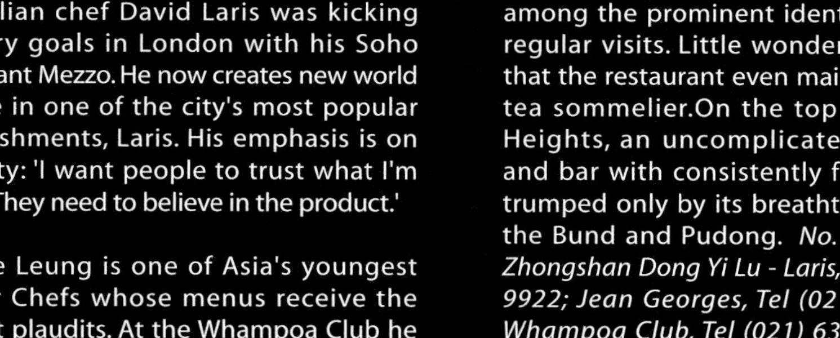

Before he moved to Shanghai, Greek-Australian chef David Laris was kicking culinary goals in London with his Soho restaurant Mezzo. He now creates new world cuisine in one of the city's most popular establishments, Laris. His emphasis is on integrity: 'I want people to trust what I'm doing. They need to believe in the product.'

Jereme Leung is one of Asia's youngest Master Chefs whose menus receive the highest plaudits. At the Whampoa Club he transforms traditional Shanghai recipes into his own tours de force. Ja among the prominent identi regular visits. Little wonder, that the restaurant even main tea sommelier. On the top f Heights, an uncomplicated and bar with consistently fir trumped only by its breathta the Bund and Pudong. *No. 3 Zhongshan Dong Yi Lu - Laris, T 9922; Jean Georges, Tel (021 Whampoa Club, Tel (021) 632 Heights, Tel (021) 6321 0909*

Shintori Null-2

Shintori Null-2

This uniqueness of this Japane derives not only from its creat menu, but also from its sp breathtakingly minimalist interio movie theatre. The use of spac - intimate small tables clustere balcony wings, fringed with priv private eating areas, overlook a space with an over-proportioned for family and group gatherings. focus is on the former stage wh perform their culinary acrobat open kitchen. *803 Julu Lu, Tel (021*

Eastern China

JIANGSU • ZHEJIANG • SHANDONG

The region is one of striking visual and economic contrasts. The colourful fertile plains around the lower reaches of the Yangtze River have prospered throughout Chinese history as the proverbial land of fish and rice. Further north, Shandong has emerged as one of China's top provincial economies

Grand Metropark Hotel Nanjing

The Grand Metropark Hotel Nanjing (former Hilton Nanjing) with 561-rooms, is located next to the Nanjing Museum, and offers their guests a wide variety of recreational and entertainment facilities. The spacious rooms equipped with high speed Internet access, well equipped bathrooms and special amenities will make your stay a memorable one. Our Grand Ballroom, with a capacity of 1200 people is equipped and decorated to cater for fine banquets and international conferences, while the hotel's tradition of culinary excellence and dramatic presentations complete the magic for any event.

中国南京中山东路319号　319 East Zhong Shan Road Nanjing,210016,P.R. of China
电话Tel: (86-25) 8480 8888　传真Fax: (86-25) 8480 9999
电子邮件E-mail: sales.njgm@metroparkhotels.com　网址：www.metroparkhotels.com

CTS 香港中旅酒店管理有限公司管理 *Managed by* China Travel Hotel Management Services H.K. Ltd.

JIANGSU PROVINCE

Nanjing

In times past Nanjing has been the capital of eight dynasties and many bloody battles. Although it has since lost its elevated position, it can still claim to be the capital of Jiangsu province, one of China's most prosperous areas, famous for its silk industry and fish farming. The location of the city is strikingly attractive, swept on its northern flank by the Yangtze River and surrounded by mountains. The warm face and peaceful atmosphere of the city belies the fact that is the commercial hub of the lower Yangtze basin. Besides being a handsome modern metropolis of tree-lined avenues, the city is also a commercial powerhouse for multinational industry.

The city boasts a wealth of historical sites and expansive recreational areas that converge in the verdant and elegant eastern suburbs. The main draw of the Zhongshan, or Purple Mountain, area is the graceful granite and marble mausoleum of Dr Sun Yat-sen. The environs also entertain theme parks, a beautiful botanical garden, as well as the tomb of the first Ming emperor.

In the centre, Nanjing's answer to the Forbidden City in Beijing was opened to the public in 2000. The Presidential Palace is a magnificent complex of renaissance, art deco and traditional Chinese style buildings, accompanied by a classic Chinese garden that once housed all the Nationalist government ministries between 1927 and 1937.

Many sections of what was the longest city wall in the world, 600 years ago, have been renovated. Inside the wall, a magnificent new provincial museum was completed in 1999. A museum laying testament to more modern and sombre times - documenting the 'Rape of Nanking' in 1937, in which some 300,000 were massacred, can be found to the southwest of the city.

To the south of the city, a buzzing Ming and Qing style recreation area has been built on the shores of the Qinhuai River. Centred on a reconstructed Confucian temple, the teeming alleys are heavy with the smell of local snacks and offer opportunities to buy curios, clothes, pets and flowers.

To the west, the monumental Yangtze River Bridge straddles the great north-south natural barrier and remains an important symbol for the strength and unity of the Chinese nation.

Wuxi

Wuxi acquired its name, which means 'no tin,' when deposits of the metal ran out around 2,000 years ago. This no doubt caused an economic downturn and the city remained in the doldrums until the seventh century, when the Grand Canal was built through it. That put Wuxi on the map as a port for shipping produce from the surrounding countryside.

Like other ancient towns on the Grand Canal, Wuxi has a touch of Venice, with its narrow waterways, narrow beam boats and picturesque architecture. As elsewhere, modernisation has remoulded the city over the last few years. Nevertheless, a walk along Nan Chang Road and over the divine Qing Ming Bridge brings one to a quiet residential area where time has stood still.

Wuxi is an extremely popular resort. Its attractions are found around Lake Tai - China's third largest natural lake. Traditional fan-sailed junks ply the inland sea stopping at unspoiled islands, lotus farms, pearl farms and chestnut beds.

One of Lake Tai's islands was chosen by Central China television as the site for two outdoor film sets, and these have since become popular attractions. Tang City is composed of sturdily built palaces, courtyards, temples and streets of shops. Located on the shore, Three Kingdoms City is a recreation of a palace fortress, ship-filled harbour and battleground as they looked in 200 BC. A further attraction is the world's tallest Buddha image - some 87 metres high.

Until the 1930s Wuxi was reliant on the silk spinning and weaving industries. However, recent overseas investment has transformed it into a boomtown. The city boasts modern international-standard hotels, including The Hilton and the resplendent lakeside Taihu Hotel, capable of hosting large-scale conventions.

南京

南京市古称金陵，是江苏省的省会，它是一个有2400多年建城史的历史文化名城，东晋、东吴、宋、齐、梁、陈、南唐、明等朝代，以及太平天国、中华民国均曾定都于此，故有"六朝古都"、"十朝都会"之誉，亦是全中国最大的内河港口城市。四周群山环抱，地势雄伟，风景秀丽，素有"龙蟠虎踞"之称，是中外旅游者向往的游览胜地。市内的"南京海底世界"更是南京市民及游客参观的景点，内藏活鱼15000条，类别达300种之多。

无锡

位处于长江三角洲中部，太湖正北方、京沪铁路线上的无锡是一座具有三千多年历史的文化古城。相传古时候这里盛产铅、锡。汉初锡矿采尽，改名无锡。无锡是中国民族工业的发祥地之一，明清时代更是有名的"丝都"、"布码头"和"四大米市之一"。地处中国最大的蚕丝产地—太湖流域，丝绸业发达，工业繁盛，又有"小上海"之誉，惠山泥人是其著名的传统工艺品。至于地跨无锡、苏州等市的太湖风景名胜区更是中国国家重点风景名胜区之一。湖中大小岛屿星罗棋布，湖光山色驰名中外。

Suzhou

Suzhou, the fabled 'Venice of the East' established its present form on the commerce of the Grand Canal some 1,500 years ago. With rising prosperity and idyllic surroundings came the merchants, and later, poets, the intelligentsia and courtly officials. Today, most of the canals have been built over, and huge areas of the city rebuilt in traditional style.

The city has a rich history and is accustomed to economic well being, as well as aesthetic benevolence. The was one of China's most advanced areas during the Southern Song Dynasty (1127-1279) with its massive output of silk products, garments and arts and crafts. These industries still live on, but Suzhou's newfound prosperity comes from its modern high-tech zones.

As host to the APEC Finance Ministers Congress in 2001, the mayor confirmed his intent to develop the city as an ultra-modern metropolis. The city's former murky canals have been cleaned and new highways completed.

The most precious remnants of the past are its fine classical gardens. Most were created during the Ming dynasty by scholar-artists seeking retreat from the outside world. Combining the Confucian principle of order with Taoist principles of harmony and nature, each individual garden was uniquely designed and landscaped. The key features of garden design are water, rocks, foliage and pavilions. Bridges, walkways, moon gates and latticed windows ensured a lifetime of visual and sensory pleasures.

Only a handful of the gardens have been restored and opened to the public. The most notable gardens include the Lingering Garden, the Humble Administrator's Garden and the Master of Nets Garden. The small but perfect Master of Nets is regarded by many as the epitome of garden design, and part of it has been replicated in the Metropolitan Museum of Art in New York. The new Suzhou Museum, adjoining the Humble Administrator's Garden and designed by I. M. Pei, a descendant of one of the city's most famous families, is due to open in late 2006.

A good way to obtain a vista of the city itself is from the top of the North Temple Pagoda. The Panmen area affords views of life as it was, and has an exquisite Ming dynasty bridge crossing its canals.

Suzhou is proud to promote her heritage as the centre of the Chinese silk industry. Visits can be made to a silk-spinning factory, the Silk Museum or to the remarkable Silk Embroidery Research Institute. The Institute, housed in a wonderful garden, produces the most refined and delicate single and double-sided embroideries.

The main streets of the city centre are new, with many fine stores on Renmin Road and an interesting bazaar area around Guanqian Road.

苏州

江南水乡城市苏州古称平江，简称吴，别称姑苏。是素以富雅秀丽而举世闻名的江南古城和著名的现代化城市，农村商品经济也较发达。苏州园林为江南园林建筑艺术的精华，以湖光山色、园林景致著称于世。苏州又是江南著名水乡，苏州古城仍保持着宋代水陆并行、河街相邻、桥梁棋布的格局和小桥、流水、人家的水乡城市风貌，是中国河桥最多的城市。苏州手工艺特产有苏绣、玉雕、苏扇、桃花坞木刻年画，佳肴美食和苏式糖果糕点、碧螺春茶(中国十大名茶之一)、太湖银鱼及阳澄湖闸蟹，更是脍炙人口。绚丽的苏州丝绸亦久负盛名，畅销全球百多个国家和地区。

承苏州古典园林的幽雅
融苏州活力城市的魅力

Sharing the elegance of Suzhou's classical gardens, with the charm of a city with a vigorously growing economy.

竹輝飯店是擁有356間（套）客房、中西餐廳、酒吧、娛樂及會議設施以及超大面積停車場的四星級飯店。不管是商務、會議、旅游和休閑，都會有您值得品味的印象。

The Bamboo Grove Hotel is a 4-star hotel with 356 well-appointed rooms and boasting a choice of restaurants offering both Chinese and Western cuisine, together with a welcoming and relaxing bar area. A comprehensive range of recreational and service facilities are also available together with a spacious parking lot to compliment our efficient conference, business and leisure accommodation.
Our team is dedicated to making your stay with us successful and memorable.

Add: No.168.Zhu Hui Road, Suzhou, China (Post Code 215006)
地址:中国苏州竹辉路168号(邮政编码:215006)
Tel 电话: 86-512-65205601 Fax 传真:86-512-65208778
E-mial: bghsz@public1.sz.js.cn http://www.bg-hotel.com

ZHEJIANG PROVINCE
Hangzhou

The city skirts the shore of a wide, shallow lake rimmed by green and gentle hills where the famous Longjing tea is grown, alongside mulberry bushes that are used in silk production. Marco Polo cited Hangzhou, with its stately palaces and mansions, as 'the finest and most splendid city in the world.'

The main attraction for visitors is the majestic lotus leaf carpet of West Lake, whose blue mists and soft hills have inspired artists for centuries. Strolling the lake's circumference is a popular diversion, as are leisurely boat rides to the islands and shores, dotted with historical buildings and other attractions. The city also has a fine botanical garden and several fine parks. Dragon Well Spring, in the outskirts, is a natural wonder, as are the lush tea bushes of nearby Longjing (Dragon Well) Village. A tea museum gives an insight into the history and etiquette of tea drinking. The city also has many other excellent museums, including the Zhejiang Provincial Museum, with its comprehensive collection of bronzes and coins.

A short outing from the city is needed to visit the 800-year-old Buddhist Lingyin Temple set in a woodland setting next to the Feilai Fang, or 'Peak That Flew There.' According to legend this limestone outcrop was originally part of an Indian holy mountain, which miraculously relocated itself in China. Spectacular 10th century Buddhist sculptures are found carved into the hills of Feilai Fang.

The Hangzhou metropolitan area was enlarged in 2001 by annexing two neighbouring cities, making it number two

in terms of commerce and industry in the Yangtze Delta area. Hangzhou is one of the largest garment distribution centres in Asia - producing huge quantities of synthetic garments as well as being a huge market for the silk garment trade. The city first hosted the West Lake Expo back in 1929 and again is hosting it as an annual event. Hangzhou boasts excellent conference facilities and hotels, including the Radisson Plaza, the Shangri-La, the Hyatt Regency and The World Trade Centre Grand Hotel.

Numerous high-class restaurants have also opened in Hangzhou's own Xintiandi area as the corner stone of a development that will see the world's first air-conditioned, open air, mall. Hangzhou can be reached by train from Shanghai in around two hours.

杭州

浙江省省会杭州是中国历史上著名的六大古都之一。杭州，古称钱塘，后称临安，是一座有二千多年历史和文化的古城。自古就有"上有天堂、下有苏杭"的赞誉。杭州诸山多泉水，尤以虎跑、玉泉、龙井称著，又因绮丽的西湖而誉满中外，一年四季适宜旅游，是世界闻名的风景游览城市。杭州素刀、王星记扇子、天竺筷子、绸伞等传统名产均受中外旅游者欢迎。而该市的国际级18洞杭州高尔夫球场更是爱好此道者不容错过的好去处。

杭州维景国际大酒店座落在美丽的西子湖畔，为杭州市金融、商业中心所环抱，典雅的异国氛围融汇在传统的中国风格之中，带给您至上的享受。

The Grand Metropark Hotel Hang-zhou is located in the city's financial and business center by the West Lake. A fine blend of Chinese tradition and exotic elegance embraces every room.

（原杭州五洲大酒店，THE FORMER HANGZHOU CONTINENTAL HOTEL）

地址：中国浙江省杭州市平海路2号　Add：2 Pinghai Road, Hangzhou, China

邮政编码 Postcode：310006　电话 Tel：(86-571)87088088　传真 Fax：(86-571)87077618

香港中旅酒店管理有限公司管理

CTS *Managed by China Travel Hotel Management Services H.K. Ltd.*

Ningbo

The Portuguese gave the city an international flavour when they began trading there in the 16th century. A further boost came in 1842 when Ningbo was made a treaty port. Unfortunately, the city was overshadowed by Shanghai, which grew to become China's premier trading city by the turn of the 20th century.

Only in recent years has Ningbo re-emerged as a booming business centre, with a population of 5.5 million. Much of the new impetus was provided by two of its native sons, shipping tycoon Sir Y. K. Pao and movie baron Sir Run Run Shaw - both having amassed huge fortunes in Hong Kong.

The development has now gained momentum with the assistance and sanction of both the Chinese authorities and a host of investors, including many overseas Chinese. The port of Beilun is undergoing a multi-billion dollar expansion, which will make it China's main shipping facility for the new generation of container ships. The port handling capacity has doubled in the last five years. Meanwhile, opposite the port, Daxie Island has developed as a technical and economic zone.

High-tech industries are expected to lead the city into the future. To meet the requirements of a new generation of visiting and resident business people, new international hotels and luxury villa estates have been established. Meanwhile, the airport has been rebuilt and an expressway connects the city to Shanghai.

However, all this activity has not been allowed to overshadow Ningbo's past, and the city fathers have taken positive steps to protect their heritage. This has involved projects such as the restoration of Moon Lake Park and the renovation of a traditional temple-market complex. Probably the most impressive renovation so far has been the work carried out to the 16th century Tianfeng Library. Its theatre has been completely rebuilt according to the original design to incorporate intricately carved walls and a gilded, spiral-domed ceiling.

宁波

宁波市位于宁绍平原东端，濒临东海，是中国南北航线的交汇点，亦是东南沿海重要的水陆交通枢纽之一。宁波是浙江省粮、棉、水产品的重要生产基地之一，有不少土特名产和传统工艺品载誉海内外，故有"四明八百里，物产甲东南"之称，主要有宁波冻鹅、猪油汤圆、绣衣、泥金彩漆器、骨木镶嵌家具、余姚杨梅、奉化水蜜桃、宁海蛏子和牡蛎等。宁波市主要名胜有一阁(天一阁)、三湖(东钱湖、慈湖及月湖)和三寺(天童寺、阿育王寺及保国寺)。

SHANDONG PROVINCE
Jinan

Despite Jinan's modern aspect, it stands on the site of one of China's oldest settlements. By the 4th century, Jinan had become a military outpost and trading centre. The town expanded during the Ming dynasty. In 1898 Germany obtained the right to build the Shandong rail lines and the city was opened to foreign trade in 1906. It consequently experienced rapid industrialisation under the dominion of the Germans, English and Japanese. Today, as the capital of Shandong province, Jinan hosts a population of around 3 million.

Jinan is famous for its natural springs, although what exists of the complex today lacks the magnificence that poets once eulogised. The most famous is Black Tiger Spring and its stone pools are a popular bathing spot.

The main downtown area lies just south of the large Daming Lake, edged with willow trees and sprinkled with water lilies. The park around the lake contains quaint gardens, pavilions and bridges. The Shandong Provincial Museum contains a number of fine Buddhist carvings, as well as exhibits from the excavations of two nearby Neolithic sites.

Another attraction worth visiting is Thousand Buddha Mountain, about five kilometres south of the city. Leafy paths wind up the mountainside, with the main route lined by painted opera masks. Near the top of the mountain behind the Xingguo Temple superb 6th century Buddhist carvings are to be found.

Jinan is the major transit point and communications centre of Shandong province. The city also has an international airport with connections to Japan, South Korea and Hong Kong as well as all major Chinese cities.

Qingdao

The port city of Qingdao, in the east of Shandong province, is unlike any other city in China. From certain aspects the city looks more like a Bavarian village than a thriving industrial metropolis and commercial hub. Countless European vistas unfold as one walks its quiet and dignified lanes. Qingdao was, and remains, China's largest and most sophisticated sea-side resort with fine beaches flanking acacia-lined avenues.

Qingdao was a sleepy fishing village until it was ceded to Germany and flourished as a port and centre of industry. The German influence dates back to 1898, when they acquired a 99-year lease from the Qing government. Qingdao had a Chinese and European business section, with a garrison of 2,000 soldiers to protect its independence. Although the German control only lasted until 1914, it had a dramatic effect on the development of the city. The Germans built a deep-water navy base and embarked on the construction of railways. They also set up the Tsingtao brewery in 1903, and it still produces fine quality beer today. Following the Germans, the Japanese occupied Qingdao from 1914-1922 and in the late 1930s. Qingdao is now China's fourth largest port, with a population of over 2.3 million.

A good place to begin a tour of the old German town is in the area to the east of the twin-spired Catholic Church. Red-roofed buildings, with decorative wrought-iron balconies, line the cobbled streets. The former residence of the German Governor, the most outstanding example of Bavarian architecture built in 1905, is now open as an hotel known as 'The Guest House.' Qingdao's biggest attractions are its sandy beaches and each seems to have its own speciality or mood. They are now all linked by a coastal walkway which crosses a beautiful park dedicated to the poet Lu Xun.

August is the time to visit for beer lovers - great quality tipples flow at the renowned annual beer festival. Laoshan, the source of the mineral water said to give Tsingtao beer its distinctive flavour, is 40 kilometres outside the city. Laoshan, one of China's most famous mountains, is also home to the impressive Huadong Winery, which is open to visitors and can be reached by a spectacular coastal road. Qingdao also hosts an annual wine festival in September. The city is preparing itself as host for the 29th Olympics sailing events in 2008 involving a massive redevelopment of the Fushan Bay area.

济南

济南市是山东省的省会，地处鲁中丘陵和鲁北冲积平原的交接带上。市区南部是山麓丘陵，市区北部是平原低地。黄河改由山东入海以后，在市区的北面奔腾而过。济南市区气候温和，土质肥沃，农业很发达。

济南拥有众多的泉水，自古享有“家家泉水，户户垂柳”之誉，因此被称为泉城。主要旅游胜地有趵突泉、大明湖、千佛山和柳埠古迹。

青岛市

青岛市位于山东半岛南部，胶州湾东南岸。青岛港水域宽广，终年不冻不淤，是中国第四大港，被列为五大外贸口岸之一，乃重要的外贸出口基地。青岛三面濒海，碧山青水，风光旖旎，气候宜人，以其独特的自然景观和众多的名胜古迹驰名中外。有"东方瑞士"之称的青岛亦是避暑以及疗养胜地。青岛市文物古迹丰富，城市景观优美，是具有多重文化背景的旅游区。主要旅游景点有青岛市海滨风景区、石老人国家旅游度假区、崂山风景名胜区、琅琊台风景名胜、大泽山风景名胜区和田横岛等。而该市著名特产有青岛啤酒、崂山矿泉水、即墨老酒 、高粱饴、贝雕画等。

青岛值得游览的地方很多，而前海海滨风景区更是游人不容错过的好去处。位于青岛市区南端、东起燕儿岛，西抵团岛，是一个岬角、海湾相间分布的基岩海岸带。岬角上或植松柏，或建别墅，景色优美。海湾多积沙成滩，滩平沙细。现已辟建四处海水浴场，其中汇泉湾第一海水浴场最负盛名，是中国接纳入浴人数最多的海水浴场。该区自开发建设以来，已建成众多旅游景点，如栈桥海滨公园、小青岛公园、观海山公园、观象山公园、信号山公园、小鱼山公园、鲁迅公园、中山公园、百花苑名人雕塑园、基督教堂、天主教堂、天后宫、水族馆、湛山寺及八大乡疗养度假区等，成为景观荟萃的黄金旅游带。

Southwest China

GUILIN • GUIYANG • KUNMING • LHASA

Twenty years ago, southwest China was a relatively isolated area of the country visited by few foreigners other than those studying either the fauna of the region, or its many ethnic minority groups. Today this is far from the truth. The area has become both a tourist attraction and a growing commercial centre

Guilin

Guilin landscapes have been popular with sightseers for over one thousand years and today its visitor numbers are only topped by Beijing. Once the capital of Guangxi province - which moved south to Nanning in 1914 - Guilin has always been a prosperous commercial centre, profiting from its proximity to the Ling Canal. The waterway was built in the second century BC to connect the two major river networks of the Pearl and the Yangtze. Guangxi has been designated as an autonomous region as over 35% of its population belong China's largest minority grouping, the Zhuang nationality. Guilin is a small town by Chinese standards, with a population of around 700,000.

The city, previously drab and dishevelled, has undergone massive civic reconstruction since 1999. The city centre has a theme park feel - with spectacular new pagoda structures hosting entertainment and food outlets, western-style buildings housing modern shops, and a spectacle of fairy-light illuminations at night. Low-rise buildings partner attractive tree-lined avenues, and the expansive city lakes have been joined together and linked by new bridges of fantasy European and Chinese design. To the north of the city, an area little visited by foreign tourists, pick-your-own farms and barbeque sites pepper an area crowded with spectacular hills that will become better known as the area develops over the next few years.

Spanning the Li River, the recently completed Liberation Bridge provides a vital link for the bisected city. On the Zhongshan Road in the city centre, the new People's Square forms a canopy over a massive clothes market below. New bars and restaurants have proliferated around the waterfront. The neighbouring area has been pedestrianised and is full of small and inexpensive eateries offering everything from Italian to local snack foods. The city has a real holiday feel about it and promenades along the shores of the Li River are a real delight.

The main purpose, however, in visiting Guilin is not to view the city, but to revel in its landscape of unusual limestone mountain formations. These were created over 300 million years ago when the whole of the region emerged from the sea-bed exposing the rock to bombastic erosion from wind and rain. The resulting, spectacular, karst scenery with its pinnacles peppering the river plain has poetically and artistically enriched

桂林

中国著名的风景游览城市桂林位于广西东北部漓江西岸，湘桂铁路线上，是一座具有二千多年历史的文化古城。自从秦代凿通湘运河(灵渠)以后，即成为“南连海城、北达中原”的军事重镇，因当时城内多玉桂树，故名桂林；宋代至新中国成立以前，一直为广西政治、军事、文化中心。桂林属岩溶喀斯特地貌，山峰秀丽天成，洞奇石美，千姿百态；漓江明洁如镜，碧水萦回，两岸奇峰林立，田野似锦，构成一幅壮丽画卷，素有“桂林山水甲天下”之誉。两洞(芦笛岩、七星岩)、三山(叠彩山、伏波山、独秀峰)、一条江(漓江)堪称桂林山水的代表。桂林市旅游业发展完善，国际级饭店如假日、漓江及喜来登桂林文华等均提供旅客高水平的住宿及餐饮服务。此外，桂林著名特产有“桂林三宝”(辣椒酱、腐乳、荸荠)、三花酒、酥糖、米粉、罗汉果、竹篦、美术陶瓷等。

贵阳

贵州省地势险峻，自然风光引人入胜，作为该省首府的贵阳市海拔超过1000米。这里气候温和，人口逾180万，其中15万人为少数民族人口。贵阳老城区历史悠久，可以上溯至明朝年间，但直到20世纪下半期贵阳才逐渐引起世人的注意。15年前，贵阳开始了自己的现代化进程，但直至今日，贵阳仍然是中国东南部一个带有几分神秘色彩的地方。市区内的人民广场最近经过了重新整修，是放松休闲的好去处，广场上伫立一尊建于上世纪50年代的毛泽东像。此外，黔灵公园占地极广，公园内的弘福寺是闹市中的清静所在。贵阳的花鸟市场沿南明河延伸300多米，在当地颇有名气。

若前往贵阳旅游，绝不可错过距市区约150公里的著名风景区黄果树瀑布，景区包括18个主要的瀑布群。条条瀑布自空中飞流直下，最高落差达74米，蔚为壮观。来到贵阳的客人还能欣赏到多姿多彩的少数民族节日庆典，时间多集中在春季和初夏时分，界时全城各处将成为欢腾的歌舞海洋。

people's lives for generations. Climbing the peaks and gazing out over the Li River is a source of great satisfaction - below fishermen pole their bamboo rafts through the lazy current, while their cormorants dive for fish. Cormorant fishing, a nocturnal pastime, has been practised in the area for over 1,000 years. Rice straw tied around their necks ensures a diet of minnows, whilst the rest of their catch ends up on the restaurant table.

Solitary Beauty Peak, Guilin's best-known pinnacle, sits amidst a Ming-style university campus that was once a 14th century imperial palace. The calligraphy on the peak's rock face dates from the Tang and Ming dynasties. On the waterfront, Fubo Hill, named after a famous Han dynasty general, has many fine stone inscriptions and carvings. South of the city centre are two famous hills that resemble animals - Camel Hill and Elephant Trunk Hill. Camel Hill is perched on the eastern bank of the Li River, past Seven Star Park - so called because its peaks are arranged as the stars of the Big Dipper. The cavernous Seven Star Cave is a fairy tale grotto with its procession of stalagmites and stalactites. To the west of the city, the Reed Flute Cave affords a 500-metre subterranean amble through skilfully lit, imagined agricultural scenes and city landscapes.

An excursion along the river from Guilin to Yangshuo is an imperative for most visitors. Depending on the water level, trips usually take from three and a half hours to five hours, aboard large comfortable boats with open decks. Many of the stunning peaks, almost at arms reach, have been prescribed with poetic names such as 'Yellow Cloth in the Water' and 'Pushing Millstones Rock.' Water buffalo laze, feeding on reeds and small bamboo rafts ply the waterway linking scattered Zhuang villages.

The charming small town of Yangshuo, infested with market stalls, small shops and cafes, is a unique place where East and West meet on a satisfyingly intimate scale. For nearly two decades the town was the exclusive domain of budget independent travellers - but now it caters for group tourists as well. The nearby scenery at Gaotian, where waterlogged, terraced plains act as foreground to a ribbon of unbelievable peaks, is amongst some of the finest in China.

Guiyang

As the capital of the Guizhou Province, one of China's most rugged, beautiful and colourful areas, Guiyang is perched over 1,000 metres above sea-level. Blessed with a mild climate it is home to 1.8 million people - of whom some 150,000 belong to various ethnic groups. Even though the old-walled city dates back to the Ming dynasty it has only been in the latter half of the 20th century that it has risen to prominence - and the spectacular modernisation of the city has only occurred within the last 15 years. It still remains one of southwest China's less-visited secrets. Popular places to stroll and relax include the recently re-modelled People's Square guarded over by a 1950s statue of Chairman Mao and the vast, yet restful, Qianing Park incorporating the Hongfu Temple. Stretching for over 300 metres along the banks of the Nanming River the fascinating bird and flower market, housed in traditional styled buildings, is another impressive recent addition to the city's repertoire of places of interest.

Many visitors to the city will make a day trip to the Huangguisho Waterfalls, which are around a 150 kilometres away. The area contains 18 spectacular waterfalls cascading airborne streams up to 74 metres high that have rightfully been declared as the province's primary scenic attraction. Another main attraction are the numerous minority festivals, in spring and early summer, when the streets and squares are swarming with song and dance.

Kunming

Yunnan's gentle climate makes its capital, Kunming, appealing as a place to visit, even in the winter months. Bright blossoms adorn the streets throughout the year in 'the city of eternal spring.' Yet it is the fascinating variety of people who live in the region that provide the main attraction for visitors. As a result, many travellers use Kunming as a staging post for journeys to surrounding towns and villages.

Even if time does not permit exploration far beyond the suburbs of the Kunming itself, visitors can still learn about the minorities and see their handicrafts in museums and shops, or make a visit to the nearby Yunnan Nationality village. In addition, Kunming, located 1,900 metres above sea level, has its own pleasures - wonderful gardens and parks, many old temples and pavilions, tea-shops and markets, and excellent street snacks, including the local specialty 'crossing the bridge noodles.' Add to this a comfortable climate, unique cuisine, and bustling nightlife and the attraction of the city becomes obvious.

Historically, the city was on Southern Silk Road to India and produced fine teas and magnificent bronzes. By 1200 BC Kunming had a flourishing civilisation. Later it became a stronghold for the powerful Kublai Khan and a buffer for China against incursions from the west and south. Its role as the gateway to Yunnan has been re-established in modern times.

Travelling to, and staying in Kunming is becoming increasingly convenient, since it has become the commercial hub for all of southwest China. With over 700 flights a week, including connections to many South East Asian countries, Kunming International Airport is the fourth largest in China. The economy was given a huge boost with the development of a massive exhibition site to host the International Horticulture Expo in 1999 - one of the largest exhibitions that China has ever held. The event, which attracted over 9 million visitors, has spurred the development of new roads, apartments, first-class hotels and further expansion of the airport. In fact, Kunming is evolving into a major conference and festival centre with an annual commodity fair and an international tourism festival.

For those seeking an overall perspective of the culture of the province, a good place to begin is the Yunnan Provincial Museum. It introduces all the different minority peoples of Yunnan and displays how their lifestyles

昆明

昆明是云南省省会，这里气候温和，即使是冬季也很适合旅游。由于大街小巷四季鲜花似锦，昆明有着“春城”的美誉。除了气候，这里多种多样的民族景观也是吸引游客的重要原因。

从历史上讲，昆明地处通向印度的南方丝绸之路上，这条路是茶叶、铜器贸易的重要通道。在公元前1200年前，昆明的文明已经十分繁荣。而后，它又成为忽必烈可汗防御西方南方侵略的军事要塞。在近代，昆明作为云南门户的地位就显得更加重要。

云南省境内居住着许多回族人，他们的渊源可追溯到元朝。因此，昆明有五座清真寺，如果穿着符合要求，不乱拍照的话，游客可以造访这里。最大的清真寺位于顺亭路，这里是伊斯兰人聚居之地，各种小商店餐馆值得细细游览。

大多数造访昆明的游客都会到著名的滇池泛舟。现在，这个云南最大的湖泊周围已经开设高尔夫球场和度假区。滇池西岸座落在西山脚下，这里山势陡峭，寺院众多，美不胜收。现在，缆车已经开通。华亭寺是昆明最大的佛教寺院，寺内有一片人工湖，几座宝塔围湖而建。沿山而上就到了太华寺，这里的景色同样迷人。

昆明最著名的景点要数市区东南126公里的石林。这里的岩石耸立如林，但并非是由于化石作用，而是水流腐蚀的结果。这里的景观与桂林相似，只是规模稍小。随着夜幕降临，石林发出声音和闪光。这里还是热情好客的萨尼族的聚居地，善良的主人喜欢拿出手工艺品献给客人，并送上欢乐的歌舞。

如果想要娱乐一下，从昆明驾车只需一小时就可抵达由杰克・尼古拉斯设计的高级高尔夫球场。而昆明高尔夫俱乐部也配备豪华的设施。

vary. The museum also has a fine collection of bronzes dating from the Dian Kingdom of 1200 BC. These bronzes deserve careful scrutiny, since they are intricately decorated with scenes of daily life.

The Buddhist Yuantong Temple and its adjacent park are close to the zoo in the north of the city. This temple dates back a thousand years or so, and has been attractively restored. The park is famed for its flowering shrubs and trees: cherry in spring, rhododendrons in summer, chrysanthemums in autumn and camellia or magnolia in winter. The city has a 'Chinatown' area complete with ceremonial arches and the East and West Temple Pagodas - the oldest surviving structures in the city.

Yunnan has a large Muslim community, originating from Yuan dynasty times. Of the five mosques in the city, the largest is on Shunting Lu, which alone is well worth exploring for its interesting little shops and restaurants.

Just twelve kilometres northwest of the city, the Bamboo Temple sits in a woodland setting. Legend tells of the temple's foundation during the Tang dynasty, when two princes chased a rhinoceros to a spot where monks appeared holding staves of bamboo, which then miraculously turned into groves of bamboo. The temple is noted for its 500 luohans - finely crafted, idiosyncratic statues of holy men, created in the late 19th century. To the northeast of the city, the Copper Temple, sometimes called Golden Temple, can be reached after a dramatic climb through pine woods.

Most visitors to Kunming take an excursion on one of the numerous ferries that traverse Lake Dianchi at various points. Golf courses and resort areas now fringe Yunnan's largest lake and a large resort has developed at Yangronghai. The western shores of the lake rise steeply towards Western Hill, a range of four mountains famous for their temples and magnificent views that can be accessed by cable-way. The Huating Temple, Kunming's largest Buddhist monastery, has an imposing garden with an ornamental lake, the enclosing decorative wall of which connects several stupas. Higher up the mountain is the Taihua Temple, which also has a charming garden setting.

The Kunming Botanical Garden, outside the city limits to the northwest, is of particular interest. Over half of China's indigenous trees and flowers grow upon the mountains and valleys of Yunnan. And in fact, many flowering shrubs, such as the rhododendron and camellia, which people from the West now see as a natural part of their own landscape, were first collected in Yunnan by European plant-hunters. Close to the Botanical Garden is a colourful Taoist temple known as Black Dragon Pool. The dragons featured in this temple's legend were destructive, only being mastered by a Taoist scholar who banished nine of them and tamed the tenth. This one is said to live in the pool.

The most popular day trip from Kunming is to the Stone Forest, 126 kilometres southeast of the city. The Stone Forest is a strange place, with limestone pinnacles and rocks standing like petrified trees. Actually, the outcrops are not a fossil forest, but the result of water erosion, which left the limestone outcrops standing. These sculpted pillars are similar to the mountains of Guilin, except on a much smaller scale. As night falls the pinnacles are spectacularly choreographed with an assault of sound and light. The area is the home of the ebullient Sani people, who delight in offering their handicrafts to visitors, and often give song and dance performances in local hotels.

For the recreation minded, an impressive golf course, designed by Jack Nicklaus has been opened at Yiliang, an hour away from the city. Closer to the centre, the Kunming County Golf Club also offers excellent facilities. The area also offers a variety of other sports ranging from grass skiing to white water rafting.

Lhasa

Much of Tibet's mystery arises from its remoteness and inaccessibility. It truly is on the 'roof of the world' perched among mammoth mountains on an immense plateau drifting at four to five thousand metres above sea-level.

The capital Lhasa, or 'Sunshine City' as it is aptly referred to, with its sapping rarefied atmosphere and elusively enigmatic heritage, is now home to around 400,000 people, with an urban population of around 180,000. Nowadays, despite the rising number of Han Chinese residents, larger than life Tibetan figures dominate the city scene. The allure and promise of this magical city has also drawn in many Hui Muslim traders from neighbouring regions.

As the geographical and religious centre of Tibet, the Jokhang Temple at the core of the city, hosts unceasing hordes of dutifully prostrate pilgrims fulfilling their purpose in life. Above the city the skyline is dominated by the majesty and might of the Potala Palace.

The large-scale redevelopment of the city, which began in the 1980s, is entering a new era as enormous plans to enlarge and modernise the city are aided by the opening of the Tibet-Qinghai Railway. Around the new railway terminus, the Liuwu New Area has been established and new tourist hotels have been fashioned. The first rails were laid on the Tibetan territory in June 2004 and the first trains left Beijing on their 48 hour journey to Lhasa in July 2006. It is the highest railway in the world, with hundreds of kilometres of track above 4,000 metres, peaking at a staggering 5,070 metres. The 1,956-kilometre line, which cost in the region of US$ 3 billion, has brought the rest of China within easy reach.

But for most Tibetans, scattered in remote valleys, life carries on in a manner unchanged for centuries. On the uplands nomads raise herds of sturdy yak on the thin pastures of this harsh but awe-inspiring wilderness. The yak provides valuable meat, hides, milk and butter. Pungent yak butter-fuelled lamps proffer the most pervasive and quintessential Tibetan odour at monasteries, temples and shrines throughout the region.

A unified history of Tibet stretches back to the seventh century, when its armies occupied Nepal and took control of the Silk Road. In the ninth century, the kingdom disintegrated into feuding principalities and the Buddhist clergy grew in power, with the Yellow Hat and Red Hat sects in perpetual conflict. By the 17th century, the former asserted dominance and its leader adopted the title of Dalai Lama or Ocean of Wisdom.

Today, the spiritual, cultural and artistic life of Tibet is still centred on a home-grown form of Buddhism. Every Tibetan attempts to make at least one pilgrimage to Lhasa's Jokhang Temple and Potala Palace. Though most of the great monasteries that once thrived throughout Tibet were destroyed or badly damaged during the Cultural Revolution, many have been restored or rebuilt.

The mystical Jokhang Temple embraces a labyrinth of rooms and chapels containing over 250 statues, including a beautiful gold image of Sakyamuni and some of the finest and oldest treasures of Tibetan art. Encircling the Jokhang, the Barkhor provides an amazingly colourful circuit for a procession of chanting pilgrims in constant clockwise movement. Crowds jostle in a maze of picturesque cobbled alleyways lined with street performers, tea-houses and stalls hawking everything from prayer wheels and turquoise to jewelled yak skulls.

Lhasa is also home to the remarkable Drepung and Sera Monasteries. Northward, soaring peaks surround the Nam-tso Lake, and in the spectacular Yarlung Valley to the southeast there are numerous religious sites, including the Ganden Monastery. Connecting Lhasa to the Nepalese border, the Friendship Highway is a sensational trip - taking two or three days. Shigatse - home of the Panchen Lama and of the awesome Tashilhunpo Monastery, is passed en route. One of Asia's greatest forts still stands at Gyantse, having survived the onslaught of the British-led Younghusband expedition of 1904.

Southern China

GUANGDONG • HAINAN • FUJIAN • HUNAN

Guangdong and Hainan provinces are typical products of China's recent economic development. Guangdong has traditionally been home to the nation's most prosperous special economic zones, while sub-tropical Hainan Island has become a major tourist destination. Fujian province has long fostered relations with the outside world and Hunan is renowned

GUANGDONG PROVINCE
Guangzhou

Despite Guangzhou's relentless development and population boom due to the influx of fortune seekers from other Chinese provinces, it often surprises visitors to learn that the city still retains several centuries-old historical sites as well as many fine old colonial buildings. With its pivotal position on the Pearl River Delta, Canton, as it is known in the West, was China's key trading post for over 2,000 years. As the premier port for sea-borne trade the city flourished, often with virtual autonomy from the imperial capitals of the north. Cantonese culture has maintained its distinctive dialect, cuisine and the entrepreneurial talents that have made Guangdong the richest and most modern province in China today.

The Portuguese sent their first embassy to Canton in the early 16th century, followed by the Dutch and the British. By the 18th century thirteen business offices of foreign companies had been established on the sandy shores of Shamian Island, which in 1859 became a private enclave for European and American merchants. Here they built mansions, warehouses, banks, churches and sports grounds. The island was linked to the city by bridges that were locked at night. Many of the former colonial buildings remain and have been renovated as heritage sites - some of them housing hotels and restaurants. The island has undergone a dramatic face-lift and its open-air riverside café bars attract large crowds.

Many more come for the famous Guangzhou Export Commodities Fair, or Canton Trade Fair, which was launched in its current form in 1957. The exhibition is hosted twice a year at the Liuhua Exhibition Centre as well as the Pazhou International Conference and Exhibition Centre, with the centres being conveniently connected by subway.

With the advent of the new millennium, the physical fabric of the city has experienced fantastic change. As Panyu, Huadu, Conghua and Zengcheng counties merged with Guangzhou, this southern China city is now a huge metropolis covering over seven million square meters. Billions of US dollars were poured into the city which almost instantly appears modern, attractive and accessible. The completion of the city's first metro line in 1991 is being followed with a massive development of underground and over-ground railway systems costing around US$25 billion. A second line was completed in 2004 and two other lines are partly open. New highways and ring roads have greatly eased traffic congestion and seven bridges now cross the Pearl River. Along its banks fine new illuminated buildings and lamp-lit promenades lend a European flavour.

The fine century old colonnaded buildings, pasted with later art deco features, have been restored on Shang Xiajiu Road. The street and others like it, including the Beijing Road, have been pedestrianised to absorb the swelling masses out to shop, eat and enjoy life.

广州

随着来自全国各地寻找财富的人们大量涌入，广州在不停地发展，人口急剧膨胀。但尽管如此，它长达数个世纪的历史还是常常让游客吃惊。这里有历史古迹，也有许多殖民地风格的建筑。广州作为珠江三角洲地区的核心城市，两千年以来一直是中国的主要贸易地区。广州的兴起归因于它在海上贸易中的重要地位。由于北方的帝国对广州采取了自治政策，广东文化保留了其独特的方言、菜系和创业理念——正是这种理念使今天的广东成为了全国最富裕、现代化程度最高的省份之一。

在16世纪早期，第一批葡萄牙人来到广州，随之而来的是荷兰人和英国人。到了18世纪，外国公司已经在柔软的沙滩边建立了十三个办事处，这里在1859年成为了欧洲和美国商人私有的地盘。他们在这里建造了大厦、仓库、银行、教堂和运动场。岛屿与城市被桥梁连接在一起，这些桥梁只在白天开放。至今许多殖民地时期的建筑仍然如故，其中一些还被装修一新，当作酒店和餐厅。岛屿经历了翻天覆地的变化，河边露天的咖啡座吸引着成千上万的人们。

更多的人来广州是为了见识著名的广州出口商品展览会或广州贸易洽谈会。这洽谈会开始于1957年，每年举办两次，展览会的地点包括流花和琶洲展览中心。

随着新千年的来临，广州的城市面貌发生了巨大变化。番禺、花都、从化和增城四县并入广州，使广州成为了一座现代化大都市。广州，以其现代、迷人和便捷的面貌吸引着上亿元的投资。1999年，地铁一号线建成，随后广州又投入了大约250亿美元进行大规模的地下铁路建设。到现在，广州已开通了四条地铁线路。新的高速公路和环城公路大大便利了城市交通，珠江上已经有七座桥梁。美观的建筑如雨后春笋般涌现，霓虹闪烁的步行街更是具有欧洲风情。

城市的传说与它日新月异的发展形成了鲜明对比。传说这座城市是和五位仙人的传说有关，他们骑着羊升上了天，将谷物洒向大地，以保佑这片土地的肥沃。至今，羊城仍是广州的别称和象征。在五仙观，大堂正中的雕像正是五位骑着公羊的圣人，他们保佑广州永远繁荣。在越秀公园，绿色的山坡上、宁静的湖边、幽密的塔下，到处是太极的爱好者，这里的大型五羊雕塑更是人们拍照留念的好地方。

在越秀公园对面有座兰圃，如果清晨造访这里，你就能感受到老广州的韵味。无论是否到了兰

Exclusive Position
Exclusive View

高瞻远瞩·唯我独尊

广州市环市东路339号
339 Huanshi Dong Lu, Guangzhou
邮编 Post Code: 510098
电话 Tel:(86-20) 8331 1888
传真 Fax: (86-20) 8331 1666
电子邮箱 e-mail:sales@gitic.com.cn
网页地址 Wed Site:http://www.gitic.com.cn

On the Beijing Road pedestrians can view ancient underground relics through a glass facade. Around the East Railway Station, huge bank and commercial complexes stand like pinnacles in a sea of green as new parks are being rolled out across the vast city landscape. New suburban business parks are prospering, such as the Guangzhou High and New-Tech Development Zone in which seven out of ten businesses have foreign investment.

In contrast to the modern fairy tale of development, legend tells of the city being founded by the Five Immortals who descended from the skies, each riding a ram and holding a grain. They left the grain for the local people and blessed the land's fertility and today Yang Cheng (Rams City) and Sui Cheng (Grain City) remain as nicknames for the city and images of the horned quintet abound. At the Wu Xianguan Temple, which translates as the Temple of these Five Immortals, a statue in the centre of the main hall depicts the five gods and rams as they blessed Guangzhou to be ever famine free. In Yuexiu Park, rolling green hills contain boat lakes and gardens that are popular with Tai-Chi exponents and a large and much-photographed Five Rams statue.

An early morning visit to the Orchid Garden, opposite Yuexiu Park, offers an indulgent taste of old Guangzhou. Regardless of whether orchids are in season - and there are always examples to be seen in a greenhouse - the beautifully landscaped park, with its moon gates, and bamboo grove houses several enchanting tea pavilions, where the staff proffer precious teas in small porcelain vessels.

Guangxiao Temple's guardians stand at the entrance of Guangzhou's oldest place of worship dating back to the fourth century. Today, monks living quarters stand in grounds that contain huge trees, different worship halls and several shrines. Nearby, the Six Banyan Pagoda, dates back to 573 and its nine-tiered exterior conceals 17 storeys inside.

The extravagance of the Chen Clan Temple, one of Guangzhou's best preserved remaining examples of historical architecture, was established in the 1890s. Exteriors and interiors of all buildings are exquisitely decorated, with colourful ceramic sculptures atop all roof ridges and detailed relief wood carvings appear on giant doors and as panels in walls - both depict auspicious symbols, mythical animals and historic characters acting out legends. The remarkable tomb of the second King of Nanyue (214-111 BC) and his sacrificed attendants has been restored. Thousands of items buried with them, in surprisingly fine condition, are on display in the museum built above it.

花盛开的季节，在温室中总有怒放的花朵。在美丽的花园中，穿过月亮门，在竹林的掩映下有茶房，精致的茶具内上等茶叶飘香千里。

在光孝寺，两尊威严的铜像伫立在这座广州最古老的寺院门前。到了公元四世纪，这里成为了佛教圣地。今天，僧侣们在大树下、在大堂里、在庙宇中静修。不远处就是公元573年修建的宝塔，它九层外部结构内含了十七层建筑。

雄伟壮观的陈氏祠堂修建于19世纪90年代，是广州保存最为完好的历史古迹之一。祠堂的建筑是依照中国传统建筑方式而建，祠堂的外部装潢和内部设计均独具匠心，屋脊上都装饰有陶制的雕像，大门上刻着木制的雕刻，描述的是中国古代历史传说中故事。

比祠堂年代更久远的还有南越(公元前214至111)第二位皇帝的陵墓。这座皇陵和其中的祭品保存完好，就在南越王墓博物馆展出。同时展出的还有皇帝的金镂玉衣和首饰。广州还拥有众多近代历史古迹。孙中山纪念堂用闪烁的蓝瓦覆盖，优美的草坪表达了中国人对于这位革命先驱的尊敬。城市的另一端还有烈士陵园，那里埋葬着在广州起义中牺牲的烈士。

广州是寻找古玩、手工艺品和仿制品的好地方。白天鹅宾馆有一些廉价的古玩和手工艺品商店，而比较专业的收藏家更常去的地方是清平路。在城市的其他地方还有许多艺术品商店，出售瓷器、铜器、字画、首饰和丝绸。在北京路和天河商业区的大型商场中，一样有古董和收藏品出售。对于许多游客来说，此地最实惠的工艺品当属佛山制造的产品，包括剪纸、核雕、象牙雕刻、灯笼和陶器。

在广州各处的酒店、舞厅和练歌房里，夜生活的内容丰富多彩。虽然不如上海和北京，起步较晚的酒吧和夜总会还是别有风味。新的酒吧区正在市内形成，它的灵感来自于香港的兰桂坊，珠江沿岸六百米的地区内，到处是欧洲风情的酒吧。夜总会里各种音乐不停流淌，将夜生活推向高潮。由专业团队演出的传统粤剧定期在文化公园上演，到了节日，他们还会在寺院周围搭起临时剧场。

美味可口的粤菜全面席卷了整个城市，像广州饭店这样的连锁餐厅人满为患，从早茶到晚宴应有尽有。广州还有一系列西式餐厅可供选择，从葡式咖啡到法国酒馆应有尽有。

随着地铁一号线的建成，夜晚游览这座城市变得更加容易。地铁与香港的风格相似。位于花都的广州新白云国际机场到2010年，旅客吞吐量将达到八千万人。作为国际商业中心，广州拥有众多豪华酒店，包括白天鹅酒店和花园酒店，那里有各种名牌商品出售。

Guangzhou also contains several monuments to more recent historical figures. The majestic imperial architecture of the Dr. Sun Yat-sen Memorial Hall, with its gleaming blue roof tiles and elegant gardens displays great reverence for him. The Martyr's Memorial Garden, in another part of town, salutes the country's early Communist leaders.

Guangzhou is a great place to find antiques and excellent reproductions, as well as handicrafts. The White Swan Hotel has relatively inexpensive antique and crafts stores, while dedicated collectors will browse around the alleys in Qingping market. There are also plenty of arts and crafts stores around the town, selling porcelain, bronze ware, scroll paintings, calligraphy, jade ornaments and silk. Antiques and collectibles can also be found in the new, sophisticated department stores that have opened, particularly along Huanshi Dong Road, Beijing Road and in the downtown area of Tianhe. For many visitors the great buys found in the area are the handicrafts made in Foshan, including intricate paper cuts, olive kernel carvings and lanterns, and the glazed pottery of Shiwan.

The city's nightlife flourishes in the hotel and independent discos and karaoke lounges found all around town. Though not as developed as Shanghai or Beijing, the bar and club scene is attempting to compensate for its late start. New bar areas are springing up around town. One of the bar areas takes its inspiration from Hong Kong's trendy Lan Kwai Fong - the Bai-E-Tan Bar stretches for 600 metres along the Pearl River and has a remodelled European flavour. Clubs like the Tang Club, Yes and Big Boss offer a medley of night-time excitement from go-go girls, live bands, dance-floor techno, house and rap to slushy Canto-pop. In the more traditional vein Cantonese opera, by professional groups, is performed regularly in Nanfang Theatre, in the Cultural Park and during festivals at temporary theatres beside the temples.

The delicious native cuisine comprehensively dominates the city and chain restaurants like the Guangzhou Restaurants are popular for evening banquets as well as for morning and lunch-time dim sum. Guangzhou has a great selection of international eateries.

Guangzhou has a new international airport, which has been designed to handle 80 million passengers a year by 2010. As an international centre of commerce, the city boasts numerous luxury hotels including the Garden Hotel with its lobby loaded with goods from Bally, Gieves & Hawkes and Cerrutti 1881, amongst others others.

ESSENTIAL GUANGZHOU >>>>>>>

Culture Buffs Allow at least half a day for a visit to the spectacular Guangdong Folk Art Museum. The building itself is a cultural relic from the Qing Dynasty.
Go Chinese Visit the bustling Shang Xia Jiu walking street and shop in the Li Wan Plaza for the hottest fashions. Hunt for bargains in the Antique Building and paw over Cantonese antiques and jade accessories in Jade Street
Past Splendour Explore the historic colonial splendour of Shamian Island. Stay on till evening and take a drink, or dinner, alongside the Pearl River.
Peckish? Sample Guangzhou's very own dim sum treats - shrimp dumplings, steam pork dumplings, fried taro cake and many, many more.
Spending Time Get lost in the Yi De Lu wholesale markets - everything from food and drink to stationery and toys is there.
Taking it Easy Cruise on the Pearl River, take a hike on Baiyun Mountain, relax in Panyu and get back to nature at the Xiangjiang Safari Park. Take in a night time show at the Chime Long International Circus. Cool off in one of the city's top spas.
Trendy Feast in the Huan Shi Dong Lu area - at Latino, The Peach Blossom, and Lemon House. For that much needed drink head to the overseas Chinese village.

Cafe Amor
A genuinely cool place, full of interesting touches - and it does great coffee and good cocktails too. *1/F No. 11 Jun Yi Lu. Tel: 87654361*

Chen Jia Ci
34 En Long Li, Zhong Shan Qi Lu. Tel: 8181 4559

Chime Long International Circus
All the fun of the circus - animals, magic and acrobatic tomfoolery. *Yingbin Road, Panyu. Tel: 8479 6600*

Comrades
A popular place for live jazz and hip hop DJs. *165 Tao Jin Lu. Tel: 8737 1886*

L.A. City Billiards Bar & Restaurant
With more than twenty billiard tables, this place has dining and cafe sections as well as a large screen sports bar. *4/F Tian Lun Garden, Jian She Si Lu. Tel: 8356 0339*

Lan Kwai Fong
Cosy seating and decor, famous for Thai cuisine, though, the signature dish is roast pigeon Cantonese style. *No. 5 Sha Mian Nan Jie. Tel: 8121 6523*

Lemon House Vietnamese Cuisine
A great place for Vietnamese food - be prepared to join the queue outside. *1/F, 11 Jian She Liu Ma Lu. Tel: 8375 3600*

Mamamia Wine Bar and Italian Restaurant
One of the most elegant and popular Italian restaurants in town with stylish private rooms. *196 Lin He Xi Heng Lu, G/F Ri Hang Hotel. Tel: 8701 3423*

Nan Fang Theatre (The Cantonese Opera House)
No. 80 Jiao Yu Lu. Tel: 8333 3155

Roof Restaurant and Bar
Great food, champagne and cigars. *8/F, China Hotel, Liu Hua Lu. Tel: 8666 6888 ext. 71891*

The Peach Blossom
Guangzhou's premier Cantonese restaurant. *3/F The Garden Hotel, 368 Huan Shi Dong Lu. Tel: 8333 8989 ext. 3315*

White Tiger Restaurant
A stylish and upmarket western restaurant with a great wine cellar. *1/F Chime Long Hotel, Ying Bin Lu. Tel: 8478 6838 ext. 6333*

Xiang Jiang Safari Park
Yin Bin Lu, Pan Yu. Tel: 8478 3333

Xi Guan Ren Jia
Old Cantonese style interior setting for great dim sum. *Shop 4DZ, 4/F South Tower, Li Wan Plaza, Xia Jiu Lu. Tel: 8138 0308*

GUANGDONG TOP SPOTS

Tang Club

GUANGZHOU

Chao Hao Restaurant

Located in the city centre, the Chao Hao has a great environment, comfortable private rooms and convenient parking. Authentic Chaozhou Cuisine is the main attraction - oyster cakes, shrimp dumplings, taro paste, pan-fried cod fish and much more. Seafood lovers, and those hunting for exotic Chinese dishes, will never run short of surprises on its menu. Cantonese dim sum is another yummy option. *6/F World Trade Tower, No. 371-375 Huan Shi Dong Lu. Tel: (020) 8769 1333*

Tang Lee Food Art

With its great lake view, this garden restaurant combines elements of traditional Cantonese cuisine and Cantonese culture. Morning tea, which can be taken at an outdoor table, starts from 8.00 a.m. and spills over into the early afternoon. At night, take dinner on a boat anchored in the middle of the beautifully illuminated lake. The restaurant's signature dishes include deep-fried pigeon and the popular Ti Zi Zhou – a rice congee with seafood. *Li Wan Hu Park, Ru Yi Fang Road, Huang Sha Da Dao. Tel: (020) 8181 8002*

Tang Lee Food Art

Kam Boat Restaurant

A Hong Kong style restaurant with great ambiance and service, as well as a selection of famous dim sum delicacies – including shrimp dumplings, turnip paste and beef balls and an almond paste desert. Novel 'cartoon style' dim sum adds another dimension to the restaurant's repertoire. *5/F Asian International Hotel, No. 326-329 Huan Shi Dong Lu. Tel: 6128 8888-8523. No. 528 Long Jin Zhong Lu. Tel: (020) 8195 5783*

Bing Sheng Seafood Restaurant

All the way from its roots as a small local restaurant into one of the most famous franchises in the city, Bing Sheng has always been a top choice for seafood lovers. The combination of a fantastic variety of fish and seafood options – and affordable prices, ensures that its restaurants are packed each and every evening. Its most famous dish, the 'Shun De Fish Sashimi' includes ten dips and a sumptuous seafood soup. *No. 33 Dong Xiao Lu. Tel: (020) 3428 6910, 3428 6911. No. 168 Tian He Dong Lu. Tel: 8751 8683, 8751 8682. 1-4/F Wu Feng Hotel, No. 438 Jiang Nan Da Dao. Tel: (020) 8447 2844, 8424 4611*

Four Season Hibiscus

Four Season Hibiscus

Featuring authentic Chinese cuisine, the Four Season Hibiscus Restaurant has recently been renovated and is now a great dining venue with luxurious rooms, elegant fixtures and fittings - and of course delicious food. Its opulent menu includes bird's nest, abalone, trepang and rare seafood offerings. *1/F Hua Tai Hotel, Xian Lie Dong Lu. Tel: (020) 8762 7913*

Four Seas International

Although a little far from town, buffet lovers should not miss this trip to experience an all-in-one dinning experience. In spite of its international flavour with Japanese sushi and sashimi, Indian curry and Brazilian BBQ, many local favourites are also on offer - dim sum, roast duck, BBQ pork, hotpot, freshly steamed seafood and more. The buffet features over 800 choices, as well as an extensive and prestigious wine list. *A2 Building, Wanbo Centre, Ying Bin Lu, Panyu. Tel: (020) 3482 2266*

Four Seas International

Sultan Restaurant Turkish BBQ

Resembling Aladdin's royal palace, Sultan's splendid and lavish interior is dripping with gold – from its table settings to its walls. The restaurant offers barbeques and grills, kebabs, hot and cold appetizers and fantastic desserts. Orders can be taken in Arabic, Turkish, English and Chinese. *1/F Bai Yun Hotel, No. 367 Huan Shi Dong Lu. Tel: (020) 8349 4170*

Sultan Restaurant Turkish BBQ

Bai Yun Xian Guan

This is an unpretentious local restaurant with good prices and big dishes. Located inside a bamboo wood alongside a lake at the foot of a mountain, Bai Yun Xian Guan (god's residence in white cloud) really pairs its name and provides an exotic dining environment which is hard to match. A great place to relax and enjoy wholesome mutton hotpot dishes in a quiet city oasis. *Lu Hu Park, Lu Hu Lu. Tel: (020) 8359 0424*

Yes

Taking a music factory concept, Yes is the most amazing night club in town. It has four different entertainment venues - Super Yes is famous for hosting world famous guest DJ's, Funky Yes is more into hip hop dance, Club Yes is an elegant place offering music from overseas and local bands and Mini Yes features a pure white dancing hall. A one stop shop for all one's night life needs. *No. 132 Dong Feng Xi Lu. Tel: (020) 8136 6184*

Kevin's Café

Full of interesting decorative and atmospheric touches, Kevin's is a conventional, yet genuinely cool place for night life with cosy sofas and lazy jazz. Kevin's offers great coffees and cocktails, as well as sublime desserts from its Luxembourg-trained pastry chef. *No. 12 Jian She Liu Ma Lu. Tel: (020) 8376 5879*

The Paddy Field

The Paddy Field

The Paddy Field is the only proper pub in town and completely lacks the tackiness you sometimes expect from 'Irish' bars. The wooden fixtures and fittings help give it a great atmosphere, the pints are decent and the food is far better than average pub grub. It's the homesick expatriate hub of the city - with prominent notice boards announcing events and club activities. The Paddy Field is also renowned for its wicked parties. *G/F Central Plaza, No. 38 Hua Le Lu. Tel: (020) 8360 1379*

SHENZHEN

Ju's Fusion Restaurant

Abalone always features at the top of the list of a fine Cantonese dining experience - and Ju's culinary master Li Ju has earned the accolade of the 'King of Abalone.' Additionally, Ju's Restaurant offers a gastronomic and cultural tour emphasising fresh and healthy dining. With 280 seats in the main dinning hall and eleven VIP rooms, the restaurant provides a classical and extravagant dining environment. *2/F 999 Royal Suites & Towers Shenzhe. No. 1001 Shen Nan Dong Lu, Shenzhen. Tel: (0755) 2513 0999*

Ju's Fusion Restaurant

Trattoria Italiana Da Angelo

The restaurant's stunning contemporary décor is accented with Etruscan themed paintings and Roman statues. This is little Italy in China, where everything is either imported from Italy, or homemade by its Italian maestros. *G12, Princess Plaza, Tai Zi Lu, Shekou Shenzhen. Tel: (0755) 2682 5927*

Trattoria Italiana Da Angelo

360° Bar, Restaurant Lounge

A high-rise sensation with magical views of the city lights, 360° Bar, Restaurant Lounge can claim to be the top romantic destination for a night out. The place to luxuriate on a comfy couch and to enjoy a meal or drink, whilst taking in a panoramic view of Shenzhen and Hong Kong through a glass wall. Conveniently located close to the Shenzhen-Hong Kong border, and near the train station, this is a perfect place for a short stop either before or after a long journey. *31/F Shangri-La Hotel, 1002 Jianshe Road, Shenzhen. Tel: (0755) 8233 0888*

V Bar

V Bar, Shenzhen's top nightspot features a stage set behind the bar and a large ball-shaped screen. Shenzhen's finest in-house band, who play popular dance hits, help keep the place packed most nights with a mix of locals and hotel guests. It also has a large patio by the poolside and a terrace overlooking the three of the city's major theme parks. *2/F Crowne Plaza Shenzhen, No. 9026 Shen Nan Da Dao, Shen Zhen. Tel: (0755) 2693 6888*

DONGGUAN

Thai Basil Restaurant

Located in the Dongguan Bar street, Thai Basil's green decoration sets the scene for fine Southeast Asian cuisine prepared with fresh, seasonal ingredients served up in elegant and comfortable surroundings. Apart from Thai food, Indian, Singaporean and Malaysian dishes are conjured up in a kitchen presided over by Indian and Thai chefs. *Bar Street, Dongcheng Road South, Dongcheng District, Tel: (0769) 2245 4988*

ZHUHAI

Cohiba Bar & Grill

The South American carnival persona of Cohiba comes from its mix of flavourful cuisine, including an all day Western breakfast, and the tangy sounds of its Latin American band. It's also got a large outdoor terrace, replete with pool tables. *No. 203 -209 Shui Wan Lu, Xiang Zhou District, Zhu Hai. Tel: (0756) 889 2444*

Thai Basil Restaurant

Jin Yue Xuan Seafood Hotpot Restaurant

Set right next to the ocean, this Chinese Restaurant combines great visual enjoyment with exquisite seafood-inspired Cantonese cuisine. Its main dining room, decorated in classical and traditional Chinese style, affords great sea views. *1-3/F Block B, Ri Hua Commercial Plaza, No. 265 Qing Lv Nan Lu, Xiang Zhou District, Zhu Hai. Tel: (0756) 813 3133*

Jin Yue Xuan Seafood Hotpot Restaurant

WWW.CROWNEPLAZA.COM

3.2 million dollar project

2 days of intense negotiations

5 outstanding deals

14 hours before your flight

1 perfect opportunity to unwind

ust relax at our stylish Venice oasis.

his is where, at the end of each day, you will find a respite from the fast-paced, usiness lifestyle you lead. *The Place To Meet* is Crowne Plaza Shenzhen.

r reservations, visit www.crowneplaza.com or call toll-free numbers in China 800 830 4088, 400 88 40 888 (mobile)
ddress: No.9026 Shennan Road, Overseas Chinese Town, Shenzhen 518053, P.R.China
el: (86-755) 2693 6888 Fax: (86-755) 2693 6999 E-mail: cpsz@cpsz.com

CROWNE PLAZA®

SHENZHEN

深圳威尼斯皇冠假日酒店

THE PLACE TO MEET

999 Royal Suites & Towers
Suite is what u deserve

Awarded
"The Best Interior Design Business Hotel"
&
"The Best Serviced Apartment Hotel"
at the China Hotel Golden Pillow Awards 2006.

Located in the heart of Shenzhen's business and entertainment area (Lowu district) Offering 298 suites,the 999 Royal Suites & Towers has the cozy,yet elegant atmosphere of a boutique hotel along with 24 hours Butler Service. An ideal destination for both business and pleasure.

Reservation Hotline
86-755/25130999
Ext/88888
No.1001 East Shennan Rd,Shenzhen 518002,China
Tel: (86–755) 2513 0999   Fax: (86–755) 2513 0839
www.999royal–suites.com   sales@999royal–suites.com

东方银座酒店，为您送上五星级酒店家居式服务，让您时刻享受真正自在的私人空间。地处交通枢纽，座落在深圳福田区商业中心，与地铁站竹子林出口相连接，到会展中心只要10分钟，到罗湖车站和深圳国际机场分别只有15分钟和20分钟的车程。

Come and experience our five-star hospitality at Swiss-Belhotel Suites and Residences, Shenzhen. You will enjoy an impeccable and truly personalized service that is second to none···Be at the heart of everything! Located at the Central Business District of Futian,Shenzhen. Next to the Zhuzilin Metro Station, Just 10 minutes to Convention & Exhibition Centre, 15 minutes to the Luohu Railway Station and 20 minutes to Shenzhen International Airport.

Unirez by Pegasus

Amadeus	UZ SZX155
Apollo / Galileo	UZ 75969
Sabre	UZ 6160
Worldspan	UZ 9155

Shennan Boulevard West,Futian District Shenzhen 518040,China (Exit B2 at the Zhuzilin Metro Station)
中国深圳市深南大道西(竹子林地铁站B2出口) 邮政编码：518040
T电话 (86 755)8350 0888 F传真(86 755)8302 9333
E电邮 reservation@sbsrswiss-belhotel.com www.sbsrswiss-belhotel.com
Hong Kong Sales Office 香港办事处
Room 1421, 14/F, Albion Plaza, 2-6 Granville Road, Tsimshatsui, Kowloon, HongKong
香港九龙尖沙咀加连威老道2-6号爱宾商业大厦14楼21室
T电话 (852)2834 4223 F传真 (852)2834 4229 E电邮 saleshk@swiss-belhotel.com

WWW.SBSRSWISS-BELHOTEL.COM

Shenzhen

As the city absorbed much of Hong Kong's manufacturing industry, and then became a Special Economic Zone, it sprawled out into what now is a well-planned settlement of over 4 million people. The sleek skyscraper skyline of the centre in the Luohu and Futian districts, or so-called Middle Area, bustles with shoppers and restaurant go-ers. New government offices, museums, gardens and a cultural centre are located here. The train station is the busiest place in the area providing express links to Hong Kong, Shanghai and Beijing as well as subway links to the east part of the city and the famous Overseas Chinese Town.

Hong Kong visitors regularly take short breaks here on weekends and public holidays and often head for resorts scattered along the western coast of the area, where the range of recreational facilities has grown as quickly as the commerce in the city. The resort hotels have a fine range of sporting and recreational facilities, at considerably less cost than in Hong Kong. Shenzhen also boasts some of the best golf courses in China. Stretching across Shenzhen and Dongguan, Mission Hills is the world's number one golf club. Designed by 10 world-renowned golf players, it's an international golf community that combines golfing with relaxation, business and lifestyle.

Shenzhen's theme parks also attract swarms of visitors. Sprawling Splendid China, on the edge of Shenzhen Bay, illustrates the glories of China's centuries old culture with miniatures on a scale of 15:1. The adjacent 20,000 square metre Chinese Culture Park is a perfect complement. It contains life-sized buildings as they are found in various provinces. The materials and construction are strictly authentic, as is the food served in the restaurants. Combining Chinese history and culture with state-of-the-art sound and lighting the Dancing with Dragon and Phoenix night show extravaganza is not to be missed. The nearby Window on the World features miniaturised international monuments from East and West set in landscaped gardens. The area, which is lucky to see snow once in a century, also accommodates a large indoor ski-slope.

Shekou, which started as an industrial zone many years ago, has also become a major residential area for expatriates. The Sea World Square and the nearby Princess Plaza are saturated with a sea of domestic and international restaurants, bars and night clubs.

深圳

深圳经济特区，深圳位于广东省南部沿海，是中国最早的经济特区城市，1980年特区成立以来，旅游业发展神速。“锦绣中华”、中国民俗文化村、世界之窗更被誉为中国三大文化旅游景区。而邻近的“欢乐谷”更拥有一个设备齐全的水上乐园，是游客不容错过的好去处。此外，境内还有内伶仃猕猴自然保护区、福田红树林保护区，以及赤湾左炮台、宋少帝陵等古迹。

A TOUCH OF LEGEND

Proximity to the Lo Wu border crossing, train terminus and future underground mass transit system, Sunshine Hotel is a complete 5-star facility ideally located in the heart of the business and financial district of Shenzhen. Renowned for its personalized quality services, luxurious accommodation and facilities, the hotel has been praised as the leading five-star hotel in Shenzhen.

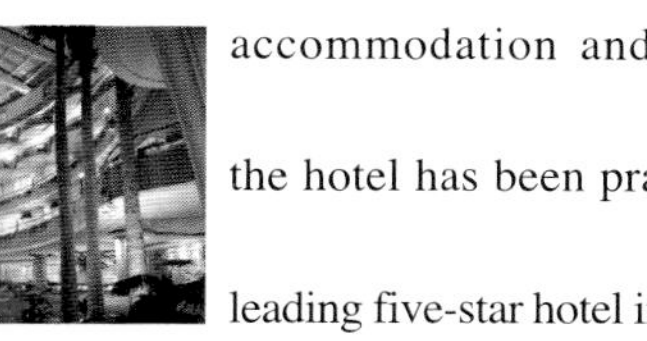

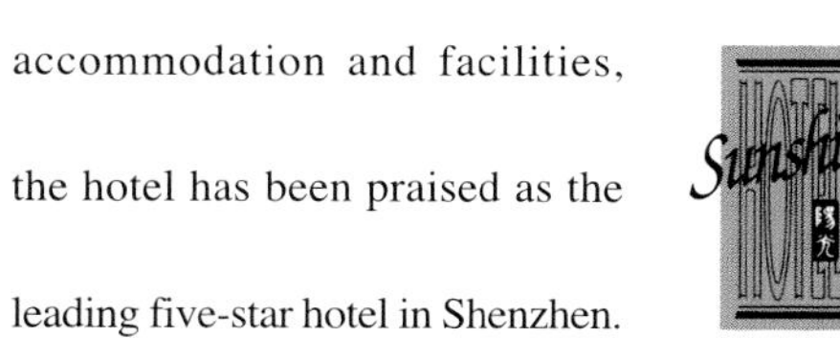

位於深圳市商業區心臟地帶之『陽光酒店』，位置優越，鄰近羅湖關口，火車站及未來之地下鐵路車站近在咫尺，盡握天時地利。佈置高雅亮麗，氣派非凡的酒店大堂，優良先進之設施及完善週到的服務，令陽光酒店傲視同儕，成為五星級商務酒店之典範。

陽光酒店
Sunshine Hotel

中國廣東省深圳市嘉賓路1號　1 Jiabin Road, Shenzhen, China.　郵編／Postal Code: 518005　電話／Tel: (86-755) 8223 3888　圖傳／Fax: (86-755) 8222 6719
電子信箱／E-mail:rez@sunshinehotel.com　國際電腦網絡／http://www.sunshinehotel.com　免費訂房熱線（國內）／Toll-free (Domestic): 800 830 2302

香港辦事處／Hong Kong Sales Office：香港灣仔駱克道353號三湘大廈35樓 35/F, Sunshine Plaza, 353 Lockhart Road,Wan Chai, HK　電話／Tel: (852) 2575 5989　傳真／Fax: (852) 2803 4311　電子信箱／E-mail: ciemgt@netvigator.com

Relax

We will take care of the rest.

No matter for business or leisure, you will find that Holiday Inn Donghua Shenzhen is a relaxing oasis eager to cater to your every need and desire.

Toll-free Reservations Number:
Mainland China 800 830 4088
400 88 40 888(for mobile phone users)
Address: Donghua Park, Nanyou Road,
Nanshan District, Shenzhen 518054, P.R. China
Tel: 86-755 2641 6688
Fax: 86-755 2664 5282
E-mail: hiszhen@public.szptt.net.cn
Global Website: www. holiday-inn. com

For reservations, please call our Asia Pacific Reservation Centers: Hong Kong 800 965 888, Australia 1 300 666 747, Malaysia 1 800 80 1881, Indonesia 001 803 656 888, Philippines 1 800 1651 8888, Singapore 1 800 787 1221, Thailand 001 800 65 6888, Taiwan 886 2 2776 5702

Zhuhai

The transformation of Zhuhai, from a fishing village into a booming commercial and industrial centre in a sea-side garden city setting has been staggering. Designated as a Special Economic Zone in 1980, it now houses 1.2 million residents in an area of 121 square kilometres, including dozens of coastal islands. At its heart, just across from the Macau border is Gongbei, with its huge high-rise and hectic shopping streets - like a slice of Hong Kong.

Zhuhai is, perhaps unexpectedly, the jewel of China's tourism crown, receiving more international visitors than anywhere else in the nation. Many frequent visitors cross the border from Macau. Large numbers of overseas Chinese, who trace their roots to the Foshan region of Guangdong province, also visit the city. In addition, the zone attracts tour groups from all over China who come to pay their respects at Dr Sun Yat-sen's birthplace in nearby Cuiheng and proceed to Zhuhai to shop for imported goods. Some go on to cross the border into the former Portuguese territory of Macau.

Another slice of history inspired one of Zhuhai's attractions - New Yuan Ming Yuan - a reproduction of Beijing's Yuan Ming Yuan Palace, which was destroyed by British and French soldiers in 1860 during the Second Opium War. The new construction contains staterooms, pavilions and courtyards, where throughout the day old ceremonies, musical concerts and dances are performed. There are also restaurants as well as a cinema show depicting the burning of the palace.

There are some excellent hotels in Zhuhai and neighbouring Zhongshan where day trip or overnight visits offer a wide range of recreational possibilities - several resorts offer outdoor pools, saunas and such sports facilities as tennis courts, horseback riding, rifle shooting and bowling as well as discos and karaoke lounges. Shui Wan Road Bar Street is the city's popular night out places with restaurants and bars in both western and Chinese styles.

For some visitors the great attraction is golf. There are championship courses in Zhuhai itself and in Zhongshan, where China's first modern golf club opened in 1984 with a par-72 course designed by Arnold Palmer. A second adjoining 18 holes, designed by Jack Nicklaus, has also been added. But it is the Zhuhai International Circuit that has put the spotlight back on Zhuhai City. The circuit was designed by Jacques Villeneuve.

珠海

位于广东省南部，珠江口西岸的珠海市，面临南海，陆连澳门，水通香港，距广州137公里。全市共有大小岛屿一百四十个，有“百岛之市”之称，盛产海鲜、糕蟹、龙虾、石斑、鱿鱼等水产品，畅销海内外。珠海海湾优美，奇峰异石众多，气候宜人，拥有现代化的高级宾馆及酒店。珠海风光绮丽，旅游点包括香洲湾、九洲城、濂泉洞等风景区及仿古建筑圆明新园，将北京圆明园重现于世，九十九个景点令人眼界大开，皇庭气派，湖光山色。此外，珠海赛车场更被指定为主办中国格兰披治大赛车的场地。

HAINAN ISLAND PROVINCE
Hainan

A favoured winter resort of northern Chinese, Hainan Island has the credentials to rival any other tropical holiday destination in Asia. Sunny days, balmy nights, white sand beaches, good diving, diverse wildlife, interesting minorities, traditional fishing villages and great seafood are transforming the island into the next Hawaii. It's becoming a playground for China's new rich as well as a growing tide of Russian tourists. New resorts, condos and villas are hastily being erected to lure Chinese and international buyers. Many, including South Koreans, Japanese, Russians and even some Americans, are now looking to the island for their idyllic second homes.

Plush resorts dot Sanya on the southern coast, overlooking white-sand beaches lined with coconut palms. Just 30 kilometres away the Yalong Bay National Resort is the island's premier destination. It's a world-class resort with a matchless crescent-shaped beach and is host to every kind of water sport including water-skiing, jet-skiing and scuba diving along coral reefs. It also offers tennis, hiking and rock climbing and a superb 36-hole golf course designed by Robert Trent Jones Jnr. II. The area also boasts the Sea World Aquarium, a butterfly park, a shell museum, a large Guanyin stature at the shore, and a cluster of top-notch five-star hotels. A number of these hotels contain world-class spas. And the spa business is very hot in Hainan. Of particular distinction is the Mandara Spa at Sheraton Sanya Resort, and the Tea Tree Spa at the Holiday Inn Resort Yalong Bay.

The Tianya Haijiao, a boulder-strewn beach just outside Sanya, is a major attraction for Chinese tourists. It recalls the old days when Hainan was a place of exile for those who offended the emperor. It was considered as the end of the earth. Over the years exiles expressed their despair by carving inscriptions on the boulders littering the southern-most point in Hainan.

Over half the island is covered by lush forest and the hilly terrain of the interior is home to exotic plant species, rare animals and over 20 minority nationalities. Tongshi, at the foot of Qizi Shan and Wuzhi Shan is home of an excellent ethnic museum and nearby pine-clad mountains can easily be reached for hiking. Roads snaking past vaulted thatched houses around communal courtyards, where the Li and Miao minorities preserve their traditional way of life, are regularly encountered, as are ethnic tourist villages offering entertainment and crafts buying opportunities.

海南

对于生活在北方的中国人来说，海南岛可谓是最理想的冬季度假胜地。它有着同地区其他假日目的地难以比拟的优势，比如阳光明媚的白天，温暖怡人的夜晚，白净光滑的沙滩，各种各样的生物，风情各异的民族，传统古典的渔村以及生猛可口的海鲜　　这一切都使海南成为中国的夏威夷。

在南部沿海，有一个豪华的度假胜地——三亚，在那里，白色的沙滩在椰树的掩映下闪烁发光。距离亚龙湾国家度假区仅仅30公里，就是该岛最迷人的旅游胜地了。亚龙湾有着世界一流的条件，适合各种水上运动，比如滑水，冲浪以及珊瑚潜水。这里还拥有各式各样的运动设施，比如网球、远足、攀岩以及由罗伯特·特伦特二世设计的三十六洞高尔夫球场。该地区还有令人惊艳的海底世界、蝴蝶公园、贝壳博物馆以及顶级的五星级酒店。

在这类酒店中配备了世界顶级的水疗设施，在海南，水疗热正在流行。在这些水疗中，万豪酒店的泉尤为引人注目，这里提供应有尽有的符合亚洲文化和习俗的按摩和塑身服务。它的特点在是在按摩中使用了岛上丰富的自然资源，比如咖啡和热带水果。

对于中国游客来说，天涯海角是最吸引人的旅游胜地，这是三亚地区一个岩石遍布的海滩，它使人不禁想起，在古代，触犯了皇上的人要被发配到海南来。从北京看来，这里是想像中最远的地方，也被认为是世界的尽头。多年以来，被发配到这里的人在这海南岛的最南端的岩石上提诗写字，抒发郁闷绝望的情绪。

海南岛的一半地方被郁郁葱葱的森林覆盖，岛内地形多山，是多种罕见物种和超过二十个少数民族的栖息之地。棋子山和五指山脚下的铜时可谓是一个民族博物馆，而其附近松林覆盖的山丘又是理想的攀登胜地。沿着茅草覆盖的房舍，山路蜿蜒，在这里，经常能够遇到黎族和苗族的乡民，他们仍旧保持着传统的生活方式。淳朴的村民会为您献上丰富多彩的娱乐节目和手工艺品。

海南全岛温泉遍布，在兴隆尤为多见。这里有两个风景秀丽的植物园和一座现代化的东南亚主题公园。这里有青山秀水、热带雨林和椰子树林。第二代马来人、越南人和华人聚居在此，以种植咖啡和茶树为生。许多植物都是任游客采摘的。兴隆的许多旅馆都备有温泉可供洗浴。

海南的省会海口，意为大海入口，在19世纪末期就已成为重要贸易地区。在日新月异的发展中，这座城市仍然保持着旧日的习俗——市民们聚集在露天咖啡座下品尝优质的当地咖啡，传统的市场一直开放直到深夜。海口是全岛的经济中心，这里有鳞次栉比的银行大厦、香港时装的分店以及数个世界一流的国际酒店。

博敖，距离海口之东100公里处，水陆纵横、湖泊众多，美不胜收，是各国领导人们探讨亚洲经济和发展方向的理想场所。这一变化促进了当地的发展，现在，博敖不仅有优秀的酒店，还有崭新的高尔夫球场。

海口有两个关于著名流放者的著名古迹。其一是海瑞墓。海瑞是16世纪祖籍浙江的官员，敢于直言，反对腐败。他在海南的墓地最近刚刚重新修葺一新，1589年树立的墓碑和雕刻依然如故，而在人造瀑布旁，又加建了雕刻精细的宝塔。五公堂是另一清朝古迹，纪念五位因直谏皇帝而被流放的人。

海南岛的自然资源极其丰富，包括铁、金、石油和天然气。海口和三亚都有国际机场，可直达香港特别行政区、东南亚以及中国许多城市。另外，这里还允许香港的船舶做短暂停泊。2003年初，一座铁轨渡口建成，将广东省湛江市与海南岛连接了起来。符合国际标准的酒店、西式餐厅、游泳池以及健美中心如雨后春笋般出现，在海口和三亚，还建立了新的高尔夫球场。

海南鸡饭名扬全国，不容错过。鸡饭佐料丰富，美味可口。在椰子丰收的季节，椰奶是最受欢迎的饮料。这里的其他特产还包括海鲜火锅等等。

Beach, sand and sun, welcome to Haikou, Hainan Island.

The Sheraton Haikou Resort is a 346 room Beach Front property, minutes from the city's commercial and entertainment districts and two International Standard 18 Hole golf courses. The 7 Food & Beverage outlets and recreational facilities (SPA, Gym, Hot-spring pools, water sports, Games Room) will delight even the most discerning travelers looking for a piece of Paradise.

With over 1300 square meter (11,000 square feet) of meeting space, the Sheraton Haikou Resort is the ideal venue for board meetings to conferences and events that require the perfect blend of work and play.

Come and enjoy the Sheraton Haikou.

Call 800-810-3088 directly in China.
Visit www.sheraton.com/haikou.
Best rates, guaranteed.

MEMBER OF STARWOOD PREFERRED GUEST®

199 Bin Hai Road, Haikou City 570311, Hainan Province, P.R. China
Telephone: +86 898 6870 8888 Fax: +86 898 6870 6999 Website: www.sheraton.com/haikou

Hainan has an abundance of hot springs. Spa resorts are particularly plentiful in Xinglong, which lies close to two beautifully landscaped botanical gardens, and a modern Southeast Asian theme park. The county is blessed with mountains, tropical rainforests and coconut groves. Second-generation Malay and Vietnamese Chinese communities live in this area and were responsible for introducing coffee and tea plantations to the island. Many plantations are open to visitors. Many hotels in Xinglong have spring water pumped into their pools and bathrooms.

The capital Haikou, meaning 'mouth of the sea,' came to prominence as a trading port in the late 19th century. Still under constant development it remains laid-back in many ways - residents gather for the excellent local coffee in open-air cafes, and traditional markets stay open until late at night. Its role as the economic hub of the island is evident from the glass-clad bank buildings, branches of Hong Kong fashion boutiques and several first-class international hotels.

Boao, 100 kilometres east of Haikou, with its myriad of waterways, lakes and streams of unparalleled beauty, has become a favourite spot for policy makers to discuss Asian economic and development issues. Its new importance has spawned the development of excellent hotels, including The Westin, the Sofitel and a superb golf course.

Haikou harbours two interesting monument sites to some of the better-known exiles. The Tomb of Hai Rui, a 16th century magistrate from Zhejiang province and outspoken critic of imperial excesses and corruption of his day - hence his residency in Hainan - has been recently re-landscaped. The Five Figures Temple is a sprawling Qing dynasty complex, built to honour five exiled imperial critics.

The island is spectacularly rich in natural resources including iron ore, gold, oil and natural gas. There are international airports in Haikou and Sanya, both with regular flights from Hong Kong and Southeast Asia as well as many Chinese cities. In addition there are regular cruises from Hong Kong that drop anchor for a few hours. Access was further improved in early 2003, when a rail ferry was introduced connecting the island with Zhanjiang in Guangdong province. New hotels of international standard, complete with western restaurants, pools and health clubs, have opened in prime areas and there are now two golf courses, near Haikou and Sanya. Food-wise, Hainan chicken is famed all over China and should not be missed - soup from the boiled chicken is used to cook accompanying rice and the chicken is eaten with a tangy ginger and spring onion dip.

FUJIAN PROVINCE

Fuzhou

As capital of Fujian province, Fuzhou has been an important political centre for over 2,000 years and served as the temporary capital of China during the Song and Ming dynasties. Located near the estuary of the scenic banks of the Min River, which discharges its waters into the East China Sea skirting Taiwan - Fuzhou has long been an area whose descendants have travelled far and wide.

The city is richly spread with banyan trees and historical sites. The huge, tranquil West Lake Park mirrors the city's traditions and ambitions. Two 'opposing pagodas' have been an essential element of the city scenery for over one thousand years. The White Pagoda stands on the southern slopes of Yu Hill, whilst the Black Pagoda sits on the Black Mountain. They can both be climbed for resplendent views over the old and new. Near the city the Gu Mountain is a major focus for visitors. At its heart lies the remarkable Yongquan Temple, nestling amongst more than one hundred sites, displaying the finery of Chinese civilisation embodied in architecture and rock carvings.

Xiamen

Once an island, now linked to the mainland by a causeway, Xiamen was at the centre of one

of China's most action-packed opium and tea-trade sagas - in the days when it was known as Amoy. Once again this port and bustling commercial city is thriving. Its clean air and healthy economic environment have attracted many multinational companies and overseas investments. Behind its modern façade, now enhanced by night time LED displays, a wealth of historic buildings remain, from sea-side hotels to Victorian shopping arcades.

In the 1840s, foreign traders transformed the tiny islet of Gulangyu into an International Settlement - much like Shamian Island in Guangzhou - building grandiose mansions, churches, warehouses and a city hall based on the US Congress building. Many of these historic structures have been renovated. The islet's residential population, noted for its love of music, is dwindling with the redevelopment - but a piano museum remains. The dignity and tranquillity if the island, with its delightful small beaches, remains intact and electric carts are the only permitted form of powered transport. Needless to say there are great opportunities to eat fresh seafood and there are plentiful international restaurants operated by foreigners.

The original SEZ occupies the western part of the city, with smart office buildings, factories, warehouses and wharves. The DELL company's enormous interest in the area is never far from sight. There are smart newer high-tech looking department stores and office towers - but also large areas of the old town have been renovated, with traditional shop-houses being repaired and repainted to better display merchandise. New internationally-managed hotels have facilities and services to match the best in Asia. Xiamen has an international airport and numerous international golf courses, including one designed by Greg Norman.

福州

福州是福建省首府，2000年来一直是重要的政治中心，宋明两朝曾是中国的临时都城。福州坐落在风景如画的闽江入海口处，闽江就从这里汇入中国东海。福州人氏遍布世界各地。

福州市内随处可见古老的榕树和历史古迹。宽广宁静的西湖公园代表着这座城市的文化传统和发展雄心。福州一处著名的风景是两座“遥遥相望的宝塔”，已有两千多年历史。其中白塔耸立在于山南麓，乌塔则位于乌山，登塔可尽览市内新老交融的美景。福州市附近的鼓山也是一处重要的旅游景点，著名的涌泉寺就位于山腹中，四周分散着一百多处历史遗迹，这些古迹充分反映出中国古代文明中建筑和石雕艺术的灿烂辉煌。

厦门

厦门市位于福建东南沿海金门湾内，鹰厦铁路终站。厦门港港阔水深，国际机场极为现代化，是中国对外贸易的重要港口。境内归侨、侨眷众多，是中国著名侨乡之一，市中心商厦临立，百货大楼随处可见，一派欣欣向荣的景象。农业以种植业为主，水产养殖和海洋捕捞业较发达。工业属轻型结构，以罐头、食品、纺织、机械、电子、化工、造船、建材、轻工等部门为重要。厦门旅游资源丰富，有山、海、池、岩、洞、寺、圆诸胜，处处可以赋诗入画，被誉为“山无高下皆行水，树不秋冬尽放花”。主要旅游风景区有普陀寺、鼓浪屿，集美学村、狮山、胡里山炮台。

晋江宝龙大酒店是晋江市唯一的国际豪华级酒店，以舒适、豪华的居住环境，为独具慧眼的商贸及旅游人士提供细腻而优质的服务，令您在享受现代化设施的同时又能沉醉于室内园林般的幽雅氛围。

酒店位于风景如画的江滨公园之畔，交通便捷，可步行或乘车抵达繁华的商业及购物区。酒店距泉州市中心9公里，车程约为15分钟；距泉州晋江机场4公里，车程只需5分钟；距泉州火车站13公里，车程约为25分钟。

晋江宝龙大酒店
POWERLONG HOTEL JINJIANG

中国福建省晋江市泉安中路1558号　邮编：362200
No.1558 Quan An Middle Road, Jinjiang City, Fujian Province, 362200 P.R China
电话/Tel：(86-595) 2808 8888　传真/Fax：(86-595) 2808 8999
客房预订电话/Room Reservation：(86-595) 2808 8855
宴会预订电话/Banquet Reservation：(86-595) 2808 8222
电子邮箱/E-mail：jinjiang@powerlonghotel.com
网址/Website：www.powerlonghotel.com

诚信 Honesty　恭谦 Modesty　创新 Creativity　敬业 Devotion

Powerlong Hotel, Jinjiang is the city's leading and only international deluxe hotel. It offers 5 star deluxe accommodations. Discerning travelers desiring the utmost in quality service and comfort will find an excellent combination of ultra modern facilities and indoor garden atmosphere.

Situated in the heart of the Jiang Bin Park and major commercial, shopping district of Jinjiang City, Powerlong Hotel is a mere 15 minutes By taxi to Quanzhou downtown city is 9 kilometers,5 minutes away to the Quanzhou Jinjiang Airport is 4 kilometers and 25 minutes by taxi to the Quanzhou Railway Station approximate 13 kilometers.

一流的广东经典名菜
An exquisite cantonese cuisine
(1F-2F)

极具特色的国际自助餐
International casual dining
(1F)

以精湛手艺制作的定食套餐
An exquisite Japanese buffet
(1F)

激情尽在宝龙会
Enticing environment night club & KTV
(2F、3F&4F)

无限享受
A celebration of taste
(-1F)

富丽堂皇的宴会
Classic banqueting
(3F)

尽善尽美的会议服务
Unparalleled service
(4F)

HUNAN PROVINCE
Changsha

Prospering from its location on the fertile Hunan plain fed by the Xiang River, Changsha has been populated for over three thousand years and has historically featured as a major agricultural trading centre. In the early twentieth century European and American traders established modern industries, schools and factories and again today the provincial capital has established itself as a commercial and business centre. First class hotels and excellent communication facilities have partnered the rekindled prosperity.

The mountainous countryside setting, dotted with lush rice paddies and traditional adobe brick houses, sprouted the seeds of modern China as Mao Zedong was raised in the nearby Shaoshan village. In the 1960s millions flocked to pay homage to the great helmsman and his childhood home is still meticulously preserved. Immutable stone tablets inscribed with his poems rest on the mountain slopes, whilst more ephemeral Mao memorabilia is in abundant supply.

Mao studied and later taught at the Hunan No. 1 Teacher's Training School in Changsha. His former home and office of the Communist Party Committee is now a museum. Exhibits at the Hunan Provincial Museum not only cover revolutionary history, but also contain many treasures excavated from nearby Western Han tombs at Mawangdui, including a spectacular 2,000 year-old mummified remains of a woman swaddled in twenty layers of silk.

Other city attractions include the Yuelu Park, densely populated with ancient trees and the majestic Hunan University campus, which evolved from a Song dynasty academy. Fine views of the city can be observed from the Wangxiang Pavilion. The Tianxin Pavilion area, incorporating the last remnants of the city wall, affords a fascinating insight into local life.

长沙

拥有3000多年历史的长沙座落于肥沃的湖南平原上，受湘江水的滋养，农业十分发达，曾是重要的农业贸易中心。20世纪早期，来自欧洲和美国的商人在这里建立起现代化的工业、学校和工厂，如今这座湖南的省会城市已成为主要的贸易中心，市内酒店林立，设施便利。中国的一代伟人毛泽东就生长在群山环绕的韶山村里，这里有肥沃的稻田和散发着浓浓乡土气息的农舍，中国革命的火种就在这里点燃。毛泽东童年的居所受到妥善的保护，坚实的石头桌子上还刻着他描绘山坡的诗句，在这里你可以阅读到详细的毛泽东生平事记，每年都有无数游客来到这里一睹伟人踪迹。

毛泽东受教于长沙湖南第一师范学校，毕业后留校任教。他在共产党委员会的办公室和住所如今已改建为博物馆。另外，湖南省博物馆馆藏除革命时期的文物外，还包括从马王堆出土的汉代墓葬文物，其中最著名的是一具已有2000年历史的汉代女尸。

长沙市内其他景点包括古木参天的岳麓公园和演变自宋代书院的湖南大学校园。登上市内的望乡亭可欣赏全城景色，而天心阁和古城墙更为长沙增添了一抹迷人的色彩。

TALK INFORMS

BE BETTER INFORMED

WITH SOUTH CHINA

CITY TALK MONTHLY

Published since 1992, City Talk is part of the "Talk" network of city-living magazines in China.
Please send subscription, editorial, advertising enquiries to media@ismaychina.com

Hong Kong

With its established status as an international financial and trading hub, China's original 'Golden Egg' is the place where today's clichéd expression 'East meets West' was fittingly conceived

Naturally, China's national flag and the SAR bauhinia flower flag now fly where the Union Jack had previously. Although colonial red post boxes have been painted green and the word 'Royal' removed from several institutions, road names and buildings named after British governors and monarchs remain.

With its long reputation as global trading port and its large southern Chinese population, Hong Kong has always been inextricably linked to China in both economic and cultural terms. Family ties across the border are very strong - a fact borne out by the huge investments made in China by Hong Kong tycoons wishing to return some of their good fortune to the land of their birth. A major part of all foreign investment in the mainland comes from Hong Kong. Manufacturing industries have long straddled the border between Hong Kong's northern New Territories and the mainland to the point that Shenzhen has virtually become a suburb.

Combatant with the meteoric rise of Shanghai and China's entry into the WTO, Hong Kong's executive role as a bridge between China and the outside world is bound to diminish in the future. But, resilient as ever, the Stock Exchange flourishes and Hong Kong vows to bite back as huge infrastructure projects are planned and executed.

Signifying its status as the region's premier host of international trade shows, a huge new convention centre has opened on Lantau Island. The AsiaWorld-Expo, the size of nine soccer pitches, is already heavily booked. And to cater to complaints that Hong Kong lacked a suitable venue for indoor concerts and sporting events, the exhibition centre also boasts the city's biggest indoor arena, able to seat up to 13,500 people. The existing curvaceous Hong Kong Convention and Exhibition Centre in Wanchai, scene of the 1997 hand-over ceremony, will continue its function as the downtown venue. The new centre, costing around US$300 million is only minutes away from the International Airport and Hong Kong Disneyland. The Hong Kong Disneyland opened in September, 2005. The world-class theme park and resort will be Disney's first theme park in China offering magical experiences for the entire family ranging from Broadway-style shows and signature Disney attractions to vibrant fireworks and parades.

The first phase of the development will have 2,100 hotel rooms, as well as an area for retail, dining and entertainment, and is expected to initially attract 10 million visitors a year.

In an effort to increase tourism revenues, quotas for arrivals from the mainland were lifted in early 2002. The effect has been

香港

紧邻广东省南部，珠江口东侧的香港，是远东地区海空交通运输的要冲，扼中国华南门户。香港由香港岛、九龙、新界以及大小二百多个岛屿组成，总面积1066平方公里，人口达六百多万，其中百分之九十八为中国居民。香港清朝时归广东新安县管辖，1842年鸦片战争后，英国通过强迫清政府签定的《南京条约》、《中英北京条约》、《展拓香港界址专条》等三个不平等条约占去整个香港地区，自1898年起“租用”香港。租期99年。1984年9月，中英两国政府经过一系列谈判签署了有关香港问题的联合声明；1997年7月1日中国恢复行使对香港的主权，成立香港特别行政区，享有高度自治权，现在香港特别行政区正在此“一国两制”的环境下，繁荣发展，成为中国南方一大国际都会。

香港是世界上一百三十多个自由港和自由贸易区中的佼佼者。它对外实行自由贸易，逐步形成了一个以加工工业为基础，以对外贸易为主导，以多种经营为特点的国际工商业城市。现在香港已为远东地区主要的国际工业中心、贸易中心、金融中心、航运中心、旅游中心和信息中心；而对外贸易、制造业、房地产建筑业、旅游业并列为香港经济的四大支柱。此外，香港除了被称为“东方之珠”，更拥有“世界商品橱窗”、“购物天堂”及“美食天堂”的美誉。而位于港岛中区的兰桂坊、新(苏豪区)更是中外青年人娱乐吃喝的好去处。

香港旅游景点众多，有浅水湾、香港仔、鲤鱼门、海洋公园、青马大桥、太平山顶、黄大仙庙、圆玄学院、沙田万佛寺、锦田吉庆围、尖沙咀星光大道及今年9月开幕的迪斯尼乐园等。

startling as throngs of mainland tourists, richly garbed and stashed with hard currency, queue to buy gold and indulge in all the opulent pleasures found in the former colony.

In the past Hong Kong has promoted itself as the 'City of Life' - not an understatement as its just about seven million population all appear to be on the streets at the same time and place, its densely populated and animated harbour never rests and its cobweb of night-time lights routinely transform the city into an awesome spectacle. The night-time scene has recently been augmented by a spectacular multi-media show, A Symphony of Lights, combining lights and narration involving 19 key buildings on Hong Kong Island. Their façades are decked out in lights that, at the flick of a switch, glow in a myriad of colours depicting Hong Kong's colourful and bustling atmosphere. On special occasions, such as at Christmas and at the Chinese New Year spectacular pyrotechnics are also featured.

An additional red carpet spectacle to compliment the sound and light show was rolled out in April 2004 when the Avenue of Stars opened on the Tsim Sha Tsui promenade. The Avenue honours celebrities of the Hong Kong silver screen over the past 100 years. Measuring 440 metres from end to end it presently showcases 100 film celebrities with a plaque bearing their names, palm print and signatures. It has already become a tourist site of international renown as well as a rest and recreation venue for local residents – pulling in around seven million visitors during its first six months. Alongside, the Tsim Sha Tsui Promenade Beautification Project, due to be completed by mid-2006, is well underway, New landscaped areas will be created for outdoor activities and performances and al fresco dining are carefully being sculpted.

Today's Hong Kong, a vibrant, culturally enriched modern metropolis has little in common with Hong Kong of 1842 when it was conceded as a spoil of the Opium War. But Hong Kong's history did just not begin then. Many hidden treasures, including a Han dynasty tomb and a large number of Neolithic artefacts, place the territory far back in Chinese history. Under the same emperor who built the Great Wall, Hong Kong became part of the Chinese empire, but remained sparsely populated until the 12th century. The fertile areas of the New Territories and the rich advantages of the harbour attracted migratory peoples including the Tankas, the legendary boat dwellers still evident today, the Hoklos and the Hakkas from the north. Walled villages became a distinctive feature of a territory redolent with rebellion and piracy.

The legitimate piracy of the opium trade brought massive wealth to Great Britain and great suffering to China. Following the Opium War humiliation was heaped on China as Hong Kong and other Chinese ports, including Shanghai, were turned over to the British imperialists. Hong Kong Island, or the 'barren rock,' was ceded in perpetuity. With almost no fresh water or vegetation, and a thin population limited to small communities of fishing and farming families, the colony's only apparent advantage was a deep, sheltered harbour that was ideally placed for growing trade between China and the rest of the world.

Hong Kong's geography grew with the addition of the Kowloon peninsula in 1860 and the 99-year lease of the New Territories in 1898. However it was little more than a modest country cousin to treaty ports such as Shanghai and Tianjin until they were closed with the Communist Revolution of 1949.

With a manufacturing boom in the 1950s and 1960s, its population rose from 1.8 million in 1947 to more than 4 million in 1970. Massive public housing estates were built, and new towns gradually developed in the rural New Territories. When Deng Xiaoping's economic reforms began, the territory came into its own. With a well-developed banking and finance system, high-tech communications and an experienced, international business community, it was an ideal point of liaison between China and the rest of the trading world.

In response, the SAR's infrastructure was broadened with a new international airport, new container terminals, a third cross-harbour tunnel and extensions to its showpiece mass transit rail network. The opening of the Tsing Ma suspension bridge linking Kowloon to Lantau Island, one of the highest profile projects in recent years, provides a direct link to the new airport at Chek Lap Kok by both road and rail. The US$1.16 billion bridge breaks many existing engineering records - at 1.34 kilometres, it is the longest two-tiered suspension bridge in the world - and the heaviest, with 49,000 tons of steel.

Despite not being the bargain basement it used to be, shopping remains the most popular pastime for locals and visitors alike - and there are still plenty of bargains to be had. The city offers an extraordinary range of shopping opportunities from the lovable Stanley market to downtown luxury malls; from the bastion of the British high street, Marks & Spencer's to Sogo of Japan. The main shopping areas are located in Tsim Sha Tsui, where the colourfully illuminated signs of the Nathan Road never fade, and in Causeway Bay where the streets are proverbially packed like sardines.

For up-market shoppers Hong Kong's mega-malls - containing stores, offices, entertainment facilities and restaurants, appear as self-contained mini-cities complete with climate control. In Central and Admiralty most designer labels can be found with the confines of the Prince's Building, The Landmark, Alexandra House and Pacific Place. In Kowloon, Harbour City, Hong Kong's largest complex sits like a fortress over the sea - its battery of luxury hotels, offices, stores and delicatessens providing sanctity from the marauding masses outside.

The recently completed International Finance Centre complex (ifc) comprising top-class shopping malls, restaurants, offices and the six star Four Seasons Hotel is a commanding statement of Hong Kong's 21st century ambitions. Its stunning main 88-storey tower is now the city's tallest building.

Hong Kong's markets proffer soothing comfort to the palatially organised malls and stores. On the southern shores of Hong Kong Island the Stanley Market is awash with tourists and locals alike seeking anything from brand labels, to Chinese paintings and trinkets. Back in Kowloon, the Temple Street Night Market is a hectic, haggling maze of pirated goods and cheap fashions. The nearby Ladies Market used to be the exclusive domain of female shoppers, but now hardy sales-people proffer tourist souvenirs and clothing. In the same area are markets with a distinctive Hong Kong flavour - the Yuen Po Street Bird Garden parades parrots and shrill songbirds in bamboo cages - the Goldfish Market sells slithers of good fortune, whilst the Flower Market conjures a concerto of dazzling colour.

The most up-market destination is the refurbished Victorian splendour of Western Market featuring peasant arts and crafts as well as fabrics and antique watches. For aficionados the nearby Hollywood Road area offers a treasure island of quality antiques and curios - from old Hong Kong postcards and Mao badges to Tang Dynasty horses and ancient cloisonné vases.

The urban face of the SAR changes daily but its drama remains - the bustling harbour with its backdrop-synergy of skyscraper-covered mountains; the rugged island of Lantau crowned by the giant bronze Buddha that rises over Po Lin Monastery; Cheung Chau and Lamma Island's vehicle-free laid-back pace; and the New Territories, where traditional walled villages and ancestral temples continue to exist alongside the New Towns.

Hong Kong's glittering glass towers, mirroring each other, often blind the visitor to the massive natural attraction that lies beneath. Over seventy per cent of the area is either covered with lush vegetation, mountains or used for farming. Hong Kong also has over 260 rugged outlying islands - mostly devoid of human habitation, apart from the intrepid hiker. Large areas of Hong Kong Island itself are still barren of human assault and the city prides itself on its vast number of well-managed country parks. Nestling above the modern pinnacles of Central, the Hong Kong Zoological and Botanical Gardens offer a quiet retreat for all forms of wildlife and humankind. Rare pink dolphins nose dive in near proximity to the fine, safe beaches that sweep the fringes of the entire territory.

Man-made attractions, including Ocean Park and the waterfront Cultural Centre-Space Museum and Museum of Art have proliferated over the last three decades. A permanent

exhibition of Hong Kong, yesteryear is now on display in the Museum of History.

Victoria Peak offers lofty panoramic views across the harbour to Kowloon and beyond into a hazy no-man's-land. The seemingly perpendicular tram ride to the mountain's summit is a quintessential Hong Kong experience. The peak has always been a symbol of social standing - wealthy British merchants used the funicular railway, built in 1888, as a modern form of conveyance to their elite residences. Today new high-class residences have again appeared and a seven-storey Peak Tower opened in 1997 - brimming with shops, eateries and attractions, including Madame Tussaud's Wax Works.

Dragon Boat racing, a unique action-packed sporting occasion steeped in tradition takes place in June. This old Chinese festival attracts the best oarsmen in the world to compete in international status contests. Sports-wise, Hong Kong and horse racing are synonymous, with vast sums wagered at two of the most modern tracks and opulent grandstands in the world. The Hong Kong Jockey Club is by far the world's largest non-profit race club - donating over a billion Hong Kong Dollars to charities and community projects each year. The famous Credit Suisse First Boston Sevens rugby championship is hosted annually at the Hong Kong Stadium. The major pastimes for the well-to-do are golfing and yachting - fine golf courses and St. Tropez-like marinas abound.

The city is one of the world's great gourmet palaces, embracing an exotic fusion of flavours from the East and West. Just about every national cuisine on earth is represented in Hong Kong. With almost ten thousand restaurants, the thought of food is never far away. The quintessential Hong Kong dining experience literally 'touches the heart'- that is how 'dim sum' translates into English. These light snacks are served for breakfast or lunch in local teahouses as well as in first-class Chinese restaurants. The most popular dim sum items include shrimp dumplings (har gau), pork dumplings (siu mai) and barbequed pork in steamed bread (cha siu bau).

The city is the world capital for Cantonese cuisine and small local restaurants with their glossy glazed poultry and game in illuminated windows accompany some of the classiest and most sophisticated restaurants in Asia. Favourite up-market haunts for dim sum include Spring Moon at The Peninsula, Shang Palace at The Kowloon Shangri-La and Man Ho at the JW Marriott.

There are half a dozen, or so, eating centres covering the downtown areas of Causeway Bay and Tsim Sha Tsui, and beyond to Stanley and Kowloon and across the Victoria Harbour to Lamma Island. The trendiest places to eat are around Central where steep inclines add charisma to the Lan Kwai Fong area. Its veritable pile of ebullient non-stop eateries, bars and clubs spill over on to adjoining streets where every night is party night. Nearby the more sophisticated SoHo, short for the area South of Hollywood Road, offers an inimitable range of intimate dining experiences. The latest elite supplements to the Hong Kong culinary scene are to be found in the landmark ifc 2 development on the Central waterfront and at the Landmark Oriental Hotel and the Four Seasons Hotel.

Hong Kong also has a mature and electric night-scene with clubs and bars to suit all tastes - from the jazzy intimacy of the Music Room Live to the lusty youthfulness of Queen's and the traditional pub comforts of The Dickens Bar in the Excelsior Hotel. In Wanchai, the home of legendary Suzie Wong, the bars and clubs wait for sunrise to quell their passions - just as they have done for decades. Partaking of afternoon tea is another British institution that is alive and well in Hong Kong. The magnificent lobby of the Peninsula Hotel delivers cream teas and cucumber sandwiches accompanied by the sweet sounds of a fine classical ensemble. Other favourite afternoon warrens to watch the world and his wife include The Verandah at The Repulse Bay Hotel and the MO Bar at The Mandarin Landmark Oriental Hotel.

ESSENTIAL HONGKONG >>

Breathtaking Take a night time stroll on the Kowloon promenade and its Avenue of Stars. Cross the Victoria Harbour on the legendary Star Ferry and take the equally legendary Peak Tram ride up Victoria Peak.
Away from it all Stroll the mountain trail down from Victoria Peak to Hong Kong Park. Go island hopping – visit Cheung Chau, Lamma and Lantau islands.
Delights Indulge in a seafood dinner on the shores of Lamma Island. Dine in style at one of the city's top hotels. Imbibe afternoon tea at The Peninsula Hotel and cocktails at the Repulse Bay Hotel.
Noisy Go party in the Lan Kwai Fong district. Shop till you drop in Causeway Bay, at the Ladies Market, Stanley market and at Sam Shui Po. Sample Sunday afternoon dim sum in one of the city's huge restaurants. Catch a Cantonese opera performance at the Temple Street Night Market. For the young at heart, play a day away at Disneyland. Spend a night and some cash at the Happy Valley races.

Club 97
This hip and chic club, with house/techno music has become a Lan Kwai Fong landmark. *9 Lan Kwai Fong, Central. Tel: 2810 9333*

Disneyland
Hong Kong Disneyland Resort Lantau Island

Flagstaff House Museum of Tea Ware
In Hong Kong Park. Tel: 2869 0690

Gaddi's
This fine dining French restaurant is considered one of the last formal establishments where jackets are required for men - the food is a legend. *The Peninsula, Salisbury Road, Tsim Sha Tsui. Tel: 2315 3171*

Hari's
Besides the usual cocktails, this bar offers a staggering 18 different martinis. *Mezzanine, Holiday Inn Golden Mile, 50 Nathan Road, Tsim Sha Tsui. Tel: 2369 3111 ext. 1345*

Hong Kong Museum of History
100 Chatham Road South. Tel: 2724 9042

Hong Kong Space Museum
10 Salisbury Road. Tel: 2721 0226

Jumbo Floating Restaurant
Perhaps the ultimate tourist event, dining on this floating restaurant is an experience of imperial proportions. *Shun Wan, Wong Chuk Hang Road, Aberdeen. Tel: 2553 9111*

M at The Fringe
Amazing décor, ambience and reinvented menus from the creative hand of Michelle Garnault. *1/F, 2 Lower Albert Road, Central. Tel: 2877 4000*

One Harbour Road
Fine Cantonese cuisine - from dim sum to Chinese soups - and a host of other delicacies. *Grand Hyatt Hong Kong, 1 Harbour Road, Wanchai. Tel: 2588 1234*

Spring Moon
Inside the legendary Peninsular Hotel - the 1920s retro-Chinese styled restaurant, created by famous local designer Kenneth Ko, is undisputedly one of the best. *1/F The Peninsula, Salisbury Road, Tsim Sha Tsui. Tel: 2315 3160*

The Peninsula
Salisbury Road, Tsimshatsui, Tel: 2920 2888

The Repulse Bay
109 Repulse Bay Road, Tel: 2292 2888

Vong
The highlight of this place is the onyx-lit, semi-circular bar where champagne is poured and martinis shaken. *25/F Mandarin Oriental, 5 Connaught Road, Central. Tel: 2825 4028*

HEAVENLY BITES

Amigo

Scroll down Amigo's hall of fame and you find uncountable names of celebrities, presidents, royalty and senators that have visited the restaurant since it opened in 1967. Amigo is a real classic. Don't be mistaken by its Spanish name, though. Amigo is a genuine French restaurant that serves nouvelle cuisine Françoise. Every dish is sophisticatedly made to perfection including the Pate De Foie-Gras Truffle De Strasbourg, Bisque D'Homard and the made in heaven soufflé. *Amigo Mansion, 79A Wongneichong Road, Happy Valley, Tel (852) 2577 2202/8993*

Grissini

Modern dishes may draw the attention of young customers, but it is always good to know that there are some old-school restaurants that vow to protect traditional recipes as national treasures. Grissini is definitely one of them. This elegant Italian restaurant with dim candle lights, rusty walls and mahogany flooring somehow resembles how real Italian culture should be - romantic, enthusiastic and intimate. *2/F, Grand Hyatt, 1 Harbour Road, Tel (852) 2588 1234*

Grissini

Harlan's

Self-confident and seasoned with arrogance, food & beverage tycoon Harlan Goldstein has finally opened his very own in Hong Kong establishment. Originally from Manhattan, Harland has travelled the world and catered for the elite on his travels. Harlan's blend of technical perfection and social understanding are delivered in his fascinatingly diverse menus. *2075 Podium Level 2, IFC Mall, 8 Finance Street, Central, Tel (852) 2805 0566*

Spoon

The reason why internationally renowned chef Alain Ducasse named his most talked-about restaurant 'Spoon' is simple. The spoon is the only utensil common to all culinary cultures - and international food is the theme for this very modish restaurant. Spoon is all about creativity. Just take a look at the menu - besides the traditional a la carte selection, diners are pointed towards creating their own salads and pastas. *Intercontinental Hotel, 18 Salisbury Road, Tsimshatsui, Kowloon, Tel (852) 2313 2256*

Spoon

Harakan

Minimal cooking and absolute enticement is what this latest Japanese bistro has to offer. Harakan brings serenity a world away from its hectic location in the heart of Causeway Bay. Greeted by a huge cherry blossom tree transported all the way from Japan the stage is set for a poetic harmony of minimal wooden décor of and skillfully artistic food. Their signature dish of Harakan Delux Sushi Set – comprised of red snapper, cod roe, grilled urchin & squid, blowfish, spicy tuna, sweet prawn with taro, silver fish and Japanese sea-eel is an ocean of freshness. *G/F Sunning Plaza, 10 Hysan Avenue Tel (852) 2882 8616*

Jewel

An 18th century Indian door and some very good-looking bouncers greet you at Jewel. This chic club with an Indo-Asian theme is the popular spot for those who are dressed to kill. As is the club itself with its terrain of coconut tress, silk cushions, comfy velvet couches, some equally sleek teak furniture as well as some very plush Javanese stone wall carvings. Playing mainly Hip-Hop and R&B, the club has a variety of Martinis for clubbers to indulge in. *G/F 37-43 Pottinger Street, Central, Tel (852) 2541 5988*

Drop is known for its great cocktails and its long queues of expectant customers. Those who get in never grumble, for Drop has it all – the right drinks, the right group of people to party with - and the best of all, the right music to keep those hips shaking all night long. Drop brings some funky groovy tunes to party animals over weekends, with occasional R&B and Hip-Hop to spice it up - the bar even managed to release its own enormously successful CD last year. Martinis are hot on their drinks-list topped by a trio of Dirty Martini, Lychee Martini and Chocolate Martin. *Bsmt, On Lok Mansion, 39-43 Hollywood Road, Central, Tel (852) 2543 8856*

Felix

Serving Pacific Rim and New Age American cuisine. Felix, on the 28th floor of the opulent Peninsula Hotel, should be a destination on every traveller's list. Designed by Phillippe Starck, the restaurant is a perfect combination of wood flooring, metal furniture and some very classy tableware. *The Peninsula Hotel, Salisbury Road, Tel (852) 2315 3188*

Drop

Hutong /Aqua

Above the Dior and Gucci outlets at One Peking Road are a number of stylish restaurants - including Hutong and Aqua. Very fashionable and very chic, Aqua provides innovative cultural cross-over by serving both classic Italian and contemporary Japanese dishes. The little Italy of Aqua Roma is famous for their crunchy antipasti and savoury al dente risottos, while Aqua Tokyo, the Japanese bit of the restaurant, captures essences of Japanese cuisine by serving jet-fresh sushi and sashimi, Tarawa crab tempura and Robatayaki grill.

Hutong

A completely differen story is told downstairs at Hutong. Elegantly dressed with Chinese Ar deco, Hutong is one of the most beautiful Chinese restaurants in Hong Kong. Carved antique wood screens, billowing Chinese silk curtains, rec lanterns and bird-cages successfully bring light and sound from the Imperia Palaces of ancient China Serving authentic northern Chinese food, the restaurant recounts the history behind each and every dish they serve. *One Peking Road, Tsimshatsu Kowloon - Aqua Tel (852) 3427 2288; Hutong Tel (852) 3428 8342*

Aqua

Isola

A hip new restaurant in a hip new building. Think white - this 7,000 square feet space is composed of contemporary textured whiteness - absolutely lovely for afternoon tea or a romantic dinner with dazzling views over the Victoria Harbour. From international to Italian classics like their signature appetizer of Misticanza con aragosta, carciofi, funghi e mango (made from lobster, artichokes, mushrooms and mango) Isola's defines beauty in a fresh aspect. *Levels 3 & 4, IFC Mall, Central, Tel (852) 2383 8765*

Macau

Suddenly this small outpost in southern China has been thrust to the forefront of growth in the Pearl River Delta with the arrival of Las Vegas casinos, fantasy theme parks and record tourist arrivals. But the temples, fortresses and unparalleled cuisine continue to beckon

Macau has been gracefully imbued with a unique identity through its long historic association with Europe and its role as a major point of contact with the world through seafaring activities. This truly multicultural enclave, with a population of around 450,000, has its urban centre on the Chinese mainland and encompasses the two charming communities of Coloane and Taipa – now one island after extensive land reclamation. At its heart, the magnificent neo-classical architecture is reminiscent of Lisbon.

In 1557, Portuguese merchants were amicably allowed to set up a trading post on this tiny peninsula. The next century saw the port of Macau flourish, as it became a major entrepôt on the Maritime Silk Route. As one of the richest places on earth, it was the gateway to China, not only for traders, but also for Christian missionaries. However, the golden age ended around 1640, and when Hong Kong was occupied in 1842, the foreign community migrated to the new British colony.

Undaunted, Macau had a card up its sleeve – quite literally. In order to raise revenue, not just in Macau but also in their colony in Timor, the Portuguese overlords issued licences for gambling houses. Today's galloping economy is still tied directly to tourism and gambling, with the great majority of visitors coming from the Mainland and Hong Kong. In 2002, the gambling market was liberalized and now Macau sees Chinese and US operations competing cheek-by-jowl, in a unique and exciting experiment which will culminate with the completion of 'Asia's Las Vegas' on the Cotai Strip.

While there is no doubt that most of the swelling numbers of tourists in Macau come to gamble at its casinos, the local government is keen to promote Macau as a destination with historic and cultural attractions as well. In 2005, the 'Historic Centre of Macau' was finally inscribed on UNESCO's World Heritage list, and it is this side of Macau – a little corner of Europe in Asia – that most non-gambling visitors come to soak up.

Downtown, the principal attraction is the Jesuit Cathedral, St. Paul's, of which only the fabulously carved façade and part of the crypt remains. Started in 1602 and taking twenty-five years to complete, it was cruelly ravaged by fire in 1835. Senado Square, with its magnificent fountain and pedestrianised quiescence, is the city showpiece – enclosed by age-old edifices including a 17th century monastery. The former Leal Senado building, which now houses the Institute of Civic and Municipal Affairs, was built in 1784 and remains the most outstanding example of traditional Portuguese architecture in Macau. The nearby area is also the best place to shop for antiques and curios.

Yet there is much more to Macau than its historic Portuguese buildings. Locals still

澳门

中国南部的小城澳门一跃成为珠江三角洲经济增长的前沿地带，但与此同时，古老的历史遗迹和无与伦比的美食却依然保持着无法取代的魅力。

澳门总人口约45万，包括澳门市区以及路环和凼仔两个岛屿。 1557年，葡萄牙商人最先涉足这里，进入17世纪澳门逐渐繁荣，成为海上丝绸之路一个重要的贸易口岸，各国商人和传教士都取道此地进入中国。

1842年以后香港取代了澳门在殖民贸易上的地位。为增加收入，葡萄牙统治者在澳门发放赌博许可证，但政府对赌博业的管理直到1961年澳门旅游娱乐有限公司(STDM)获得独家经营许可证后才走上正轨。

澳门经济的飞速发展与旅游和赌博产业密不可分，赌场上交的利税占政府财政收入的75%。STDM曾垄断澳门赌博市场40余年，但经过2002年的投标，如今由STDM、永利渡假村集团和银河娱乐场股份有限公司三分天下，相信中美赌业巨头将在“东方蒙特卡洛”实现双方共赢。未来澳门将继续保持并扩大目前的国际娱乐产业。

澳门美食云集，在完美融合中葡特色的基础上形成了自己的风格，所选原料均来自南美、欧洲和非洲。薯茸青菜汤、咸鳕鱼干、甜品木糠布丁、蛋挞和葡萄酒都值得亲口尝试，建议您前往外港新填海区(NAPE)大快朵颐。可以说，在澳门无论是在路边小咖啡馆，还是历史悠久的大酒店，你都能品尝到永不褪色的澳门风情。

澳门的欧式古建筑数量众多，其中耶稣会圣保罗教堂最为著名。教堂始建于1602年，历经25年时间方才建成，1835年遭大火烧毁，如今仅留存教堂门楼和部分地穴，保存有少量16至19世纪文物，地穴中埋藏着在战争中死去的教徒遗骸。

当地人信奉神灵，澳门的中式庙宇数量众多，其中最著名的是妈祖阁。妈祖阁历史可上溯至600多年前，沿用至今的观音堂始建于1627年，供奉大慈大悲观世音菩萨，仍保留着明朝的中楣，1844年中美首个贸易友好条约正是在此签订。

澳门的博物馆包罗万象，是当地的亮点。澳门博物馆建于大炮台城堡遗址上，以互动手段展示澳门的历史。位于内港的澳门海事博物馆在亚洲首屈一指，展现了澳门昔日航海的辉煌历史。格伦披治大赛车博物馆代表的着澳门的当代追求。位于澳门文化中心内的艺术博物馆共有七间展厅，完美融合了中西影像和艺术品。澳门葡萄酒博物馆主要记录和展示葡萄栽培和葡萄酒生产过程，并提供多种酒类供参观者品尝。

worship at a number of temples around the city. The A-Ma temple, after which Macau was named, contains a 400-year-old Kun Iam shrine. Dating from the 19th century, the lovely Lou Lim Ioc Gardens echoes classical Suzhou style. The nearby Old Protestant Cemetery convulses with capitulation over the fortunes of Macau's early foreign adventurers and their fall to tropical diseases and murderous plots.

With such a history, it is not surprising that Macau is a city of museums. Besides St. Paul's sits the dazzling Macau Museum, built on the foundations of the 16th century Monte Fort. Asia's leading maritime museum on the inner harbour presents exhibitions of Macau's seafaring past, whilst the Grand Prix Museum serves as an indicator of more modern pursuits. A great destination for the whole family is the new and extremely entertaining Communications Museum, an example of Macau's increasing confidence in the cultural sector. Similarly, the Museum of Art has started to host a more and more diverse range of exhibitions, while the territory's Arts Festival and Music Festival are growing stronger with each year that passes.

Macau's islands also offer cultural attractions. On Taipa's old Praia waterfront, a row of five restored houses, dating from 1921, display many fascinating aspects of Macanese and Portuguese history, as well as providing a venue for local artists and musicians. Taipa Village is still steeped in tradition, but elsewhere the island has been the site of much modern construction, including an airport, the Macau University campus, the Macau Jockey Club and Racecourse and a 15,000 seat sports stadium which was used for the 2005 East Asian Games. Coloane, meanwhile, remains largely rural and unspoiled. The island is protected from the commercial development found over the rest of the territory and offers plenty of room for tranquillity and recreation.

Dining out is one of the best ways to enjoy Macau, and the territory is a food-lover's paradise. Macanese cuisine embodies an inimitable combination of Portuguese and Chinese cuisines. A great place to explore the world of culinary offerings is at the New Reclamation Area (NAPE), with its wide selection of restaurants, cafes, bars and lounges.

The area lies in the shadow of the 20 metre high bronze statue of Kun Iam, the Buddhist goddess of mercy, which shines like a bright beacon in the night sky. Nearby is another new landmark: Fisherman's Wharf. This theme park, which houses shops, restaurants, bars and entertainment facilities, comes complete with its own volcano, and is an example of just how far Macau is willing to go to attract even more visitors.

In recent years, the face of the city has been radically altered and its sleepy Mediterranean image reformed as the city brings itself into the modern world – a world very much tied up with the fortunes of mainland China. The international airport opened in 1995, and services have rapidly expanded to include destinations across the region, augmenting Macau's importance as an economic gateway into China.

ESSENTIAL MACAU >>>>

Step Back in Time Visit the spectacular façade of St. Paul's Cathedral, the symbol of Macau, before heading to the wonderful Macau Museum, housed in the nearby Monte Fort. To explore the territory's Chinese heritage head to the Inner Harbour's A-Ma Temple, from which Macau reputedly got its name.

Get Tarted Up Stop off at either Margaret's Café in downtown Macau or Lord Stow's Bakery in Coloane Village to sample Macau's most famous snack – the Portuguese egg tart.

Village Life Wander amongst the quaint Portuguese buildings of Taipa Village, visit the restored houses on the waterfront, and go snack shopping along crowded Rua do Cunha – Taipa's food street.

Island Hideaway Get away from it all by heading back to nature amidst the greenery of Coloane. Cool off at one of the island's two clean, quiet beaches before visiting one of many seafront cafes and restaurants.

Try Your Luck Take your chances – or watch others winning or losing a fortune – at one of Macau's bustling casinos. The Lisboa offers a glimpse of the territory's gambling past, Sands its present, and the emerging mega-casinos on the Cotai Strip its future.

High Life The commanding views from the top of the Macau Tower should appeal to everyone, but only the brave will want to attempt the SkyJump: a death-defying adventure activity which involves leaping from the tower's outer rim, 233 m. above the ground!

THE BEST OF THE WEST

In the past, fine dining in Macau often meant pricey Cantonese seafood. Now however, there is much more on offer at Macau's top restaurants than shark's fin and abalone, and establishments offering world class international cuisine have begun to spring up across the territory.

None has received more praise than Robuchon A Galera at the Hotel Lisboa. Since it was opened by internationally acclaimed chef Joel Robuchon in 2001, this elegant restaurant has become known as one of the finest in the region, offering unparalleled levels of French cuisine and service. As you would expect, you'll pay for the privilege of dining here, but the fixed price executive lunches offer a surprisingly reasonable way of exploring Robuchon A Galera's culinary masterpieces.

For the best Italian food in town, head to the Mandarin Oriental's romantic Mezzaluna. In a setting which takes its inspiration from the casual elegance of a Tuscan villa, Italian chef Igor Bocchia conjures up a host of creative dishes using authentic Italian ingredients. His food represents an imaginative take on Italian cuisine, and his pizzas in particular – cooked in a wood-burning oven in the restaurant's open kitchen – have made Mezzaluna a firm favourite for many.

A TASTE OF HOME

With its Portuguese heritage, it is hardly surprising that Macau is home to a host of restaurants which serve up a taste of the old country, and the Macanese cuisine that it inspired. Throughout the territory, you'll find unpretentious eateries, complete with chequered table cloths, taverna-style wooden furniture and big jugs of sangria, where you can enjoy home-style Portuguese and Macanese food.

Next to the A Ma Temple on the peninsula, for example, there's A Lorcha – a small but phenomenally popular Portuguese restaurant which serves up satisfying meat dishes and wonderful seafood, including clams with coriander, garlic and olive oil. Tucked away in a sleepy Taipa backstreet, meanwhile, A Petisqueira appears to have been transported to Macau straight from a small Portuguese village. So does its food, and this petite restaurant is often heralded as one of the most authentic eateries of its kind. Finally, on Coloane, there's the legendary Fernando's. Come here with a group of friends, and as the wine flows and your table fills up with the restaurant's hearty fare, you'll quickly understand why this place is so popular. Bookings are not taken at weekends, but don't worry – having a drink and some chouriço at the bar is an enjoyable pre-dinner ritual, and all part of the Fernando's experience.

Where to find authentic Macanese cuisine – indeed, what authentic Macanese cuisine even is – can become a matter of fierce debate, but most locals agree when it comes to Restaurante Litoral. Incorporating ingredients and ideas from Portugal, China and beyond, some of this intimate eatery's recipes have been in co-owner Manuela Ferreira's family for more than a century. Eat here, and you'll appreciate why the small but proud Macanese community is so keen to preserve its culinary heritage.

AFTER DARK

The Docks, a collection of waterfront watering holes near the Kun Iam statue, is the territory's best known area for nightlife, but options for nights out are quickly increasing. The New Orleans section of Fisherman's Wharf is now a popular choice when the weather is good, with alfresco jazz performances, a fantastic view of the Friendship Bridge, and a collection of bars and restaurants. Today you can even find nightlife in quaint, quiet Taipa Village. Since its opening in December 2005, the Old Taipa Tavern has become a firm favourite with Chinese and foreigners alike, offering the comforts of a proper pub, such as decent pints and a big screen for sporting events, as well as a restaurant which serves much more than the standard pub fare.

Of course, many visitors spend their nights at the card table, but joining them at the casinos doesn't necessarily mean gambling all your money away. At Sands, for example, you can take in an eclectic and increasingly confident line-up of entertainment downstairs at Xanadu, or head to the third floor Winner's Circle, for a quiet drink and a stunning view over a sea of slot machines and card tables. It's a safe bet that with the opening of the big new casinos, Macau's nightlife will open up too.

DINING OUT

A Lorcha
289 Rua do Almirante Sergio
Tel: (853) 313193 / 313195

A Petisqueira
15A and 15B Rua de S. João, Taipa Village
Tel: (853) 825354

Fernando's
9 Praia de Hac Sa, Coloane Tel: (853) 881047

Mezzaluna
2/F Mandarin Oriental Macau, 956 – 1110 Avenida da Amizade
Tel: (853) 567888 / 7933861

Restaurante Litoral
261A Rua do Almirante Sergio
Tel: (853) 967878

Robuchon A Galera
3/F Hotel Lisboa, Avenida de Lisboa
Tel: (853) 577666

NIGHT LIFE

Bar Nova Guia
Mandarin Oriental Macau, 956 – 1110 Avenida da Amizade
Tel: (853) 567888 / 7933831

Moonwalker
Vista Magnifica Court Tel: (853) 751326

New Orleans
Legend Wharf, Macau Fisherman's Wharf
www.fishermanswharf.com.mo

Old Taipa Tavern
21 Rua dos Negociantes, Taipa Village
Tel: (853) 825221

Winners' Circle
3/F Sands, 203 Largo de Monte Carlo
Tel: (853) 883388

Xanadu
1/F Sands, 203 Largo de Monte Carlo
Tel: (853) 883388

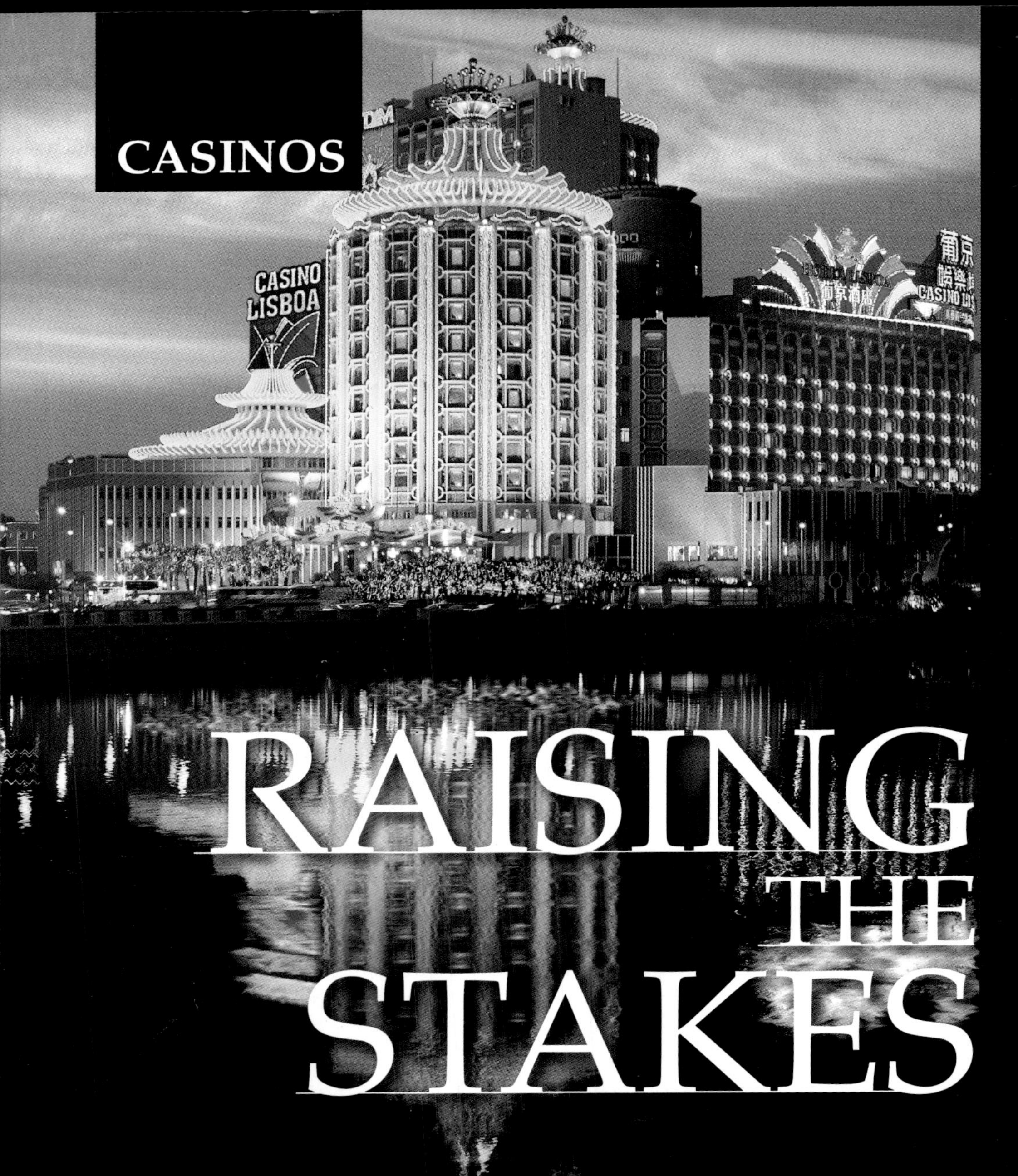

RAISING THE STAKES

Write about the gaming sector in Macau and the situation will probably have changed before the ink has even dried. It's no exaggeration to say that new casinos are appearing as if from nowhere, as it isn't only the buildings that are new – in many cases, so is the land they are being built on. Land reclamation is taking place throughout Macau, but its most high profile example is the Cotai Strip, a whole swathe of land which has emerged from the sea to connect the islands of Taipa and Coloane, and will be home to what is being touted as "Asia's Las Vegas."

The massive US$2.3 billion Venetian, scheduled to open in late 2007, is perhaps the most eagerly awaited project, but it will not be alone. The Galaxy Cotai Megaresort, City of Dreams, and many other grandiose developments, are at various stages of planning or construction, and Cotai is being developed as a major destination not just for gambling, but for dining, shopping and entertainment. Alongside the casino-hotels themselves, the strip will also feature a 15,000 seat arena, and a 1,800 seat theatre built specifically to house a new show by Cirque du Soleil.

With rooms numbering in the thousands rather than the hundreds, the resorts on the Cotai Strip make operations like the US$240million Sands look almost small. Indeed, Macau's first American-owned casino was built as an experiment of sorts, to see how a Las Vegas-style gaming outfit would fare in Macau's essentially Chinese market. Sands has been a resounding success – it essentially paid for itself in less than a year – but it has not been alone, with a number of other organizations from the US and Hong Kong also taking advantage of the liberalized market. Thus the peninsula has also seen its fair share of construction, as Wynn Macau, MGM Grand, Galaxy StarWorld and the new Grand Lisboa take shape.

But as more and more new establishments open their doors and start taking bets, will there be enough gamblers to go around? Fortunately for the casinos, the Individual Travel Scheme, which allows tourists from selected mainland cities to travel to Macau without having to join a tour group, is gradually being expanded. Macau saw a total of 18.7 million visitor arrivals in 2005 – a 12% increase compared to 2004 – and it is predicted that arrivals in 2006 could reach 21 million.

Even so, with such a large number of rival gaming operations, casinos still have to go all out to attract punters. The sleazy, smoky gambling dens of the past are increasingly giving way to brighter, breezier entertainment complexes, with non-smoking areas, spas, upscale restaurants and theatres featuring in many of the newly-opened casinos.

Some operations have gone even further to distinguish themselves from the pack, and Macau is now home to an increasing number of themed casinos. Pharaoh's Palace, in the Landmark Hotel, features massive columns covered in hieroglyphics and imposing busts of ancient Egyptian rulers, while at Taipa's New Century Hotel, Greek Mythology pays homage – as you might expect – to the gods of ancient Greece. The Emperor Palace Casino, meanwhile, makes references to London and the British monarchy, and downstairs, outside the entrance of the Grand Emperor Hotel in which it is located, you can even witness Macau's very own version of the changing of the guards.

In its lobby, the Grand Emperor also houses what it proudly describes as the world's first "golden pathway," and in Macau's increasingly competitive gaming sector it is fascinating to see how new entrants try to outdo their rivals. Take a tour round a new casino and you are likely to be shown any number of "firsts" – technological touches and little gimmicks which are new to Macau and are intended to provide that little edge over the competition. You can now find card tables linked up to computer systems, computerised versions of games which themselves use real cards, and even height-adjustable slot machines – although, strangely, however clever the machines get, they never seem to tell you how to win.

The Cotai Strip is likely to offer up even more extreme "firsts" – City of Dreams will apparently house what would be the world's first underwater casino – and looks certain to dispel Macau's image as an ex-colonial backwater. Incredible changes have taken place since gambling was legalized in the territory just over one hundred and fifty years ago, but the next few years are likely to bring even more.